SELLING
RADIO

SELLING RADIO

THE COMMERCIALIZATION OF AMERICAN BROADCASTING

1920–1934

Susan Smulyan

Smithsonian Institution Press
Washington and London

Editor: Duke Johns
Designer: Kathleen Sims

Library of Congress Cataloging-in-Publication Data

Smulyan, Susan.
   Selling radio : the commercialization of American broadcasting, 1920–1934 / Susan Smulyan.
     p. cm.
   Includes bibliographical references and index.
   ISBN 1-56098-686-7 (acid-free)
   1. Radio broadcasting—Economic aspects—United States—History. 2. Radio advertising—United States—History. 3. Corporate sponsorship—United States—History. I. Title.
HE8698.S6 1994
384.54'3'0973—dc20   93-12833

British Library Cataloguing-in-Publication Data is available

Manufactured in the United States of America
01 00   5 4 3

∞ The paper used in this publication meets the minimum requirements of the American National Standard for Permanence of Paper for Printed Library Materials Z39.48-1984.

For permission to reproduce illustrations appearing in this book, please correspond directly with the owners of the works, as listed in the individual captions. The Smithsonian Institution Press does not retain reproduction rights for these illustrations individually, or maintain a file of addresses for photo sources.

CONTENTS

ACKNOWLEDGMENTS   vii

INTRODUCTION: WHO PAYS FOR RADIO?   1

1 TOWARD NATIONAL RADIO   11
The Urge for Distance 13 • Formation of a National Audience 20 • Roots of National Radio Service 31

2 THE RISE OF THE NETWORK SYSTEM   37
Funding Broadcasts 39 • Technological Options for National Radio Service 42 • Super-power 44 • Shortwave Rebroadcasting 48 • Wired Networks 52 • Beyond the Technological Imperative 57

3 ARGUMENTS OVER BROADCAST ADVERTISING   65
Early Stations 66 • Opponents 68 • The Campaign for Broadcast Advertising 72 • Promoters 73 • Campaign Rhetoric and Strategies 75 • Changes in Broadcasting 81 • Radio Advertising to Women 86

CONTENTS

4 TWISTING THE DIALS: CHANGES IN RADIO PROGRAMMING 93
Early Radio Programming 94 • Pre-network Sponsored Shows 98 • Transitional Programming 111 • Vaudeville Comes to Radio 117 • Electrical Transcriptions versus Networks 122

5 DRUNK AND DISORDERLY: THE BACKLASH AGAINST BROADCAST ADVERTISING 125
Timing of the Protests 127 • The Protesters and Their Agendas 132 • Industry Response to the Protests 139 • Congressional Attempts to Reform Commercial Radio 142

CONCLUSION 154
Changes 155 • The Rest of the Story in Radio 155 • The Rest of the Story in Television 163 • The End of the Story 165

NOTES 169
INDEX 216

ACKNOWLEDGMENTS

I am grateful that my friends and colleagues are often one and the same. This unusual but wonderful situation makes it impossible to separate my personal and professional debts. The work for this book took place at four institutions. I want to thank John Blum, Hans and Geraldine Frei, and Jean-Christophe Agnew at Yale University; Bernard Finn, Elliot Sivowitch, Carl Scheele, Carlene Stephens, Barbara Smith, Carolyn Goldstein, and especially Steven Lubar at the National Museum of American History, Smithsonian Institution; Linda Pritchard, Ann Eisenberg, and Jim Schneider at the University of Texas at San Antonio; and Mari Jo Buhle, Paul Buhle, Bob Lee, Pat Malone, Jim Cullen, and Kathy Franz at the Department of American Civilization, Brown University. Many other students, colleagues, and friends have helped me in many ways and on many projects not related to this book, while a few people, such as Rick Farrell, Judy Babbitts, Bruce Sinclair, and Terry Murphy, transcend categories. Thanks to all.

Financial support for this project came from a Smithsonian Institution predoctoral fellowship; a National Association of Broadcasters grant for research; a University of Texas at San Antonio faculty research grant;

an American Historical Association Albert J. Beveridge grant for research; and a National Science Foundation postdoctoral research fellowship.

My family—Ruth and Harold Smulyan; Lisa Smulyan; Michael Markowicz; Betsy Smulyan; Ted Haber; the next generation; and most especially the previous one, Ben and Bertha Finkelstein—have made my work and my life possible and fun.

INTRODUCTION

Who Pays for Radio?

"When the first radio station began in 1920, no one knew how to make money from broadcasting." For about ten years I've begun all discussions of my work with that sentence. I learned early that most people want the one-sentence version of my project, although I also have available a paragraph, a fifteen-minute, and now a 223-page version. As a sound bite, though, that first sentence serves quite well. This book examines how radio in the United States became commercialized, or financed by selling time. It tells the story of an important technological and economic system that most Americans accept today without question as foreordained, despite the misgivings that were overcome and the struggles that were needed to achieve this illusion of naturalness. Nothing about the process was inevitable, and every step involved conflict.

Broadcasting's programs and structure, developed in radio, help define our perception of life in the United States. Television situation comedies show families fulfilling the American dream, their success measured by the products consumed. During the half-hour sitcom, frequent commercials reinforce broadcasting's position as the most visible archetype of

1

American consumer capitalism. With the help of advertising, television pays its own way, makes enormous profits through the sale of time to sponsors, and brings programs into viewers' homes without government subsidy or interference. A few distributors (the networks) hold exclusive contracts with local stations and provide most of the advertising and programming Americans watch.

To understand how this situation came about, we must look back to a time when business leaders, government officials, and the radio audience wondered about the answer to a common question: Who pays for broadcasting? The familiar shape of American broadcasting first developed during the 1920s in broadcast radio and was later adopted by television. Three factors shaped American broadcasting's form and content: the desire for national radio; the choice of a particular technology—wired networks—to provide radio service to the entire nation; and dislike and distrust of radio advertising on the part of both listeners and businesses.

During the first fourteen years of broadcasting, listeners, broadcasters, advertisers, and educators fought for control of radio. Listeners wanted national radio service. The telegraph, railroads, electric lights, and telephones had prepared Americans for technologies that might change concepts of time and space, unite the nation, bring the outside world into the home, and be operated privately.[1] Wired networks became the provider of national radio through a combination of technological, economic, cultural, and political factors, which brought with them a specific broadcasting structure and particular kinds of radio programs.

At the same time, however, the use of radio advertising to pay the expensive wire rentals provoked early and continuing protests from educators and others who hoped radio would do more than sell products. An anonymous poem published in *Radio Revue* magazine in 1930 illustrates these concerns:

"Sponsoritis"

Dame nature has a "funny" way
Of spoiling our enjoyment
For everyone who lives today
Has his or her annoyment;
And each disease beneath the sun
Has diff'rent germs to bite us

Now RADIO's developed one—
They call it "SPONSORITIS."

It's thriving like a healthy weed
Or fungus newly grafted,
And mercenaries sow the seed
Wherever sound is wafted
The artists rave then grow morose
Because of laryngitis,
And "fans" then get a stronger dose
Of this same SPONSORITIS.

No use to try to save the wreck
Or prophecy [*sic*] disaster,
For he who signs the mighty check
Is boss and lord and master;
When there's a program spoiled or botched,
It's money bags who fight us,
With heavy hearts we've stood and watched
The spread of SPONSORITIS. . . . [2]

More surprisingly, broadcasters and advertisers also distrusted the notion of radio advertising and had to be convinced it could work. The protests against radio sponsorship influenced what was heard over the airwaves despite the ultimate success of the networks' promotion of broadcast advertising. The continuing protests, as well as the programming forms and organizational structure that responded to them, influenced television. Any understanding of American commercial television must grow out of an examination of its beginnings in commercial radio.

I phrased my introductory sentence to challenge the widespread assumption that the commercialized system is a necessary evil—if you want television, you have to put up with commercials. But my research quickly raised questions about why and how, with all the evidence of conflict I found, contemporary American broadcasting could present itself as the inevitable application of capitalism to communication. Italian Marxist Antonio Gramsci was one of the first to examine how capitalist economies evolved a shared ideology. Gramsci's theory of hegemony argues that power and social control in advanced bourgeois societies derive from more than economic factors. As Carl Boggs has written, "Gramsci observed that ruling elites always sought to justify their power, wealth, and status *ideologically*, with the aim of securing general popular acceptance of their domi-

3

nant position as something 'natural' . . . and thus unchallengeable." Boggs explains that "ruling ideas must become deeply-embedded in the fabric of social relations and national traditions" until they appear as "common sense," able to mystify "power relations, public issues, and historical events."[3]

I seek to examine how the commercialized broadcasting system in the United States became "naturalized." Other scholars, notably Stuart Hall, have extended Gramsci's idea that hegemony is not imposed, but rather continually struggled for, and looked at popular culture as a site of such conflict.[4] Not only the content of broadcasting, but its economic and technological structure as well as people's conception of it, are part of the capitalist hegemony Gramsci described and a site of the conflict Hall posits. Although developed in European and English contexts, these paradigms have proven extremely useful for understanding American broadcasting.

Unraveling the truth about broadcasting's history is a difficult and politically charged task. In *Media and the American Mind*, Daniel Czitrom has concluded that "the everywhere-ness, all-at-once-ness, and never-ending-ness of the media are powerful barriers to understanding, or even acknowledging, their history."[5] The media's attempts to distort its own enterprise range from the early radio industry's labeling of its organizational structure as "the American System of Broadcasting" up to current network slogans. Early historians of radio, writing from a progressive point of view, saw advertising as the most sensible way to finance broadcasting and as a fateful and fated development.[6] Contemporary scholars who believe in the inevitability of commercialization are often those who accept with equanimity its results.[7] This approach minimizes or trivializes the strong opposition that broadcast advertising aroused. On the other hand, the concept of inevitability can also stereotype the nonprofit alternatives as perfect and the commercial possibilities as evil. The broadcasting system did not simply have to be one or the other, privatized or government-sponsored. Many different mixtures were conceivable within the given cultural and technological parameters.

In addition to deconstructing the notion of commercial inevitability, broadcast historians must also consider the question of technological determinism. It might seem that radio, as a new communications technology, demanded a particular organization, yet historians of technology challenge the concept that each new machine carries its own destiny within itself. When Steven Lubar and Brooke Hindle call for historians to examine the contexts of technology, they ask that we recognize the influence of social and cultural forces on technology.[8] This book take a particular approach to the history of technology, one that explores how social and cultural choices affect technology at the same time that technology affects society and culture. I seek to understand how technological change happens and how it can be controlled, because I reject the idea that each machine had to be designed or used in a particular way. I also believe that by understanding the design and use of machines in the past, we can better understand the machines we meet everyday. Finally, just as other technologies have often been used by those in power to extend their power, a few large radio companies consolidated their control even as they faced technological limitations and interacted with listeners, advertisers, and the federal government.

Several scholars have examined American broadcasting and advertising as a product of resistance, as well as of powerful industries imposing a profitable system. Czitrom outlines the cultural and intellectual influences on the American media, and Susan Douglas, in *Inventing American Broadcasting*, considers the social construction of early radio: the impact of technology, popular culture, entrepreneurship, and the radio operators themselves on radio in its earliest days.[9] My work picks up at the moment Douglas's leaves off in the early 1920s, and reviews the technological, economic, organizational, and cultural factors that shaped American broadcasting's next stage of development.

Commercialized broadcasting should be considered as advertising as well as technology and entertainment. When I began studying radio, there was no history of print advertising with which I could compare my research on radio advertisements. Since then, however, Roland Marchand's *Advertising the American Dream: Making Way for Modernity, 1920–1940* has made my work easier and richer by providing the details of the interwar period's advertising industry and products. Radio advertising proves the point, made convincingly by Michael Schudson in *Advertising, the Uneasy Persuasion*, that advertising is not intuitive but needs to be sold and resold to manufacturers by the advertising industry.[10]

While my introductory sentence raises important considerations of theory and fact, it omits questions of historical methodology. I have found few casual listeners interested in such issues because most believe—along with many historians—that good history simply exists without the need for an explanation of how it was conceived or written. For those readers with concern for such issues, I should note that I am a cultural historian of popular entertainment forms who insists on examining producers, texts, *and* audiences, as well as the economic and technological links among them. As a cultural historian I maintain a primary interest in the radio programs themselves and how they were produced. Yet I entered the profession at a time when social historians seemingly had a lock on political correctness, and literary critics on methodological chic, and my work reflects the changes that the new social history and literary theories have brought to all American historians.

I began my research thinking I would focus my study on the radio programs themselves. But I came to believe that historians can learn little from a popular culture form divorced from its context. Some studies of popular culture focus on the "text"—in this case, the radio programs—without any regard for the economic, organizational, or cultural forces that shaped it. As a result, they miss deeper forms of reflectivity and influence.

Treating radio programs as literature, even when applying the most sophisticated literary theories, often misses the point of broadcasting. In one approach, literary and film critics, writing in a field broadly termed "reader-response criticism" and using a wide range of analytic theories, examine texts and readers to understand how the act of reading may create, or re-create, meaning. Text-centered examinations of how meaning is constituted by readers may provide historians with a method for investigating audiences not available for interview. I have learned from this approach, but I believe its narrow focus is insufficient for the complex historical story I hope to tell.[11] My work considers the production of radio programming and how meaning was invested in it by broadcasters and advertisers. Advertisers may "construct" an audience in a more deliberate fashion than do film directors or authors; in commercialized broadcasting, the material sent over the airwaves exists primarily to gather and retain an audience for the advertising.[12] In exploring the commercial mass media, one needs to understand both the technology and the institutions that control and profit from it, in order to understand the form itself and the audiences for that form.

When studying audience interaction with popular culture, we cultural historians have felt at some disadvantage compared with our colleagues in social history. Social historians working in the tradition of British cultural studies see audiences as active participants in the making of popular culture, and have used sociological and anthropological tools to gauge audience attitudes. Many influential British studies have involved ethnographic interpretations of contemporary audience reactions and have differed somewhat in their political and qualitative focus from those conducted by American communications scholars who address similar issues.[13] Using social history methods proves difficult, however, in studying early broadcasting. For example, social scientists might be interested in the available statistical surveys and letters from early radio listeners, but both sources of evidence have serious flaws. Listeners often wrote to radio stations, but the letters that survive were culled to support the broadcasters' contention that radio constituted a perfect advertising medium. Audience surveys commissioned by advertising professionals contained similar biases.

By considering the audience in relationship to those who produced the radio programs, I can provide a more nuanced picture than is possible with social science methods. I can ask and answer such questions as: How did the radio and advertising industry "construct" listeners? On what assumptions did they base their production of radio programs and advertisements? Were those assumptions valid? Additionally, it is important to recognize that advertisers and broadcasters did not see their audience as monolithic, but paid attention to its racial and gendered makeup. For example, broadcasters kept black entertainers off the airwaves for fear of offending white audience members, and advertisers, knowing that men controlled radio listening, worked to bring women into the broadcast audience. The audience may have been mass, but it was always differentiated. And I am just as interested in what producers thought about radio programming and audiences as I am in what the audiences thought. In this study I examine some of the sources and apply some of the evidentiary standards of social history, but I use them as a cultural historian.

In the end, any isolation of a single element—whether by historians of technology focusing on modes of distribution, literary critics examining texts, or social historians looking only at audience members—misses a synergy: the culture produced by the interaction of all the elements. I examine the entire popular culture equation of producer + text + audience, and the links among the three components, and move back and forth among the components and the links. I believe it is this holistic approach that marks what I do as cultural history.

The chapters in this book move chronologically from the beginning of broadcasting in 1920 until the passage of the Communications Act of 1934, under which broadcasting is still regulated. Chapter 1 examines the forces that caused both listeners and radio manufacturers to think of radio as national. Listeners realized that national programming offered professional performers, coverage of important events, and exciting material not presented by local stations. National radio solved difficult economic problems for broadcasters and radio receiver manufacturers, who worked to refine the technology needed to send a radio signal across the country.

Technological, economic, and cultural factors influenced the choice of a particular technology to provide national radio service. Chapter 2 describes the technologies available and the ultimate decision to provide national radio over wired networks. Wired networks had a deciding influence on the development of broadcast radio because network radio brought expensive charges to rent wires and thus the need for broadcasting, as well as receiver sales, to make money. Broadcast advertising could generate the large profits needed to support a wired system, but ambivalence about radio advertising emerged early and remained. Chapter 3 outlines the arguments over broadcast advertising. The omnipresence of the question, "who is to pay for broadcasting?" showed that many did not immediately accept commercialized broadcasting as the best answer. Potential advertisers and the advertising industry itself doubted that advertisements over radio would work. The networks' attempt to sell radio advertising to advertisers, and broadcasting's resulting acceptance of basic advertising assumptions, had important consequences for the form and content of radio broadcasting.

Wired networks, the need to promote broadcast advertising, and the eventual public acceptance of radio advertising shaped the programs themselves, as discussed in chapter 4. Other forms of national radio service might have presented different performers, formats, and material. Networks dumped local musicians in favor of vaudeville artists who had long performed for audiences scattered across the country and replaced regional sponsors with large companies seeking a national market—companies who had the money to cover the vaudeville stars' fees.

The increasing commercialization and monopolization of the airwaves by the networks was met in the early 1930s with renewed resistance. Chapter 5 relates how the commercialized broadcasters moved quickly, with a paranoia that became characteristic, to smash the backlash, succeeding in destroying most of the nonprofit alternatives. The 1934 Communications Act, which failed to mention advertising or networks, marked a sweeping victory for commercialized radio. The book's conclusion reviews the changes and continuities in broadcasting between 1934 and the present.

The negative results of the acceptance of networks and broadcast advertising were evident as early as the 1930s. Commercialized radio, funded by the sale of time to advertisers, proved rigid in form and less responsive to its audience. Advertisers soon dominated radio and, because of the long-held uncertainty about listener response (a continuing worry today for television networks, which distrust current ratings systems and experiment with "people meters"), advertisers' impressions of what listeners liked actually controlled programming. Advertising forced radio to appeal to mass, rather than specialized (even if quite large), audiences. Advertisers believed they knew the pattern that over-the-air commercials should take. To accommodate the advertisements properly, the format of radio programs became inflexible. A few artists used the rigidity as a spur to creativity, like poets working within a strict sonnet form. But for most it severely restricted programming possibilities. Radio became a way to sell products, and most programs merely filled the time between commercials, just as they do in current television offerings.[14] Programs joined commercials in trying to manipulate the audience—not to entertain or educate or uplift, unless those actions would help sell.

The acceptance that networks and broadcast advertising found in the 1934 Communications Act, combined with developments in radio programming, ultimately determined the form of television. The strange relationship between Americans and commercialized mass media began with radio. Although most realized broadcasting was not as good as it could be, they came to know that they had very little control over specific programs (despite broadcasters' claims to the contrary) and came to use radio and television for various purposes unforeseen by broadcasters and advertisers. For example, programs can serve as a basis for community when listeners or viewers call radio talk shows, join fan clubs, or simply discuss a miniseries's plot and characters at work the next day. Such behavior is not part of the rationale for commercialized broadcast programming, which is supposed above all to entice people to buy products. Americans today simply accept commercialized broadcasting—sometimes using it and sometimes being used by it.

In addition to exploring why and how broadcasting became profitable, we should also consider how this society could have used radio's potential to the fullest. Many Americans in the 1920s disagreed with the idea of making money from radio at all. The struggle against broadcast advertising started before 1920 and continues today in organized pressure groups such as Action for Children's Television, in classrooms where students learn to critically evaluate their connection to television viewing, and in individuals' perceptions of the mass media and their own interaction with it. From radio's beginnings many listeners, educators, and critics disliked broadcast advertising and displayed their opposition both actively and passively. In the end the resisters had less influence than did the powerful radio and advertising industries. Yet examining these resisters is important—not only for what they did, but for their missed opportunities. An examination of the initially foot-dragging advertisers can provide similar insights; realizing that advertisers were reluctant participants in the commercialization of radio obliges us to think about their part in broadcasting as more tenuous and open to change than one might expect. For a significant period, the broadcasting system was unformed and relatively flexible. We must learn to recognize such moments during the introduction of other new technologies and push harder to shape new institutions for the benefit of many people rather than for the profit of the few.

The development of radio broadcasting offers lessons about how a new technology fits into American society and culture and who controls that fit. Some people in the 1920s wanted radio to help reinforce ethnic and regional ties, but instead broadcasters and advertisers tried to reduce listeners to the lowest common denominator, that of consumer. If succeeding technologies will be similarly up for sale to the highest bidder (to be resold as "consumer goods"), then the promise of technology will remain unfulfilled. A study of the commercialization of radio provides at once a historical perspective on the beginnings of our most ubiquitous mass medium, television, and one of our least understood institutions, advertising; a case study of a culture adopting, and adapting to, a new technology; and a striking example of conflict among different groups who seek to influence popular culture and the dissemination of entertainment and information.

1

TOWARD NATIONAL RADIO

The Distance Fiend
A. H. Folwell

He was a distance fiend,
A loather of anything near.
Though WOOF had a singer of opera fame,
And WOW a soprano of national name,
He passed them both up for a Kansas quartet
A thousand miles off and hence "harder to get."
New York was too easy to hear.
He was a distance fiend . . .

He was a distance fiend,
Alas, but he died one day.
Saint Peter obligingly asked, would he tell
His choice of residence—Heaven or Hell?
He replied, with a show of consistency fine:
"Good sir, you have hit on a hobby of mine,
Which place is the farthest away?"
He was a distance fiend.[1]

These two stanzas of a poem first published in *The New Yorker* (and then reprinted in the largest radio magazine) satirized the obsessions of long-distance fanatics in the first days of broadcasting. Such "distance fiends," with their interest in broadcasts from faraway places, served as a bridge between the earliest radio hams and members of the later broadcast audience. The special thrill of early radio for all three groups lay in the listener's ability to hear distant stations. In 1923 *Radio Broadcast* magazine identified one of the attractions of broadcast radio as the "ability to astound our friends by tuning in a program a thousand miles away" and concluded that there "is something fascinating about hearing a concert from a long way off, and the pleasure does not seem to wane with familiarity."[2]

The excitement aroused by long-distance broadcasts seems difficult to recapture today, in an era when we can instantly communicate internationally by phone and fax, turn on the seven o'clock news and casually watch videotaped footage from outer space, and fantasize about intergalactic communication ("E. T. phone home"). Yet in the early 1920s many Americans found broadcasting a miracle and the prospect of becoming part of a national radio audience enthralling. When radio broadcasting began, people all over the country wanted to eavesdrop on distant places, hear reports from faraway locations, or listen to sporting events and country music from their original venues. Both intellectuals and ordinary people were in the process of changing how they thought about time and space, a change that led to a belief that radio could, and should, connect the nation. In addition, the managerial systems, economic structures, and technical expertise already in place to run railroads, electrical lighting, and telegraph systems made it possible to imagine a nationwide radio system even before the technology existed to make such service possible.

The development of national broadcasting clearly brought the most benefit to the corporations that controlled radio. Yet the institution of national radio service reflected a more complex process than the imposition of such a system on an unaware public. A primarily local radio system could have functioned well, and at first that was how radio developed, but other forces encouraged the concept of radio as national in scope. Listeners demanded the chance to hear radio from distant locations and for everyone in the country to hear the same program at the same time, while the radio industry maintained a belief that it was destined to serve more than local audiences. The consensus on national radio service became an important building block in the construction of the American commercialized broadcasting system.

THE URGE FOR DISTANCE

Before large corporations or individual Americans imagined radio broadcasting, a group of skilled hobbyists already talked to each other across the nation using radio. Amateurs counted on the new technology to link individuals feeling isolated in an increasingly industrial society.[3] They proved that there was an interest in national radio service, and they showed how receiving and transmitting signals provided a means of long-distance communication.

Radio thus began as an active rather than passive enterprise. Susan Douglas has vividly described the middle-class, urban white men and boys, the first "hams," who experimented with radio transmission and reception in the decade before World War I, and she has explained why radio started as a principally male activity. Using inexpensive crystals as detectors, oatmeal boxes wound with wire stolen from construction sites as tuning coils, and telephones as headsets, the young hobbyists learned from each other, from magazines, from Boy Scout manuals, and from trial and error to build their own equipment. They designed receivers and transmitters to pick up distant signals and to communicate with each other using their varying skills at Morse code.

These amateurs set up a national network to send messages across the nation. Founded in 1914, the American Radio Relay League (ARRL) connected the 200 various radio clubs and stations from coast to coast. As Douglas writes, "it was the amateurs who demonstrated that, in an increasingly atomized and impersonal society, the nascent broadcast audience was waiting to be brought together."[4] The ARRL network, outlawed during World War I but revived in 1919, enabled amateurs to engage in their favorite activity, communicating with other operators who lived far away.[5] Outside the radio relay, hams held contests to see who could transmit the fastest and the farthest. Douglas has demonstrated that the amateurs forged a concept of masculinity measured by mastery of the new technology rather than by physical prowess. In the process, they "revealed that many middle-class Americans were hungering for a sense of what people in different cities or states were like, what they thought and how they lived" and showed that "these Americans had a feeling that there was more information available to them than they routinely received."[6]

Immediately after broadcasting began, many others joined the hams in their hobby of listening to information sent over the airwaves. The development of the audion and its availability to amateurs after World War

I made the transmission of words and music possible. Listeners no longer needed a knowledge of Morse code—knowledge the young hams had enjoyed developing but which limited the number of radio hobbyists. In addition, amateurs found transmitters more difficult to build than receivers. When each radio fan did not need to be both a sender and a receiver, more people became interested in radio.

As soon as one of the hams, Frank Conrad, a Westinghouse engineer, began to air a regular program of recorded music from a well-made transmitter in his Pittsburgh garage, lots of Americans wanted to listen. They sent sons, or the kid next door, or the war veteran down the block who had learned about radio in the service to buy the materials needed to build a radio receiving set. Conrad's employer, Westinghouse, noticed that it sold more equipment when Conrad broadcast. To further encourage sales, Westinghouse moved Conrad's transmitter to the top of its factory, applied for a federal license, and established regular transmitting hours as station KDKA. Transmissions such as Conrad's to many listeners, rather than the prewar use of radio to communicate between two people, changed radio into a potential mass medium.

Many of the habits and interests of the earlier hams carried over into radio listening as stations built by newspapers, feed stores, municipalities, colleges, and radio equipment manufacturers sprang up across the nation. Because ready-made receivers were not yet available, new listeners needed help to assemble a receiving set from those friends or neighbors who understood radio. Much like the early hackers who helped spread an interest in computers, the prewar hams eagerly helped others build receiving sets and, in the process, indoctrinated them into the culture of radio listening. Hearing a local program was fun, but receiving a transmission from far away was more fun. Long-distance reception proved both your radio skills and the strength and quality of your equipment.

Avid long-distance listeners found programs distracting, since they listened to each broadcast just long enough to verify station call letters and locations. Because of the technical problems involved in early radio, many stations came in clearly for only a few precious minutes; it was a listener's nightmare that such a moment might be given over to music. In January 1924 *Radio Broadcast* reprinted an irate letter:

Dear Sir,
I am making an appeal for many of my B. C. L. (broadcast listener) friends who like to "fish" for distant stations. We are greatly disappointed in the

stations which fail to announce their call signal after each part of the program. It is most annoying to wait through several long pieces, and then hear—"The next selection will be _____ ." WHY *can't* and WHY *don't* all stations give their call signal, and also their location, after every item?

The magazine added that "an effort to correct the annoying omission of call letters by station announcers would undoubtedly be widely appreciated."[7]

Advertisements for receiving sets reflected the obsession with distant radio stations. The January 1923 issue of *Radio Broadcast* featured ads headlined "Concerts from 14 Cities in One Evening," "How Far Can I Hear with MR-6?" and "How Far Did You Hear Last Night?" One advertiser wrote that the "lure of distant stations grips the radio fan" and that "even the seasoned old timer gets a thrill when he brings in a station way across the continent, or sits, in awe, as a clear Spanish message comes thru from Cuba or Mexico." To illustrate how easy radios were to use, the advertisement noted that "a ten-year-old girl in Michigan brings in New York, Denver, Atlanta, Dallas, and other distant stations."[8] Another ad featured a map of the United States with arrows, representing radio waves, converging on Wisconsin from every part of the nation; the copy bragged that during one month in Wisconsin alone "come reports of De Forest MR-6 Receiving Sets getting California, Colorado, Kansas, Texas, Tennessee, Georgia, Kentucky, Pennsylvania, and New York—distances up to 1,500 miles." The copy concluded that "if you want the best radio has to offer—the songs, the stories, the news of the world—more clearly than you have believed possible and from farther away—you can't go wrong on De Forest!"[9] Another ad boasted that "one Radio Expert called the new J. R. H. Model the 'ears to a nation.' It is wonderful to think that all the family can enjoy concerts from near or afar," and added that "all stations come in as 'clear as a bell.'"[10]

With a typical American penchant for quantification, radio fans compared distances heard. The most organized approach to long-distance listening came in the three "How Far Have You Heard?" contests sponsored by *Radio Broadcast* magazine and aimed at the distance fiends, by this time called DX'ers. The first contest announcement, in the November 1922 issue, described the "loose talk" about the great distances heard on simple equipment and noted that "whenever you receive over distances in excess of 500 miles at night or 150 miles by day . . . let *Radio Broadcast* tell its readers how you have done it. For letters published a very liberal rate will be paid."[11] In each of the next four months the magazine published accounts of listening achievements and equipment design submitted by readers. Headlines included "Theodore Bedell, Jr., Has Made an Enviable Record with a Receiver He Built for Ten Dollars" and "64,660 Is the Best Aggregate Mileage So Far."[12] One featured radio fan listed all the stations he heard, but added that he gave little attention to local stations.[13] *Radio Broadcast* announced the results of the first contest and explained the rules for a new contest in the April 1923 issue; Russell Sheehy of New Hampshire won the first contest with an aggregate mileage of 111,540.[14]

During the three following months, May, June, and July 1923, *Radio Broadcast* reminded readers of the second contest and its rules. The August, September, and October issues printed entries and reports on many of the contestants and their equipment. The winner, a "porto rico [*sic*] fan," regularly heard stations on the West Coast, 3,525 miles away, and his article, "A Neighbor at Three Thousand Miles," explained how he had amassed an aggregate of 172,071 miles.[15] Third-prize winner Abbye M. White of Hanover, Pennsylvania, showed that early radio listening had been constructed as a male hobby when she wistfully began her entry:

> Rather fearfully I venture into your contest, for I do not know if we of the fair sex are allowed in or not. But your rules say nothing against it so here I am.

White finished her description:

> I can travel over the United States and yet remain at home. Nightly I visit most of the larger cities in the United States and get much interesting entertainment and instruction.[16]

The third contest began in March 1924 and solicited entries in two divisions: "Ready Made Sets" and "Home Made Sets." Earlier, the editors had worried about the lack of entrants using ready-made sets and had decided "that the purchaser of a ready-made set is generally interested primarily in the entertainment," while the listener who built his or her own set was often "out after distance" and "learns more about fine tuning."[17] The trend toward already assembled sets took the edge off long-distance listening and, indeed, *Radio Broadcast* magazine gave diminished attention to the third contest. The winner of the ready-made division compiled an aggregate mileage of only 85,510, with a best single jump of 2,480 miles, as compared to the winner from the homemade set division, who managed to rack up 121,535 miles, with a best single jump of 3,000 miles.[18] The smaller play given by *Radio Broadcast* to the third contest also reflected changes in the magazine's focus. Coverage of the earlier contests featured lengthy technical descriptions and diagrams of interesting receiving sets. By the summer of 1924 *Radio Broadcast*, like many radio listeners, exhibited as much interest in what was heard on the radio as in how, and from where, the radio signals were received.

The proliferation of radio stations had begun to limit long-distance listening early in the 1920s. But the average fan's devotion to receiving signals from across the nation, in spite of the growing interference of competing local stations, led to a new institution, the "silent night." An early Kentucky broadcaster explained the tradition:

> Christmas came—our first. . . . I heard *Silent Night* so often that I became silent-night-conscious, and felt myself wanting to move about on tiptoe after sundown. Such a saturation of the ether may have suggested an entirely new thought to the Department of Commerce, because shortly after New Year's came this query: "What do you think of having silent nights over the country? Upon one night a week certain stations in specified areas will stay off the air, thus giving better reception of outside stations for people living close to local antennas." It was a worthy thought which we speedily endorsed, choosing for our own use—rather for our own disuse— Mondays, and on January fifteenth, 1923, we observed the first. By and large, this was one of the queerest innovations radio has ever experienced.[19]

Arguments over silent nights raised issues that reoccurred throughout the early 1920s. While many radio stations instituted silent nights, New York City stations never took up the idea. *Radio Broadcast* agreed that the concept was foolish in the nation's entertainment capital, since the "best radio programs obtainable are sent out from New York" and it would be useless to deprive listeners of this entertainment "so that a few enthusiasts may tell their fellow workers on the morrow that they heard Cuba, or San Francisco." The magazine concluded that "silent night may be observed on Main Street, but it never will on Broadway."[20] This assumption of New York's cultural superiority and the differing radio needs of rural and urban areas remained controversial.

Those listeners who lived in areas where stations interfered with each other or who did not like the programs available locally most appreciated silent nights.[21] The busy airwaves of Chicago proved a battleground as migrants to the city and long-time residents fought fiercely over silent nights. One Chicago station refused to shut down, arguing that if it did the owners of small receiving sets unable to pick up distant stations would go without entertainment. One observer granted that while radio's chief use was entertainment "its greatest potential is in the conquering of distance" and noted the value of "sitting in, by radio, on a national political convention . . . halfway across the continent."[22] Silent nights helped many radio entertainment personalities develop national audiences, and left performers and listeners alike eager for national radio.[23]

The custom of silent nights lasted until about 1927. Thereafter local stations joined networks, started selling time, and found the older institution unprofitable and unnecessary. The silent nights were, however, an important precursor of a national radio system. Radio's ability to unite listeners politically and culturally, as demonstrated by the silent nights, remained an important argument for national radio.

Throughout the 1920s listeners continued to seek the thrill of receiving faraway places, but what they hoped to hear transmitted from those places changed. Many observers noted the development of different listening habits in 1924 and 1925. As early as 1923 a *Radio Broadcast* editor wrote that "to many listeners-in, there is no particular fascination in spending half the night bringing in the call letters of some distant stations, whose programme may be mediocre, when at the same time, a good local station is providing excellent entertainment."[24] Six years later an engineer noted that "the first era in popular broadcast reception was that of novelty and of listening to distant stations. This reached a peak in the winter of 1924–25 and has decreased."[25]

Both technological limits and technological advances influenced the change in listening habits. In seeking long-distance receiving records, and even in simple listening for pleasure, listeners came up against the most intractable technological problem in early radio: interference. A 1924 article noted that "the weakest radio impulse sent out by a broadcasting station theoretically continues forever," but explained that "the fact is, there is a limit," even though its existence was often misunderstood by listeners, who thought the only "limiting factor" was the receiving set. The article asked "why can't you always increase the distance by increasing the sensitivity of your set?" and answered in one word, "static."[26] Engineers in the mid-1920s spent much of their time improving receivers and mapping radio broadcast coverage. Yet the long-distance listener, according to one engineer, "found that . . . the enormous fluctuations in night transmission usually termed fading, together with . . . natural and man-made interference, lend to his pursuit the sporting aspects of a game of chance."[27] Listeners reached a technological limit in their ability to pick up distant stations and found that stations had an annoying tendency to fade away, despite the best efforts of the listeners/technicians. The single longest distance and the aggregate mileage heard by the *Radio Broadcast* entrants actually decreased between the second and third contests.

Because engineers could not discover a way to improve long-distance reception, new radio receivers focused on improved reception quality and helped create a new type of radio fan. One historian has noted that early receivers were "designed primarily to amplify the signal as loud as was possible in order to get distant stations. Little thought had been given to tone quality or to appearance of the set." But by 1925 radio manufacturers were sending elaborate displays of radio receivers to major cities for "radio shows" in rented downtown auditoriums. These shows featured sets that looked like furniture and appealed to the whole family, not just to the radio buff.[28] Print advertisements reflected the same change. Unlike previous ads, which had claimed distance records, 1925 *Radio Broadcast* ads pictured the radio in a luxurious living room; described the set as a "radio reproducer" that "transforms mere radio reproduction into artistic recreation"; and declared that a Bristol Loud Speaker yielded "all the rich tonal quality of the singer's voice, its natural sweetness, its pathos."[29] Those who bought the new receivers were most interested in what radio could consistently bring into their home and only secondarily in receiving distant stations.

Turning away from distant broadcasts, listeners returned to their local stations but quickly realized that local programs remained at an amateurish level and failed to provide the thrill of hearing faraway events. New listeners were eager for the wonders of the radio waves—important political speeches and major musical happenings, for example—and often felt that local programs fell short of their expectations. The new audience sought easily available and reliable service featuring both broadcasts from distant places and programming of sophisticated content.

The proportion of "distance fiends" in the radio audience had thus dwindled by the mid-1920s, but they had left an important legacy. The collective memory of listeners retained the possibility, the variety, and the excitement of hearing distant people and events. The early radio fans had whetted the public's appetite for national radio. As one fan wrote, protesting the new interest in programs rather than distance:

> We are impelled by the same urge which brought about the development
> of the boat, the automobile, the telephone, telegraph, the airplane and
> every other invention which has as its object the elimination or reduction
> of the disadvantages which distance has had upon the inhabitants of the
> earth. . . . I think that it is just as reasonable to expect radio fans to try for
> distance in receiving broadcasts as it is for men to try to travel faster or by
> more direct routes. The earth is our home and no matter if at times it does
> seem large, we will eventually master it. These poor itch-crazed fans are no
> different from the pioneers of old, except that they may do their exploring
> from the comforts of an easy chair in a well lighted and warm room.[30]

Listeners wanted radio technology, like earlier technologies, to conquer space, at least partially for the sheer pleasure of being able to do so. Once the technical feat was accomplished, many listeners found the programming from distant places novel and sometimes even better than that broadcast closer to home.

FORMATION OF A NATIONAL AUDIENCE

In the early 1920s, who listened to the radio and why changed twice: amateurs who also transmitted became listeners who sought faraway stations without much interest in what they heard; these distance fiends then gave way to a wider broadcast audience interested in particular programs. Unchanging, however, was the listeners' pursuit of information and entertainment from distant locations. Farmers, sports fans, and homesick rural folks, for example, sought different kinds of radio programming with varying degrees of urgency, but all believed radio could improve their lives by connecting them with places they could not otherwise reach. Their continuing search for information contributed to the urge for a national radio system that would bring them news and entertainment from far away.

Listeners in rural areas wanted to hear broadcasts originating outside their regions for practical reasons. Farmers sought agricultural product prices, weather reports, educational programs designed to break down the isolation of farm life, and the music with which they were familiar. When early broadcasters discovered rural audiences, they began to think of themselves as regional rather than local outlets. Rural migrants, too—especially those from the South who had left their farms for the city—searched the airwaves for stations near their old homes, hoping to hear familiar music and performers.

Farmers needed a knowledge of prices in city markets because commodity brokers in their local communities frequently lied about market conditions. A "country cousin" quoted in a radio magazine told how his mother got better egg prices after the family installed a radio. When the egg buyer stopped off as usual and "told Mom that the egg market was bad and getting worse," she informed him that the New York market quotation for the day was twenty-five cents over his offer. The "old huckster's . . . mouth dropped open like a trap door at a hanging" when Mom told him "cool as a cucumber" that "we get the early morning quotations every day at eight o'clock from New York over the radio. Hereafter, you'll have to get around before that."[31]

Accurate price quotations came only from the market itself, usually located in a distant city. "If you live in Nebraska and have a load of hogs to ship to market," a broadcaster wrote, "you can know the quotations up to the last minute on the Chicago market—by radio."[32] One U.S. Department of Agriculture (USDA) official commented that because of radio, "Distance from market means nothing. The hog raiser in the Corn Belt, or the fruit grower in California, can be . . . closely informed on markets hundreds of miles away."[33] Telegraphed market reports helped, but only for those who lived near a town. *Wireless Age* noted that radio "radiates in all directions, and the most isolated places of the continent do not escape it. The farmer far removed from the centers of population is reached as easily as the big city."[34]

Weather reports remained crucial as well. Newspapers and telephones provided weather information, but it was vague and updated only once a day.[35] Ted Roush of Highland County, Ohio, wrote *Radio Age* magazine that "during harvest season we depended quite a bit on the weather forecast. We did not get any hay wet and were very successful with our harvest, never cutting down with the promise of rain."[36] Both price information and weather reports remained unavailable to farmers on a local basis and proved most reliable when provided by the federal government. The USDA supplied reports on weather and market prices to radio stations as quickly as the stations went on the air. By 1922 thirty-five of the thirty-six radio stations licensed by the U.S. Department of Commerce broadcast USDA market reports, and twenty broadcast weather forecasts.[37] A Keytesville, Missouri, farmer noted, "Radio reported hogs due to drop in two days. Shipped at once. Saved $150. In same week put off haying because of storm warning. This prevented heavy loss of hay."[38] Local stations could have rebroadcast reports received over telegraph wires, but farmers preferred the accuracy, independence, and immediacy of radio reports from regional and national centers that were guaranteed by the federal government.

In addition, the federal government sponsored several series of radio programs aimed at rural listeners, finding broadcasting helpful in carrying the USDA's instructional messages to isolated farm families. County extension agents of the USDA were instructed to encourage farmers to buy or build sets to receive the programs.[39] The USDA provided material to all types of radio stations throughout the 1920s and 1930s. Its programs ranged from those presented by local extension agents to those prepared by the department's Radio Service, which sent scripts (including "Noon-time Flashes," "Housekeepers' Chats," and "Radio Farm School") to interested stations.[40] Such programs provided important options for smaller stations with limited funds; it proved expensive for local radio stations to reach widely scattered rural listeners who needed, at the least, a regional broadcast system not unlike the regional school systems being established at the same time. In the interim, the federal government had the resources (funding and widely scattered staff) to program for rural stations that lacked money and access to performers. In return, the USDA quickly found a captive audience for its messages about how farm families should behave.[41]

Despite the scattered local informational programming and, perhaps, because of the USDA directives included on local stations, rural people persisted in listening to distant stations for the feelings of connectedness and independence they provided. Yet when the market reports, weather summaries, and county extension agent talks were over, country listeners enjoyed little of what they heard on the big city radio stations.[42] Early broadcasters sought a white, urban, middle-class audience and provided the entertainment to keep such people tuning in. Schools, churches, and businesses, who also began radio stations to add luster to their enterprises, often broadcast light classical music deemed genteel by the amateur performers on whom the stations depended for programming. While some farmers may have enjoyed such music, they proved especially responsive when the music most of them played and sang themselves made it onto the airwaves. The most popular programs on early radio featured "hillbilly music"—what we now call country music—rooted in rural white and African American folk traditions. These programs proved to be a hit with both urban and rural dwellers.

The first radio stations programmed randomly, providing airtime for virtually anyone who showed up at the studio and wanted to play. The same story happened time after time: an old-time fiddler would take his turn in front of the microphone, and listeners would flood the station with letters and phone calls begging for more such music. The popularity of these fiddlers and string bands surprised early stations in cities. Station managers thought of themselves as serving a primarily local community, with radio waves stopping at the city limits, and were shocked to find that far-flung rural Americans listened as well.[43]

Reconceptualizing their audience as a regional one, stations in the South and Midwest moved quickly to introduce programs featuring country music performers. Often called "barn dances," these musical variety shows were among the first programs to be broadcast at regularly scheduled times. While the Fort Worth, Texas, station, WDAP, may have been the earliest on the air with such a program in January 1923, WLS in Chicago (the National Barn Dance), WSB in Atlanta, and WSM in Nashville (whose program became the Grand Ole Opry) all featured country music programs within two years. The huge popularity of these shows, as evidenced by letters, listener purchases of songbooks, and attendance at special events presented by the stars, pushed station managers to think of programming for a regional audience. WSB in Atlanta, for example, adopted the slogan of the newspaper that owned the station and advertised that it "covered Dixie like the Dew."[44]

The popularity of southern rural music meant that the regional approach worked particularly well in the southern states, which were just beginning to have the urban centers necessary to support radio stations. By the 1920s white southern music had already been influenced by more than a century of varying cultural traditions and factors: British folk songs, African American music, religious revivalism, industrialization, and commercial genres such as minstrelsy, vaudeville, and Tim Pan Alley. The continuing interaction among racial, ethnic, and regional cultures cross-fertilized southern music traditions so that the music of different groups shared important traits. In addition, the white and black music of the rural South grew out of working lives and circumstances that, despite slavery and segregation, were parallel in many ways. Scholarly arguments about commercial versus folk music and white country versus African American blues tend to obscure fundamental similarities in the musics of southern rural populations. Although radio station managers in the 1920s, afraid of alienating racist whites, banned music they considered "black" from the airwaves and favored the music of certain regions over others, both African American and white listeners were familiar with the southern white music that became popular radio fare. Regional stations in southern cities could program the music of only certain white groups and yet, because of the intertwined development of country music and blues, be assured that some African Americans would also listen.[45]

The mystery is that not only rural people, but city residents, not only southerners and westerners, but northerners and midwesterners, sought out this music. Listeners used the techniques pioneered by the distance fiends to find faraway stations playing country music. The size and composition of early radio audiences are almost impossible to gauge, and the motivation of listeners remains difficult to understand (as is the case even with present-day broadcast audiences). Yet the nation's general ambivalence about rural life in the 1920s, as well as the mass migrations out of the country, may provide partial explanations for the popularity of the barn dance programs. Country music fused the conflicting responses to industrialization with the contradictory, somewhat romanticized feelings many urbanites had about rural life in the 1920s.[46] George Lipsitz has argued convincingly that the class consciousness of country music lyrics made them appealing to urban industrial workers after World War II, and the same phenomenon might well have operated in the 1920s.[47]

Many Americans had left the countryside for small towns and cities in the decades just before the introduction of radio broadcasting.[48] Best documented are the white and African American migrations from the rural South through southern towns to the urban North. Based on the 1910 census, 34 percent of the region's population left during the next fifty years. Such figures do not take into account the continuing movement of rural people who did not own land, sharecroppers who moved for better deals, or migrant farm workers who followed the crops within the South.[49] On the road, or in the cities and towns, displaced country people sought to listen to the music they had enjoyed in their rural communities; hearing it broadcast from their hometown radio stations lent it further authenticity.

By airing country music, radio entertained farm families while simultaneously reuniting rural migrants with their former homes. On the first broadcast of the "National Barn Dance" over the Sears-Roebuck station in Chicago, WLS, the performers requested a square dance caller. The station soon announced that "Tom Owen, a hospital worker, telephoned that he used to call dances down home in Missouri and he'll be right over."[50] The show's biggest star was Bradley Kincaid, a Kentucky transplant who began singing on the radio while taking classes at the Chicago YMCA. Kincaid, a graduate of Berea College, became known for his "pure" renditions of Appalachian mountain songs and remained popular in the East and the Midwest for two decades.[51] WLS listeners in Chicago and in the countryside must have nodded in recognition as these migrants to the big city performed their familiar music and routines. As Pete Daniel has observed about one of the stars of country music in the 1920s:

> Jimmie Rodgers's music about drifting and the blues became part of their heritage. As he sang in "Mean Momma Blues": "I've been from several places, and I'm going to be from here." The line reflected his life and that of thousands of fellow Southerners who drifted upriver, uptown, and the farther they removed themselves from the country, the more alluring country music became.[52]

As Daniel further notes, Rodgers's music also illustrated the intersections between the music of the black and white cultures in the south. African Americans may well have been among those listening to the country music played on the early barn dances. Programmers worked hard to keep any trace of African American music off the airwaves during the early 1920s, allowing only a little whitened-up jazz, because they thought white Americans would reject such music coming into their living rooms. The few statistics available suggest that black Americans bought fewer radios proportionally than did whites. Most observers have concluded that the large rural and poor black population could not afford the cost of receiving sets. In fact, however, black people regularly bought phonographs and race records, probably avoiding radio simply because they heard few broadcasts of equal interest. The large urban audiences for country music might have resulted, in part, from the addition of those African Americans who did have radios. African American listeners would have found much of the music labeled "hillbilly" familiar, since it drew heavily on black music traditions and on the religious and work customs shared by black and white rural southerners. Like their white counterparts, migrant African Americans sought to maintain some connections with the homes they had left behind and may well have enjoyed listening to radio stations in their southern birthplaces.[53]

The folk roots of much country music were directly related to the locations from which it was broadcast. Midwestern barn dance programs differed in content and performers from their southern cousins, with the midwestern shows featuring fewer pure folk songs and singers and more commercial, popular treatments.[54] Migrants twisted the dials to bring in the Grand Ole Opry or the WDAP Fort Worth Barn Dance in order to hear the particular kinds of music and performers they remembered. Barn dances reported fan mail from widely scattered locations.[55]

Other kinds of music also flourished on very early radio, including classical music (notably opera) and some jazz. The dynamic interaction between country music and radio, however, was unique, as early listeners used the barn dance broadcasts to help sustain a rural culture in the middle of the city.

Soon sports fans joined distance fiends, farmers, and country music fans in using radio to obtain information and entertainment from afar. *Popular Radio* began a 1923 story "Football by Radio" with the following vignette:

> Time was when the "old college grad" in a distant city hied himself to a telegraph ticker and waited for the returns of the big football games as they came over the wire, in short, colorless messages. There was an eagerness in his gaze, perhaps an attempt to catch from the face of the announcer an inkling of what had happened before he read the message aloud. But if the old grad had a touch of the philosophical in his make-up, sometimes there came the deadening thought "All this took place minutes ago. If I only knew what is happening *now*."
>
>   Today the old grad is—aurally at least—transported to the ball field by radio.[56]

The old grad wanted the results instantly, and he wanted to feel that he was present at the ballpark. Getting results over the telegraph wire was not enough; he sought out a radio broadcast to hear the progress of the game, to be part of the rooting section for his team. He hoped that adding his supportive cheers to those of his fellow alums might even improve his team's chances.

Distance fiends wanted to hear across long distances for the sheer thrill of conquering space, while farmers and rural migrants wanted specific information and entertainment and sought distant stations that could provide it. But sports fans were interested not only in changing their relationship to space, but also to time, and thus made an additional contribution to the urge for a national radio system. Radio brought sports fans three interrelated forms of information: prompt reports of the outcomes of sport events, detailed descriptions of the events themselves, and the ability to hear then as they happened. Broadcasts of sporting events thus changed the listeners' relationship to both time and space, allowing fans to follow their favorites in a way that rivaled attendance at the ballpark.

Organized sports had grown with industrialization. The explosion of interest in sports in the 1920s no doubt resulted from "commercial promotion and corporate ideologies," but as Elliot Gorn writes, "hoopla and ballyhoo not withstanding, athletic events could stir men deeply" across ethnic, social class, and regional divisions.[57] Professional and college teams were already well organized and funded when broadcasting began, and took place within a structure that emphasized "the people-place relationship." A local team's success brought glory to the town or city where it was based.[58] Attendance at professional baseball games was 9.1 million in 1920 and exceeded 10 million each year during the 1920s. Attendance and interest in baseball flourished, despite the fact that high ticket prices and the afternoon starting times put them out of reach of most working-class people.[59] Boxing, newly welcomed into the realm of acceptable commercial sports, fascinated working- and middle-class men, and championship fights were among the earliest and most successful radio broadcasts.[60]

Sports programming proved a natural for radio, which needed inexpensive programs to fill empty hours. Sporting events happening near the stations could be broadcast with minimal trouble to an audience already interested in the outcome. College sports appealed to the white middle-class males whom radio broadcasters sought to attract. Working-class fans came to love radio coverage because it increased the number of baseball games they could catch—including World Series contests, whose high ticket prices (in 1920, tickets cost between $1.10 and $6.60) and system of selling tickets first to season subscribers had made attendance difficult.[61] From the beginning the broadcasting of sporting events drew long-distance as well as local listeners.

Sports fans, like country music devotees, were affected by the great migrations. Listeners retained strong loyalties to their hometown or college teams and followed their season no matter where the fans had moved. *Radio Broadcast* noted that "there is small thrill in reading the account of a football game the Sunday after. However, you can't always get to a football game that is being played halfway across the continent." The solution lay in "an ably reported football game" that proved "an awfully close second to the real thing."[62] Not only the fans moved; sports teams themselves traveled great distances, and fans back home waited anxiously to hear about wins and losses. One advertisement for a radio receiver boasted, "They All Tried It—but it took a *Ferguson* to bring the Chicago-Dartmouth game to Concord, N.H." The letter featured in the advertisement noted that listeners had missed the first and third quarters of the game due to static and, while this had disappointed the audience, "when they found that no one else even found KYW they were very enthusiastic about the set."[63] One baseball fan noted that radio "made the world wider."[64]

Only a few boxing fans chose their favorite fighters on the basis of geography, but championship boxing matches excited interest regionally and across the country. In 1921 young businessman and radio hobbyist Major J. Andrew White felt "an important event was needed" to introduce "radio telephony to the nation at large." White noted that "this whole country has become interested in the Dempsey-Carpentier fight . . . now why can't my radio be tied up with it? Why can't I send this fight broadcast?"[65] White built a transmitting station at a train station near ringside, stringing his antenna from railroad radio towers and appropriating the dressing shack of the black Pullman porters as his headquarters. He telegraphed a description of the fight from ringside to this makeshift radio station. A "second-hand describer" read White's words over the air. The National Amateur Wireless Association, of which White was the president, set up receivers and loudspeakers at "various halls, theaters, sporting clubs, Elks, Masonic and K. of C. clubhouses," with the price of admission to hear the fight broadcast going to charity. Reports estimated the number of listeners at 300,000, some as far away as Florida, although White himself said that official receiving sets were only "scattered . . . from Maine to Washington [D.C.] and as far West as Pittsburgh."[66] Broadcasts of other fights quickly followed, with several being subsidized by companies hoping to curry favor with boxing fans.[67] As the government and radio industry shut amateurs out of broadcasting, stations made other arrangements to broadcast fights to a large geographic area, including early attempts at networking by sending matches over telephone lines to far-flung transmitting stations for retransmission.[68]

White himself became one of the best-known and most skillful radio sports announcers. The first radio sportscasters supplied listeners with "minute details," making sure no silences ever occurred. One magazine article outlined the attributes of a good football announcer: he must be a fan, familiar with the technique of the game, a "nimble-eyed reporter," an "experienced handler of the microphone," and "a craftsman of words."[69] Listeners wanted to hear the details of the games or matches in order to closely follow the competition and to compare their reactions with those of other fans and with that of the announcer.

The World Series brought all the elements of radio listening together. Like boxing championships, the World Series was an event with national appeal. Both fans following a local team and those interested in a national championship wanted to hear a description of the action and be part of the event. Baseball's appeal crossed racial, ethnic, gender, and class lines, especially at World Series time, and fans whose interest was stirred by a national contest joined those who had followed hometown teams throughout the season. Even if their team wasn't playing, one of the teams that beat them was.

In the 1920s New York City baseball teams dominated the World Series, appearing eleven out of a possible twenty times. New York radio stations, among the most technologically advanced in the nation, thus had local reasons to broadcast the games.[70] Yet despite their best efforts, the 1922 series was heard only as far away as Bridgeport, Connecticut, to the east and Syracuse, New York, to the west.[71] Like boxing championships, World Series broadcasts quickly became experiments in networking, sending programs over telephone and telegraph wires to enable the broadcasts to be heard across greater distances.[72]

In addition to helping create a group of listeners familiar with events and culture nationwide who thought of themselves as part of a large gathering, radio tapped into and enlarged an already existing national audience. Performers and producers of American commercial entertainment had conceived of a national audience long before broadcast radio began. They had been honing their acts and their ideas to appeal to the general public for several decades, as they followed the circuits established by circuses, minstrel shows, chautauquas, vaudeville, and professional and college sports teams. After the establishment of railroad lines, the number of and distance covered by traveling shows greatly increased. In 1887 and 1888 Edwin Booth, the celebrated actor, traveled 15,000 miles in eight months, giving 258 performances in seventy-two communities.[73] While there were differences between the shows available in the cities and those available in smaller towns, the differences were of degree and not of kind. Producers knew that what played in Peoria might seem dull in New York, but with small changes performers and plays appeared from coast to coast. After the turn of the century, vaudeville performers developed a good sense of what would be popular in a particular community and changed their routines to suit their location. Once national radio service was established, the vaudevillians' keen sense of what would possess nearly universal appeal made them the ultimate radio performers. The coming of silent film after World War I meant that even small changes in the entertainment product were no longer possible; the entire nation's moviegoers watched the same films. Sports maintained some regional variation: athletes at smaller colleges and high schools had different skills levels than did those at larger schools, and boxers competing for a national championship provided a different kind of entertainment than did local lads punching it out. But a genuinely national audience existed for certain kinds of sporting events even before radio.

Radio thus gave listeners a chance to repeat and intensify an experience they had already enjoyed: being part of a national audience. Listeners might still have found local radio stations satisfactory had migration been unusual, but the large movements of Americans from farms and small towns to cities in the early part of the twentieth century meant that radio had a different role to play. National radio service was not imposed on ordinary people by the radio industry; both listeners and transmitters had long tried to "connect" the nation through broadcasts. In the early years the desire for national radio bubbled up from the bottom, as well as flowed down from the top. Yet because the industry developed national service to satisfy its own needs, the listeners' preferences came to be less important in programming decisions. National radio as instituted by the radio industry featured a few broadcasters reaching many widely scattered listeners and thus often disappointed listeners who had initially sought more diverse broadcast voices. The popularity of the barn dance programs suggests that many Americans in the 1920s wanted to hear radio broadcasts from distant places in order to maintain regional, racial, or ethnic distinctiveness in their lives.[74] Country music added a working-class, rural element to early radio that it lost as broadcasting nationalized. The form and content of national radio service, once established, served the needs and desires of the large receiver and transmitter manufacturers better than it did those of ordinary listeners. The form in which national radio developed encouraged homogenous, rather than differentiated, programming. While local radio stations continued to aim specialized programming at some local listeners, national networks ignored differences, pushed aside music in favor of variety and drama, and presented and depended on a white, urban, middle-class, East Coast sensibility. Early listeners who had seen radio as a way to annihilate space, gain control over information, and maintain ties to a rural way of life, and who had demonstrated radio's ability to attract a national audience, had hoped for something different.

ROOTS OF NATIONAL RADIO SERVICE

When broadcasting began, economic and organizational precedents guided its development into a national service. Not only the needs and interests of ordinary listeners, but the economic, technological, and intellectual climate of the early 1920s pushed radio broadcasting to become national. Large companies controlled the production of radio receivers and transmitters and were therefore the first to be interested in broadcasting. These corporations had a national outlook and an interest in broadcasting to the entire country. In addition, the new search for information and entertainment from distant locations reflected changes in public attitudes toward technology and its relation to space and time.

In the decades before broadcast radio appeared, intellectuals and ordinary Americans shared a belief that new communications technologies should draw the United States together. Worries about the nation becoming fragmented into opposing camps—immigrants versus native-born and rural versus urban, for example—in addition to concerns regarding the physical and psychological dislocation caused by industrialization were commonplaces of American thought in the 1920s. The radio, telephone, and telegraph, it was commonly believed, could connect people to places and to each other.

The first scholars who studied communications seconded this belief that new technologies could reunite and improve the nation. Daniel Czitrom writes that Charles Horton Cooley, John Dewey, and Robert Park "construed modern communication essentially as an agent for restoring a broad moral and political consensus to America, a consensus they believed to have been threatened by the wrenching disruptions of the nineteenth century: industrialization, urbanization and immigration."[75] These men, writing in the late nineteenth century, saw new technologies as a means for transcending individual isolation.

By the early 1920s, when radio broadcasting became possible, ordinary Americans had joined intellectuals in accepting this role for communications technologies. As Stephen Kern outlines in *The Culture of Time and Space:*

> The present was no longer limited to one event in one place, sandwiched tightly between past and future and limited to local surroundings. In an age of intrusive electronic communication "now" became an extended interval of time that could, indeed must, include events around the world. Telephone switchboards, telephonic broadcasts, daily newspapers, World Standard Time, and the cinema mediated simultaneity through technology.[76]

The public became used to the idea that new technologies conquered time and space. Writers in the popular press viewed the future of radio broadcasting in the 1920s in much the same way as did the intellectuals: the introduction of radio broadcasting was seen as a chance to improve society. Radio could overcome the problems and anxieties brought about by the disruptions of industrial capitalism.[77] Journalists outlined utopian visions that had little impact on the form radio broadcasting ultimately took because such visions clashed with the pursuit of profits by the powerful companies that controlled radio. Yet journalists believed that their goals—overcoming isolation, reuniting an increasingly heterogeneous society, and improving morality—could be achieved if radio reached large numbers of widely scattered listeners at the same time with the same message. An article in *Collier's* claimed that radio would become "a tremendous civilizer" that would bring "mutual understanding to all sections of the country, unifying our thoughts, ideals, and purposes, making us a strong and well-knit people."[78] Popular writers clearly thought radio could fulfill its potential by providing national service.

The forms and structures taken by previous technologies influenced the way in which radio broadcasting came to be thought of and developed. The creation of a national railroad system was the first and therefore most important step in creating a national market and the economic and organizational structures needed to service it. The railroads pioneered in the innovations needed to deliver goods and services to large numbers of people. Most Americans simply assumed that complex technological and administrative arrangements could be easily put into operation—if enough managers were hired, anything could be done. The growth of railroads brought with them a new way of thinking about the nation as connected, including standard time zones, methods to precisely time and coordinate the scheduling of trains, and the possibility of moving a product efficiently across vast distances.[79] Railroads provided a model and a base on which to build the particular form of national radio system that was instituted in the United States.

Most in American government and the radio industry assumed that national radio would be regulated on the railroad model. People thought and wrote of radio in terms of transportation metaphors; writers described "highways through the sky" and "traffic cops" who kept order in the air. Because only a certain number of stations could broadcast without interfering with each other, regulation would be needed to deal with the scarcity of broadcast channels or frequencies. One legal observer noted that "it is as though we have too few tracks to accommodate our trains, or not enough streets for our automobiles, or too little ocean for our ships."[80] The radio industry believed federal regulation could benefit them by rationalizing frequency allocation, much as it had benefited national railroad companies at the expense of local companies. Radio companies favored national radio in part because they shared an understanding with government about how national radio service might be regulated in the best interest of the largest companies.

The telegraph, which grew alongside the railroads, also contributed ways of thinking, technological innovations, and managerial and regulatory precedents. A single company operated a nationwide system of wires, strung from coast to coast by the 1860s. The establishment of the news wire services meant that, along with business and personal news, the telegraph brought word of political events as they happened. In 1852 the *New York Herald* pointed out that it was no longer necessary to consider relocating the federal government to the geographic center of the country because the "telegraph has entirely superseded the necessity for any such movement."[81] In addition, the long-distance capabilities of the telegraph "forced the rapid growth of the multiunit managerial enterprise," upon which a national radio service could be modeled.[82] Czitrom believes that the form of American broadcast radio evolved from a blend of experience with the telegraph (technologically and organizationally) and the motion picture (in terms of content and form). Both earlier technologies contributed to the push for national radio coverage, yet neither provided many hints about the economic basis for such a system.[83]

Long-distance telephone service remained difficult until the invention that also made broadcasting possible. The repeater or audion, an improved vacuum tube, amplified sound waves and picked up and reproduced the voice. With the use of the audion, telephone signals would not fade at crucial moments, and radio transmission of voices, as well as of signals, became possible. Radio had still other problems to face in long-distance transmission, but 1915 brought the first long-distance telephone line from New York to San Francisco.[84] By the time long-distance telephone service was technically possible, a technological infrastructure already existed in the extensive local telephone lines. This national system of telephone wires, and secondarily of telegraph wires, played an important role in the technological evolution of a national radio system.

In addition to providing a national network of wires and the idea that communications could reach across the nation instantly, telephone service also provided another precedent for national radio service. American Telephone and Telegraph (AT&T), as the result of pressure on its monopoly position in long-distance service, in 1913 allowed individual systems not owned by AT&T to use its long-distance telephone lines. This so-called Kingsbury Commitment opened long distance to individual telephone users and showed AT&T, as well as the radio industry, that a company could maintain a profitable national monopoly without controlling every part of the enterprise.[85]

These new technologies brought both cultural dislocations and continuities. More so than the more public telegraph or railroad, telephones—a domestic, personal technology—paved the way for the use of radio broadcasting as home-based and family-oriented. At first people often felt uncomfortable with a communications technology that entered the privacy of their homes, perhaps exposing family secrets and definitely expanding family interactions with outsiders. Carolyn Marvin, in *When Old Technologies Were New*, argues that the telephone had to be "domesticated," made to seem part of ordinary family life, before it was widely adopted. At the same time, people also used the new technologies to preserve entrenched values.

Marvin shows how new technologies could fit into ordinary life without changing the ways Americans related to each other. The telephone reinforced already existing gender, race, and class relations, for example.[86]

Broadcasting thus appeared in a society already experienced with integrating new technologies into everyday life and into its economic and political structures. Changes in beliefs and management had been developed to cope with the railroad, the telegraph, and the telephone. Yet old ways of thinking and older forms of economic organization shaped the evolution of each new technology. The radio industry, for example, relied on the precedents of the railroad, the telegraph, and the telephone in working out the relationship between radio and the federal government. When broadcasting began, several national companies controlled radio through a patent pool, the Radio Corporation of America (RCA). After World War I, the federal government had urged the establishment of RCA to ensure that American firms controlled wireless technology, a control considered important to the nation's security. Once the patent issues were sorted out, private control of the production of radio receivers and transmitters seemed normal, given the American economic structure. Radio manufacturers and the government at first viewed broadcasting as an adjunct to the production of radio receivers and transmitters, and therefore did not question its privatization.[87]

As it became clear that broadcasting would be a bigger and more complex business than mere receiver production, the radio industry used the precedents of railroads, telegraphs, telephones, electric lighting, and other utilities to keep its activities regulated, but not directly owned, by the federal government. The so-called "natural monopoly" of the telegraph system had been put in place in the 1860s; one company controlled national telegraph service with the approval and aid of the federal government. Telephone service also followed this model, with AT&T allowed a monopoly if it submitted to government regulation, a practice that helped rationalize the industry. The concept of natural monopoly was based on the assumption that some technologies were destined to be national resources and thus best managed by helping them reach the most people. Radio industry leaders believed that treating radio as a natural monopoly would help it reach the most people and therefore generate the most profits on both the manufacturing and broadcasting sides, and so RCA sought federal regulation to rationalize the broadcasting business. Thus patterned on the "natural monopoly" thought to be inherent in the railroads, telegraph, and telephone, RCA would control access to both production technology and to the airwaves at the same time that it expanded service in both areas.[88]

Aside from government regulation, broadcasters came to consider national radio the answer to their organizational problems. Early broadcast radio was composed of small, struggling, unconnected units. Through centralization and the creation of a system, other technologies such as electric lighting had improved both their economic standing and their service to the consumer. Surely, by coordinating their efforts, a group of radio stations could similarly cut costs and improve programming. Just as the largest companies in the lighting, railroad, and telegraph industries had begun the movement toward systemization, so the large radio manufacturers led the way to national radio.[89]

Prodded by listeners, precedents, and their own financial forecasts, the companies controlling radio thus moved to furnish national radio service. Several crucial questions remained. Who would pay for national service, and how would it be provided? The radio industry conceived of national radio service before it knew how to make money directly from broadcasting, and before it had the technology to send radio waves across the nation. The technological, structural, and financial questions facing national radio remained intertwined. No one—not engineers, not amateurs, not distance fiends, not financial wizards, not government regulators—knew how to reliably send broadcasts across the nation or how to finance such a service.

Listeners wanted a broadcasting system that would allow them to hear distant events as they occurred. Receiver and transmitter manufacturers sought to profit from national broadcasting. But early radio still lacked the technological and economic structures to broadcast to a large geographic area. The "radio trust," as the press now called the receiver set and transmitter manufacturers, quickly began experimenting with technological options for providing national radio service. The choice of a technology to provide national service became the main factor shaping the next stage of American broadcast radio.

THE RISE OF THE NETWORK SYSTEM

The concept of national radio service existed before the economic and technological arrangements were available to make such service a reality. Even moving toward a national radio service exaggerated broadcasting's unsolved problems. But the manufacturers of radio receiving and transmitting equipment, joined together by a patent agreement, needed to tackle these problems to keep profiting from the technology. The severe financial difficulties faced by local stations meant that both the quantity and quality of programs might decline, listeners might abandon radio for a new fad, and the need for receivers and transmitters would disappear. To keep demand for their products high, the large radio manufacturers needed to ensure that broadcasts went over the air. David Sarnoff, vice-president of the Radio Corporation of America (RCA), explained that "we broadcast primarily so that those who purchase" RCA radios "may have something to feed those receiving instruments with." He added that "without a broadcast sending station, the broadcast receiver is just a refrigerator without any ice in it."[1] A national system could lower the cost of providing the ice.

In the early 1920s the radio industry believed that radio had to present high-quality entertainment since, as *Radio Broadcast* wrote, "audiences can't be held with second-rate stuff."[2] Quality programming entailed high costs. It was too important to be left to small, independent transmitting stations, and yet the costs of maintaining a large number of well-programmed stations might strain even a huge corporation. Sarnoff described the "hopelessness of attempting to pay for the services of five hundred groups of high-grade artists broadcasting nightly from . . . widely scattered stations."[3] If small stations could not afford to present programs that would hold an audience, manufacturers of radio sets would have to ensure high-quality programming or risk slumping sales. It obviously made economic sense to provide one or two strong programs from a single source rather than attempt to tailor individual programming to 500 local stations.

Yet Sarnoff shocked participants at the Third National Radio Conference in 1924 with his plan to build several "super-power" stations to provide nationwide broadcasts. The radio industry representatives at the conference, invited to Washington by Secretary of Commerce Herbert Hoover, heard Sarnoff boast that one transmitter near New York City, plus additional super-power stations as needed, would enable RCA to provide national radio service. Howls of indignation greeted Sarnoff's plan. Local stations, fearful of interference and of outright blocking of their signals, protested that super-power transmitters would give RCA a monopoly of the airwaves. Sarnoff dismissed their objections lightly, no doubt equally pleased by the controversy his plan generated and by the prominence given RCA in news reports.[4]

The U.S. Department of Commerce had carefully planned a series of four such radio conferences to provide backing for the Secretary's views on radio regulation. The first two conferences, held in 1922 and 1923, had resulted in unsuccessful legislative proposals, while by the third, issues of "interconnection" had become paramount.[5] Participants at the Third National Radio Conference thus debated questions about national radio service that had important implications for local broadcasting as well, and to which no one had answers: Who pays for broadcasting? What technology should provide radio programs? Who controls radio?

As the radio industry gradually answered these questions, national radio changed from a service that could connect different regions to a way of saving money by providing the same program to every listener. The radio companies hid the cost-cutting function of national radio behind the promise of improved programming, while the objective of national radio subtly shifted toward the provision of urban, "quality" programs to rural hicks. One of the subcommittees of the Third National Radio Conference reported that "improvement in programs is essential" and that such improved programs resulted from interconnecting "broadcasting stations, bringing the programs of the larger centers of art, music, and events of public interest to the more remote broadcasting stations."[6]

The large manufacturers of receivers and transmitters quickly experimented with technologies to provide national radio service because they had an incentive to find such a technology, as well as the financial means and the expertise to conduct the experiments. Three possibilities existed— super-power, shortwave rebroadcasting, and wired networks—and the largest radio manufacturers each invested in a different technology. Building on their already established strengths, these companies sought national radio service to maintain and improve their positions in the industry. The final choice of a technology to provide national service resulted from cultural pressures as well as from technological factors and a renegotiation of the radio trust's patent agreement.

FUNDING BROADCASTS

The question "who pays for broadcasting?" occurred repeatedly in article and chapter titles of the early 1920s, and in the recollections of observers.[7] Early broadcast radio had huge financial problems. A variety of different businesses from feed stores to newspapers founded and financed radio stations but provided them with only small budgets. Faced with the need for day-in and day-out programming, broadcasters relied first on amateur musicians and then on those professional performers they could convince to appear for free. As listeners began to turn away from long-distance listening and to seek improved programming, broadcasters faced increasing pressure and anxiety.

Manufacturers of radio sets and parts supported several early transmitting stations. David Sarnoff believed that "the expense of broadcasting is one of the 'production costs' of the radio industry. . . . it figures in the prices paid by purchasers of radio equipment."[8] Other companies saw no clear return on their investments in radio and so had no incentive to support the stations they had founded. For example, several newspapers initially sponsored radio stations but quickly found broadcasting expensive and basically unrewarding. "What is the good of a newspaper running a radio?" asked T. J. Dillon, managing editor of the *Minneapolis Tribune.* "We decided that the return in good will was not worth the expense involved."[9] Most early stations began broadcasting with little idea of how to finance either their program needs or operating costs.

Maintaining a broadcasting station became more problematic as expenses mounted. One economist thought that the high mortality of broadcasting stations was due to their large capital investment, their high operating expenses, and the absence or intangibility of their income.[10] In July 1924 the manager of a midwestern 500-watt station wrote that over the last winter "our talent cost us $700 per month, besides $200 for an operator and many other expenses too numerous to mention." He complained, "We have put about $50,000 of our money into radio during the past 12 months and we have never received back one dollar in cash returns. We no doubt have lots of good-will and are nationally advertised, but we cannot cash in on our advertising." The station could not "see our way clear to withdraw; we have too big an investment to throw it away; yet every day we stay with it, we put in more money without hope of cash return."[11] Other small stations would have found these problems familiar, although most early radio stations did not pay performers.

Early broadcasters had not expected a direct profit from programming and were surprised that anyone else thought to make money from appearing on the radio. Station managers considered singers and instrumentalists well rewarded by the publicity value of their broadcast appearances and the novelty of the experience. But first-rank performers began to demand fees for their services from the seemingly prosperous radio station owners and receiver manufacturers. When in 1922 the American Society of Composers, Authors, and Publishers (ASCAP) first raised the issue of royalties for music performed on the radio, the idea caught broadcasters by surprise.[12] Suddenly performers were demanding compensation, listeners were calling for better programs featuring currently popular songs, and ASCAP was proposing music royalties. The economic headaches of station owners and operators multiplied.

As early as 1922, David Sarnoff sought a solution to the problems of WJZ, a New York station in which RCA had a financial interest. In typical fashion, Sarnoff sought to kill two birds with one stone by increasing RCA's influence and power at the same time he bailed out WJZ. He noted that the "question of 'who is to pay for broadcasting' is a large one or a small one in proportion to the number of broadcasting stations which need be erected and operated in order to give a national broadcasting service." Pointing out that "if it were possible to cover the country with one, two or three broadcasting stations, the question of expense of operation and the matter of procuring and paying suitable artists becomes very much simplified," Sarnoff believed that the "Radio Corporation alone might be in a position to do the whole job and pay for it out of returns from sales."[13] The large radio manufacturing companies thus began to see national radio service as a cost-saving measure.

From the beginning, the issues of national radio and who paid for radio service raised questions about broadcast advertising. In another shocking and much-quoted speech at the Third National Radio Conference, Herbert Hoover declaimed that "the quickest way to kill broadcasting would be to use it for direct advertising. . . . if a speech by the President is to be used as the meat in a sandwich of two patent medicine advertisements there will be no radio left."[14] Sarnoff initially presented "superpower" broadcasting as an alternative to using advertising to finance radio. He told the delegates that it should be "the self-imposed duty of the radio industry" to distribute radio programs on a national scale and implied that these programs would be free of advertising.[15]

Some local and independent radio stations distrusted Sarnoff's offer and worried about the monopolistic implications of placing control of national service in the hands of the "radio trust." Powel Crosley, an independent radio manufacturer and broadcaster, wrote that the large radio companies obviously would gain from a takeover of national broadcasting. He worried that "as soon as broadcasting is completely controlled, a means will be devised to collect money from radio listeners."[16]

Such concerns proved justified. The radio manufacturers soon found a way to provide national service without paying for it themselves and, in fact, came to profit from broadcasting as well as from manufacturing. The opposition of the smaller broadcasters and the continuing concern over monopoly, however, did affect the eventual technological and economic shape of national service: radio networks would be structured so as to appear to support local, independently owned stations.

TECHNOLOGICAL OPTIONS FOR NATIONAL
RADIO SERVICE

The "radio trust" already knew in the early 1920s what it wanted to do, but it faced one remaining obstacle: nobody knew how to send the same signal to every receiver. Before they could guarantee and then increase their profits, the large radio manufacturers needed to find a technology that could deliver programming to the entire nation.

From the earliest battles over radio turf, the receiver and transmitter manufacturing companies had learned the importance of being quick to step into unexplored technological territory, and they were determined not to be left behind on national radio. Each component of the radio industry therefore experimented with a different technology for transmitting signals nationwide (super-power, shortwave rebroadcasting, and wired networks), in hopes of protecting and expanding its own position within the industry.

As early as the Third National Radio Conference the technological options were clear. Sarnoff had thrown down the gauntlet when he announced that RCA would use super-power to provide its nationwide programming. He based his concept of super-power on the idea that a simple increase in a transmitter's power output would send the radio signal farther. He denied that such a plan would interfere with local stations, which he believed would continue to provide community service, as local newspapers did in the presence of wire services.

Before Sarnoff spoke, delegates had heard Secretary Hoover describe two other possibilities for connecting existing radio stations. Hoover noted that "we owe a debt of gratitude to those who have blazed the way. The pioneers have been the American Telephone and Telegraph Company, in wire interconnection, and the Westinghouse Electric and Manufacturing Company, in radio interconnection through the use of short wave lengths."[17] A central source could send programs through wires to local stations for broadcast over the airwaves. Alternatively, a central station could broadcast a program over shortwaves, thought to travel farther than the medium waves radio stations commonly used. Specially equipped local stations could pick up the shortwave broadcast and rebroadcast it over medium waves.

Hoover supported interconnection because he wanted to maintain the existing local stations that were strong allies for the Department of Commerce's views of radio. In addition, Hoover sought a system that would calm fears about monopoly in the radio industry.[18] In choosing interconnection over super-power, he bet on a winning horse, but no doubt his backing influenced the outcome of the race.

Sarnoff, like Hoover, had a clear understanding of the three options for national radio service. Further, he showed his awareness of why particular companies backed different forms of national radio by pointing out AT&T's prior control of a wired network and Westinghouse's ownership of several widely scattered radio stations.[19] Sarnoff fudged on the reasons for his own espousal of super-power, failing to mention either the cost effectiveness of maintaining only a few super-power stations or his continuing drive to promote both RCA and himself as preeminent in all phases of the radio industry. His promotion of super-power notified both the delegates to the Third National Radio Conference and RCA's patent partners that RCA would fight to play a part in national radio service.

The peculiar provisions of the 1919 patent pooling agreement, in which General Electric (GE), Westinghouse, and AT&T formed the Radio Corporation of America, meant that each company had its own perspective on how to nationalize the radio audience. RCA took shape as a result of government intervention after World War I to keep a new radio transmitter design, the Alexanderson alternator, out of the control of the British-owned Marconi Company. GE, Westinghouse, and AT&T created RCA (which took over the American Marconi Company) to serve as the independent marketing arm of a patent pool. GE and Westinghouse thus manufactured RCA receivers and parts, with 60 percent of the production assigned to GE and 40 percent to Westinghouse. AT&T made and sold transmitters and controlled both wired and wireless telephony. GE, Westinghouse, and AT&T owned RCA stock and had representatives on the RCA board of directors.[20]

Under the patent agreement, AT&T controlled radio transmitters and had sole right to sell airtime to advertisers. Its interest in broadcasting also related to its control of a wired communication system, the telephone. After the opening of its own radio station, WEAF, AT&T planned a national system of telephone company radio stations connected by telephone wires, and therefore refused other broadcasters the use of telephone lines to connect radio stations. This denial of the most technologically feasible plan for national radio service obliged other companies to experiment with alternatives.

GE and Westinghouse also owned several radio stations. In seeking a technology other than the forbidden AT&T wires to link these stations, they experimented with shortwave rebroadcasting. As the marketing arm of the patent pool, however, RCA remained more concerned with protecting radio set sales than with profiting from program transmission or station ownership. To RCA executives, super-power broadcasting seemed the easiest and cheapest way to provide programming that would keep the sale of receivers high.

SUPER-POWER

The RCA super-power plan, put forward by Sarnoff as early as 1922 within RCA, proposed the establishment of several radio stations equipped with high-powered transmitters. Owned and programmed by RCA, these stations would broadcast signals nationwide and would cheaply ensure that purchasers of RCA receiving sets heard something when they turned on their radios.

One of the most influential individuals in early radio, Sarnoff had arrived in the United States from Russia at the age of nine and launched his radio career seven years later, in 1906, as an office boy with the Marconi Wireless Telegraph Company. The young Jewish immigrant learned about both the technical and business aspects of the new company in order to bridge the gap between engineers and managers. He quickly graduated from office boy to wireless telegraph operator on ships, at remote shore installations, and in the display station in Wanamaker's department store. While at Wanamaker's he took a small part in relaying the names of victims of the sinking of the *Titanic* to waiting relatives. By World War I Sarnoff was a junior executive with the American branch of the British Marconi Company. After the war he represented the company in the negotiations that led to the founding of RCA, and he secured a position in RCA when it took over American Marconi. Always more interested in prestige than money, Sarnoff worked tirelessly during the 1920s to create a role for RCA within the radio industry. The former office boy eventually became president of RCA and for decades continued to help shape the broadcasting industry.[21]

In later years RCA and NBC publicity hailed Sarnoff as a "prophet" for his predictions about radio's future, starting with a 1915 "radio music box" memo in which he predicted broadcasting.[22] This reputation depended on people remembering only Sarnoff's good guesses and forgetting his mistakes. Further, he had the power to make his predictions come true and a publicity machine to acclaim his correct guesses after he had helped realize them. Besides illustrating the limits of his predictive talents, the campaign for super-power in the early 1920s shows Sarnoff to have been a knowledgeable and wily radio insider. His advocacy of super-power was a carefully timed and planned crusade to improve RCA's position within the radio industry and to influence negotiations then taking place among patent pool members.

Sarnoff first spoke of super-power, although not by that name, in two speeches in January 1923. In these two talks he made predictions rather than taking up a cause as he was to do later.[23] Beginning in November 1923 he made a series of speeches promoting super-power broadcasting. What one observer called "the opening volley in Sarnoff's campaign for high-power broadcast services" came on November 15, 1923, in a speech to the Electrical Supply Jobbers Association meeting in Buffalo.[24] Sarnoff told these salespeople that the current number of stations was "a transient phenomenon in the march of events" since most of the stations would soon go out of business and could be replaced by a few super-power broadcasters. Sarnoff captured the appeal of national radio when he said that "no other agency can speak with a single voice to 10,000,000 people." With three to six stations, "each . . . simultaneously radiating the same program," the system would have "a power sufficient to reach every city, every town, every village, every hamlet, every home in the United States" and "an organization capable of measuring up to the responsibilities of the character of a national service."[25] Sarnoff also discussed the implications of super-power broadcasting for international communications, a subject in which RCA, because of the provisions of the patent agreement, maintained an interest.

Sarnoff gave six speeches after November 1923 and testified before the House Committee on Merchant Marine and Fisheries, which had jurisdiction over radio. In these appearances he further outlined super-power, emphasizing different aspects of the plan. He spoke of the technology as helping radio to fulfill its destiny by providing national service, and even compared super-power broadcasting with the systematization of electrical lighting.[26] In general, he presented super-power as a technological solution to an economic problem. He raised the subject of super-power stations in his discussion of "who is to pay for broadcasting?" saying that the question posed a simple "technical problem." Sarnoff argued that "as long as the present 559 broadcasting stations in this country are maintained, the situation is hopeless," and found the solution in "a few super-powered stations which will reach every home in the country."[27]

Sarnoff's speeches received some publicity. *Radio Broadcast*, referring to a 1924 Chicago speech, wrote that "to the businessman" super-power seems "probably the simplest solution of the problem and possibly it will be the final one."[28] The surprise of the Third National Radio Conference delegates stemmed from the difference between Sarnoff's previous theoretical speeches and the concrete nature of his conference proposal. He told the delegates flatly that RCA stood "ready to begin the immediate erection of a great super-power broadcasting station," followed by "the construction of another super-power station at some point where the limit of reliable effectiveness had been reached by the first station."[29]

Anticipating protests from local stations, Sarnoff said the idea that super-power would destroy local stations was "as groundless as would be the belief that a national highway would obviate the need of local roads."[30] The metaphor failed to quiet critics. Walter Strong, a representative of the American Newspaper Publishers Association, doubted whether such super-power stations could reach the distances claimed for them. C. D. Erbstein, the operator of a small radio station in Elgin, Illinois, worried that powerful national stations might interfere with the reception of local stations. Others complained about the potential for monopoly of the airwaves by the super-power stations.[31]

Pressed on the monopoly issue, Sarnoff revealed the underlying reason for his super-power crusade. "Far be it from me to hurl charges of monopoly against anybody," Sarnoff told a Third National Radio Conference committee, but currently the only method for presenting nationwide broadcasts was connecting small stations by wire. "I make no charges against the American Telephone and Telegraph Company," Sarnoff continued, "but I say it is ridiculous to assume that the development of another and independent means of communication is in the direction of monopoly." Super-power and the AT&T wires would be "independent competitive methods" for providing national radio.[32] After a year and a half of talking about super-power broadcasting, Sarnoff had finally admitted the purpose of his crusade: to put RCA in direct competition with AT&T in providing national radio service.

Sarnoff's first two speeches on super-power, in January 1923, had come at the beginning of a fight within the radio patent pool provoked by AT&T's refusal to rent wire lines to RCA. RCA had hoped to broadcast the 1922 World Series using wire line pickups, a request that AT&T refused. In January 1923 Sarnoff again tried to lease telephone wires and AT&T again turned RCA down.[33] During the spring and summer, RCA negotiated quietly with AT&T. In September RCA initiated arbitration proceedings, an action provided for by the original patent agreement. The parties signed the final arbitration agreement—an outline of issues to be discussed—on November 1, signaling the end of behind-the-scenes negotiations. Sarnoff's campaign for super-power stations began two weeks later and may have been an attempt to influence the arbiters and public opinion. On November 13, 1924, the arbiters presented a draft report of a decision that represented a victory for RCA, giving GE, Westinghouse, and RCA the right to use pickup wires and sell broadcasting time. The final resolution of the patent fight did not come until 1926, but the 1924 RCA victory brought a quick end to Sarnoff's speeches on super-power.[34] The campaign for super-power was thus a skirmish in the continuing radio patent battle.[35]

Luckily for RCA, the battle moved to other fronts, because the technology available in the mid-1920s proved inadequate for super-power broadcasting. A super-power transmitter had to throw its signal a long distance, which proved to be more difficult than Sarnoff had expected. Already established stations worried that RCA's super-power stations would interfere with other radio signals, but everyone assumed that super-power stations themselves would be unaffected by interference. A 1926 article by Alfred Goldsmith, RCA's chief broadcasting engineer, detailed the precautions taken so that the new 50-kilowatt transmitter at Bound Brook, New Jersey (the experimental transmitter Sarnoff had described at the Third National Radio Conference), would not interfere with neighboring local stations.[36] Ironically, the interference caused by other stations, plus atmospheric disturbances, impeded the transmitter. Goldsmith's article casually mentions that the signal from a 50-kilowatt station was reliable for a radius of only 100 miles.[37] Sarnoff's original dream of one or two stations blanketing the entire United States obviously assumed that super-power transmitting stations would have a much larger service range.

At the Fourth National Radio Conference in 1925, Hoover again addressed the issue of super-power, commenting that "our experience during the year has somewhat more clearly defined the geographical area within which a single broadcasting station can give complete service. . . . it will be found that the real effectiveness of a station falls within a comparatively small zone." Hoover reported that the Bureau of Standards had determined that a 50-kilowatt station would not cover more than 100 miles—thus corroborating Alfred Goldsmith's measurements.[38] As late as 1929 a review of the development of broadcasting technology noted that because of fading and interference, "it has proved impossible up to the present time to build a sufficiently powerful broadcasting station to give consistently good quality over any large portion of the United States."[39] The tendency of a super-power station's signal to fade at night and to be sharply curtailed during the day made it impossible to use super-power to provide national radio service during the 1920s.

Super-power failed to become the choice to provide national radio service for another reason beside technological impediments: super-power transmitters presented a clear threat of monopoly control over broadcasting content. In theory, a mixed system of super-power and local radio stations might have worked well for a service that provided national broadcasts and still maintained local stations with diverse programming. Yet those outside the radio patent pool worried that smaller stations would be unable to survive economically, technically, or programmatically in competition with super-power stations owned and operated by RCA. The widespread American distrust of monopoly in any form played an important role in the rejection of super-power and the shaping of the national radio system.

SHORTWAVE REBROADCASTING

Shortwave rebroadcasting occupied the middle ground among the three technological options for providing national radio service. Naturally allied with super-power broadcasting in the effort to provide national service by the use of radio waves, both options capitalized on radio's greatest appeal: its freedom from wires. Shortwave rebroadcasting also resembled interconnection by wires because both technologies would have linked many radio stations together rather than depending on a few stations to provide nationwide programming. Several companies, particularly RCA, experimented with shortwaves for international communication, but only two companies, GE and Westinghouse, attempted domestic shortwave rebroadcasting.[40]

Both GE and Westinghouse wanted to use shortwave rebroadcasting to link the broadcasting stations they had founded, hoping that interconnection would cut programming costs and provide regional and national service. In the 1920s all home radio receivers picked up only medium-wave transmissions because engineers considered shortwaves unreliable. Experimentation showed, however, that shortwaves could be used to transmit over long distances. Shortwave rebroadcasting involved sending the original program over the air on two different frequencies simultaneously—once on medium waves for listeners near the original transmitter and once on shortwaves to a distant station. The second station would pick up the shortwave signal on a special receiver and retransmit it on longer waves for its local listeners. In a 1923 *Radio Broadcast* article, "Is Short-Wave Relaying a Step Toward National Broadcasting Stations?" the magazine noted that "the possibilities of re-broadcasting are indeed staggering. A central station, located in Washington ... could carry the voice of the President to listeners in every section of our country if re-broadcasting ... were properly fostered."[41] The idea of interconnection fascinated the entire radio industry, even those stations that lacked access to the wire lines seemingly necessary for such experiments.

The technology of interconnection, both wired and using shortwaves, had been spurred by the desire to broadcast events that happened away from the studio. One GE experiment with shortwaves used them to send programs from an outside location to the regular transmitter at its Schenectady station, WGY. A 1924 photograph in *Radio Broadcast* with the headline "WGY on Wheels" showed a small truck equipped with a shortwave transmitter that "picks up programs from churches and public halls." The truck transmitter sent the events via shortwave to the regular transmitter, where they "are radiated in the regular manner. The small transmitter takes the place of the usual telephone line connection between the outside hall and the broadcasting station."[42]

Despite "WGY on Wheels," most of the GE experiments with shortwaves focused on the use of rebroadcasting to send American programs abroad.[43] GE participated in only one wholly domestic attempt at rebroadcasting, an effort aimed at obtaining publicity for shortwave interconnection, much as Sarnoff had publicized super-power. The experiment, carried out in conjunction with RCA and Westinghouse, whose shortwave rebroadcasting program was much more extensive, aimed to broadcast a 1926 Massachusetts Institute of Technology alumni dinner to various parts of the nation. A *Radio Broadcast* article reported that "WGY, connected to New York by a special circuit, broadcast the music and speeches on 380 meters wavelength and on 107 meters." Luckily, "the signals on 107 meters were so strong and clear that Pittsburgh picked them up and sent them to Hastings, Nebraska, which again rebroadcast." Finally "KGO, the General Electric Company station at Oakland, caught the three-times-relayed signals on delicate receiving apparatus and again put the dinner program into the air." The article boasted that "the only wire used was that between WGY and WJZ in New York."[44] MIT alumni gathered in seventy-five cities to listen to the ceremonies over the radio.[45] Many observers considered the transmission of the MIT Alumni Dinner as a great step forward in the evolution of broadcast technology. David Sarnoff hailed it as "the first achievement of transcontinental broadcasting without the use of wires as the transmission links between stations," pointing out that it represented the combined efforts of all members of the radio group, brought together briefly against their common enemy, AT&T.[46]

The radio companies chose MIT's alumni dinner for maximum potential publicity, drawing on MIT's prestige and the fact that its alumni were prominent in technical fields. Charles Popenoe, manager of the RCA department of broadcasting, wrote to H. P. Davis, vice-president of Westinghouse, describing the event as "a tremendous publicity feature" and reminding him that "there are no better men, as you know, anywhere than the average graduate of the Massachusetts Institute of Technology." Popenoe declared that "they do not make very much money, but they all have brains . . . and it always seems a pleasure to work out a stunt of this kind with engineers, as they realize the many shortcomings and difficulties that we have to overcome."[47] Letters among GE, Westinghouse, and RCA officials regarding arrangements for the dinner reveal the three companies eager for publicity, yet having some difficulty getting along. A letter from Popenoe to his GE counterpart suggested "a conference on the publicity so that no one company, such as was the case last time, gets all of it."[48] The memoranda and telegrams also show that many engineers doubted shortwave rebroadcasting would work and that attempts to lease telephone wire lines (even by MIT) were rebuffed by AT&T, forcing the radio companies to send the dinner over telegraph lines and shortwaves.[49]

The Westinghouse Electric and Manufacturing Company, an early pioneer in broadcasting with its Pittsburgh station, KDKA, carried out the most extensive testing of shortwave rebroadcasting as it tried to find a way to connect its stations without using AT&T's wires. Frank Conrad, the Westinghouse engineer whose broadcasts from his garage had grown into KDKA, was one of the first Americans interested in using the low frequencies for broadcasting. Early on he had sent out KDKA programs on 100 meters and had good luck with other experimenters receiving his signals.[50] But ordinary radio receivers could not pick up shortwave signals directly. Westinghouse needed a system that would enable listeners to hear distant stations without forcing them to construct different receiving sets or converters.[51]

A systematic trial of shortwave rebroadcasting began in 1923, just after the Third National Radio Conference had debated the options for national radio service. Westinghouse erected a repeater station, KFKX, in Hastings, Nebraska. Joe Beaudino, a long-time engineer with Westinghouse, recalled that the company chose Hastings since it was "not far from the geographical center of the country and by repeating KDKA's transmissions from a station at Hastings it was felt the coverage of KDKA would be greatly increased." The Nebraska station would be the first step in a new system in which "radio networks could be set up across the country . . . [with] radio broadcast stations . . . tied together by short waves." Westinghouse even offered Beaudino a job installing repeating stations with a soon-to-be formed subsidiary in charge of relaying radio programs by shortwave.[52]

KFKX went on the air November 22, 1923. The set-up in Hastings consisted of a rough frame house that housed the station and long-wave transmitter; a studio in the building of the Gaston Music and Furniture Company connected to the station (about one mile away) by telephone line; and a shortwave station on a farm about a mile outside Hastings, again connected to the station by wire. The shortwave receiver and the transmitter had to be physically separated; this was, at the time, the only way to prevent interference. Presumably KFKX also attempted to retransmit KDKA's shortwave signals to KGO, a GE station in Oakland, which could then once more rebroadcast the shortwave signal on medium waves and thus further increase KDKA's range. KFKX also originated local programs and transmitted them on Mondays and Thursdays from 9:30 to 11 p.m. central standard time. The Hastings Chamber of Commerce called KFKX the "greatest publicity asset which has ever been given to a community of its size."[53] A booklet published by the station, hailing itself as the "First Radio Relaying Station in the World," noted, however, that there was "no fixed schedule for rebroadcasting KDKA" because, as Beaudino remembered, "reception was not reliable."[54] These technical difficulties forced KFKX to close and transfer its call letters to Chicago in the fall of 1927.

Despite such valiant efforts, no shortwave rebroadcasting experiment ever operated without the use of telephone lines. Both GE and Westinghouse cared more about connecting their stations and providing out-of-studio programs to their listeners than they did about shortwave rebroadcasting. Many radio professionals remained convinced that shortwaves would eventually become useful, but in the early 1920s the radio companies continued to need AT&T's cooperation to provide national radio service. AT&T refused to cooperate, intent on providing such service itself, and eager for a prime position in the patent pool renegotiations.

WIRED NETWORKS

William Peck Banning, later AT&T's vice-president, recalled that in 1921 "nobody knew . . . where radio was really headed. Everything about broadcasting was uncertain. For my own part I expected that since it was a form of telephony . . . we were sure to be involved in broadcasting somehow." Yet "it was impossible for a while even to guess what our service duty would be."[55] By 1924 it appeared to AT&T "logical that we should undertake this business of national broadcasting. We have the necessary wire plant and are probably the only agency equipped to do a creditable job." An AT&T memo projected a "net revenue at the rate of one million dollars per year within a period of five years" with small risk.[56]

Easily understood and quickly successful, the technology of wired interconnection appealed to Secretary Hoover and to the public. During this early experimental period, however, the radio patent pool partners thought a technological breakthrough might challenge AT&T's national system of telephone wires. AT&T therefore scrambled to reinforce its already strong position by experimenting with sending programs over wires, either to studios or to connect stations, and transmitting sports, political events, and popular and classical music over great distances. AT&T acted more defensively than did RCA, GE, or Westinghouse, seeking to maintain rather than to enhance its radio interests. Because it had a profitable telephone monopoly already in place, AT&T could afford to take a more reactive approach to radio.[57]

AT&T had originally been drawn into radio with the discovery that the De Forest vacuum tube could solve problems in radio wave detection, just as it could reduce the difficulties encountered in long-distance wired telephony. In 1909 the company's chief engineer, John J. Carty, had argued for the development of the vacuum tube (a "repeater" in telephone terminology; an "audion" in radio lingo) by pointing out that "a successful telephone repeater . . . might put us in a position of control with respect to the art of wireless telephony [radio] should it turn out to be a factor of importance."[58] When radio did turn out to be important, AT&T became a partner in the radio patent pool because it controlled the DeForest vacuum tube patent. By 1924 AT&T's involvement in radio had three facets: it made and sold radio transmitters; it owned toll broadcasting stations that sold airtime, primarily WEAF in New York City; and it used and leased telephone long lines for wired transmission of radio waves, both for remote broadcasts and for the connection of radio stations.[59]

Just as with shortwave rebroadcasting, the technology leading to the experimental coupling of radio stations by wire began because stations needed more program material. Station managers, faced with a set number of hours to fill, soon realized that it would be easier to broadcast events happening outside the studio than to simulate events inside the studio or create new programs especially for broadcast. But how to get the event to the transmitter, if the participants were not in the same room as the sending equipment? The telephone immediately came to mind as a solution.

From radio's earliest days, broadcasters used telephone lines to broadcast out-of-studio events they thought would appeal to listeners. In January 1921, shortly after it went on the air and before AT&T officially refused to rent lines to its radio patent pool partners, KDKA broadcast church services from the Calvary Church in Pittsburgh. Station personnel set up microphones in the church and sent the services over telephone wires direct to the KDKA transmitter some miles away. Engineers treated the signals as if they had originated in the KDKA studio and broadcast them over the radio waves in standard fashion. Similarly, the popularity of college football games led to a 1922 WEAF broadcast from New York of both the Princeton-Chicago game (played in Chicago) and the Harvard-Yale game.[60] According to William Peck Banning's company history of WEAF, the call for quality programming brought a special Metropolitan

Opera broadcast performance on November 11, 1922, of Verdi's *Aida*, originating at the Kingsbridge Armory and sent over wires to WEAF's studio for transmission. Banning noted that "telephone engineers . . . [worked] for several days in preparing the telephone circuits for the transmission of music . . . [which] was a pioneering accomplishment."[61] A 1923 *Radio Broadcast* article listed an impressive number of recent "out of studio" events broadcast, including the World Series, football games, boxing matches, organ recitals, symphony concerts, operas, plays, banquets, addresses, church services, and a presidential message to Congress. The article noted that "the chief value of 'out-of-studio' broadcasting lies in the possibility of securing events that cannot be staged in the studio. But there is also another factor that is important; namely the atmosphere of life that is transmitted."[62]

It was only a short step from wiring a program to a single transmitter to sending it over wires to several transmitters. Western Union telegraph lines could also be used, but the telephone lines, already adapted to send voices, worked better. A program originating in the New York studios of WEAF and featuring Metropolitan Opera stars could be sent over telephone wires to stations in other cities and rebroadcast. AT&T, headquartered in New York, maintained that Manhattan provided the best—in some respects the only—entertainment. Thus, even during this experimental phase, wired broadcasts began shutting out regional programming.

As early as December 1921, AT&T was envisioning a national radio system with "thirty-eight station locations on the Bell System's main long distance routes."[63] The company regarded its first station, WEAF, founded in 1922, as a means to test the use of wires in radio and to explore the commercial possibilities inherent in national broadcasting. A company publication of April 1922 noted that if WEAF proved commercially successful "it is our plan to establish, as circumstances warrant, similar stations throughout the country." Each station could use local telephone lines and "all of such broadcasting stations may, if conditions warrant, be tied together by the long line plant, so that any one, from practically any point, may use any number or all of these stations simultaneously."[64] Long lines thus gave AT&T not only a technological edge in providing national radio service but also a conceptual advantage.

The knowledge gained from the transmission of broadcast-quality music and speech from remote locations helped when AT&T used telephone lines to send programs from one station to another for rebroadcast.

The annual meeting of the National Electric Light Association provided one of the first attempts at connecting stations by wire. Held in Carnegie Hall in New York on June 7, 1923, the meeting was sent over wires to WEAF, New York; to KYW, Chicago; to KDKA, Pittsburgh; and to WGY, Schenectady. President Harding's cross-country trip in June and July 1923 presented several occasions to connect stations. His scheduled July 31 speech in San Francisco was to have been sent to six stations, the most ambitious attempt at networking to that date. The cancellation of the speech because of Harding's illness and subsequent death deprived AT&T of a broadcast audience estimated at between three and five million people.[65]

After its experience with temporary connections, AT&T wanted to experiment with a permanent wire connection between radio stations. Col. Edward Green, an eccentric millionaire and owner of station WMAF in South Dartmouth, Massachusetts, asked to have WEAF's programs sent over telephone lines to his station for rebroadcast. Colonel Green agreed to a $60,000 annual fee, and AT&T installed a special cable between WMAF and WEAF with service beginning on July 1, 1923. AT&T offered WJAR, in Providence, Rhode Island, service over the same cable, and a three-station network came into being.[66] AT&T's Washington station, WCAP, opened in July 1923 and became part of the permanent wired system. The final network broadcast of 1923 fulfilled the dream often expressed by proponents of national radio by enabling the nation to hear President Calvin Coolidge in his first address to Congress. The December 4, 1923, speech was broadcast over the "established trinity" of WEAF, WCAP, and WJAR (Colonel Green having already dropped out), as well as on KSD, St. Louis; WDAF, Kansas City, Missouri; and WFAA, Dallas.[67]

Religious services, politics, sports, and eventually entertainment provided the programming for this experimental network. Remote broadcasts of vaudeville began on November 19, 1922, from the Capitol Theater in New York under the direction of S. L. "Roxy" Rothafel and became the basis for one of the most popular programs carried on the wired stations.[68] In 1924 "Roxy's Gang" was sent from WEAF to WJAR and WCAP. When the stars of this Sunday night program traveled to Providence and Washington, they expressed surprise that listeners "addressed a half dozen of our performers by name just as intimately as though they had been friends for years."[69]

During the first part of 1924, AT&T engineers developed a group of intercity telephone wires that could be used in off-peak hours for permanent "chain" or "network" broadcasting.[70] Yet many of the stations that were approached (twenty-one in all) rejected AT&T's offer to pay them to carry programs with advertising while requiring them to pay AT&T for the noncommercial content. Only six stations, including WEAF, WCAP, and WJAR, took AT&T up on the offer. Most stations worried that the advertising carried on the AT&T programs would annoy listeners and ruin the public goodwill the stations counted on generating.[71] The telephone company added to these problems by refusing to ask stations owned by the other members of the patent pool to join the new chain.[72]

AT&T's refusal to let other stations use its telephone lines heightened the fears of GE, Westinghouse, and RCA that AT&T wanted to cut them out of the broadcasting business. Often AT&T would not let a station use telephone lines even for a pickup, and so some stations experimented with acoustically poor Western Union lines.[73]

In a slightly different situation, a Chicago station, hoping to rent a phone line to pick up a speech by President Coolidge in honor of Washington's birthday, offered $1,000 for the duration of the speech; AT&T asked for $2,500. As quoted in *Radio Broadcast*, the Chicago station manager noted that "the regular long distance charge for the use of wires from Chicago to Washington is only $4.80 for the first three minutes and $1.60 for each additional minute." Because the President was to talk for ten minutes, "at the regular rates the cost of the wires should then be $14.80." The article described the drawbacks of using shortwave rebroadcasting in this situation, noting that "the Chicago station could not very well set up a short wave transmitter at the White House, to relay the speech to Chicago." In the end, *Radio Broadcast* took the telephone company's side in this argument, reminding its readers that "the radio receipts of the American Telephone and Telegraph Company are practically nothing at all whereas an organization like the Radio Corporation has an income from the radio public which must be measured annually in the tens of millions of dollars."[74] Whatever AT&T's radio profits and the true cost of the lines, the telephone company successfully used pricing to prevent a non-AT&T radio station from broadcasting a presidential speech.

Historians have interpreted AT&T's refusal to rent long lines as an attempt to maintain its position in the radio industry. N. R. Danielian has written, "it is obvious that the Bell System intended to put as many obstacles as possible in the way of the Radio Group's operation of broadcasting stations," while Leonard Reich has explained that "by late 1921, the AT&T directors realized the importance of blocking the proliferation and influence of stations established by rivals, especially those of the RCA group" and described the company's prohibition against RCA's use of telephone circuits as a "defensive act."[75]

By 1924 the perceived need for national radio service, and the continued inability of any one of the companies involved in radio to provide it, made a patent renegotiation necessary. The situation with regard to national radio service resembled the original problem in radio technology. No one company had enough resources (patents in the early case; broadcast stations or technological resources in the later) to provide the kind of service sought. While AT&T controlled the wires, the other companies controlled most of the outlets—the radio stations—needed to make a wired network possible. Decisions about how a national radio service would be run, how it would make money, and who would control it needed to be negotiated.

The various experiments with super-power and shortwave rebroadcasting had shown that only one technology—wired networks—was truly capable of providing national radio service. Yet although the choice of a technology seemed ordained, the economic system, the management of such service, and who would have control were far from clear. The technological experiments had grown out of the needs of the large manufacturers of receivers and transmitters, and the system for national broadcasting would also address their needs. Not even the choice of technology can be considered to have been fixed. National radio service could have been postponed with the participation of the federal government—as was later the development of television, then color television, and then high-definition television—until an alternative technology with profit-making potential for a different part of the industry was available.

BEYOND THE TECHNOLOGICAL IMPERATIVE

Even if one considers the technological choice a given, many other factors also influenced the shape of the national radio system. Several of these factors involved the radio industry's response to the public concern that had grown through the first half of the 1920s about monopoly. The radio companies increasingly found themselves defending the formation of RCA and explaining how the patent pool had averted chaos.

In 1924, for example, the public became interested in the "radio trust" when AT&T sued WHN in New York for using transmitter parts without the permission of the patent holder, AT&T. AT&T insisted it chose WHN, out of the many patent infringers, because "we decided to select a nearby station so as to minimize the costs to both parties concerned."[76] For many observers, however, AT&T's ownership of New York station WEAF (a direct competitor of WHN), as well as the curiously combined nature of radio manufacturing and broadcasting, made the case controversial.[77]

AT&T worried that the brouhaha over a radio monopoly might arouse opposition to its telephone monopoly. The louder the cries against radio monopoly, the stronger became the position of those within AT&T's management who favored withdrawal from radio and a return to the traditional activities of the company.[78] When super-power, the national radio option with the greatest appearance of monopoly control, aroused antagonism among the public and small station owners, RCA, GE, and Westinghouse also began to worry about government interference and joined AT&T in the search for a method of providing national radio service that would minimize the appearance of centralized control.

The lengthy and complex renegotiations of the radio patent agreement between 1924 and 1926 dealt with many issues, but at their heart was the question of national radio and how it could be achieved with a maximum of profit and a minimum of public fuss over monopoly. The final agreement, reached in the middle of 1926, included the sale of WEAF to RCA and the establishment of a separate broadcast organization, the National Broadcasting Company (NBC), to lease telephone lines from AT&T for pick-ups and to connect independent local stations. New York stations WJZ and WEAF would provide programs for these other stations.

This agreement solved many problems at once. AT&T withdrew from radio, thus alleviating the pressure of being regarded as a radio, as well as a telephone, monopolist; it was also paid handsomely for its withdrawal. By agreeing to lease AT&T long lines, RCA bought off its strongest competitor in the broadcasting field.[79] RCA also willingly gave up the concept of super-power broadcasting, both because it had become synonymous with monopoly control of the airwaves and because it was not technologically feasible. In exchange, RCA controlled the new National Broadcasting Company. Westinghouse and GE approved of the new arrangement because, like technologically imperfect shortwave rebroadcasting, it enabled individually owned stations to maintain their identities while increasing their profit potential.

The radio patent renegotiation set up a self-supporting wired network system administered and directed by RCA. Local stations received programming, sent over wires, from a station in New York City. Because renting the wires was so expensive, radio receiver manufacturers believed they could not fund national radio service. The new wired network thus came to be financed through the sale of time to advertisers. These and other decisions about how the wired system would be structured grew out of the relationships among the radio patent partners and were influenced by the social, political, and cultural context in which they were made.

Government approval, certifying radio's new status as a regulated monopoly and therefore a public good, remained important in instituting a wired network system. The final step in this process would come with the 1934 Communications Act, but earlier congressional actions showed that political and cultural issues remained important as the structure of broadcast radio solidified. Congress had passed the 1927 Radio Act before the ramifications of the patent renegotiation and the shape of wired networks were clear. Congressional debate over the extension of the 1927 Radio Act, two years after the founding of NBC, illustrates how the radio industry adjusted its shape to placate continuing public concerns about monopoly, as well as to forestall government interference. Such fine-tuning of the national radio system worked. The radio industry forestalled any government action, and Congress ended up endorsing (while supposing it was controlling) arrangements proposed by the industry.

The congressional debate also highlighted other political and cultural tensions in the mid-1920s that influenced the establishment of a wired network system. Members of Congress showed an awareness of the new ideas underlying the concept of national radio. The radio industry had moved away from the notion of national service as simply a means of connecting listeners. As national radio became a cost-cutting measure for large equipment manufacturers, it also became a way of presenting single events to the entire nation. Because this change was often described in political terms ("now the whole country can hear a speech by the president"), and because it implied the superiority of the urban Northeast over the rest of the nation, it aroused congressional interest.

In Congress, the questions of monopoly and regulation of national radio service became intertwined with long-standing urban-rural tensions. The Radio Act of 1927 established a Federal Radio Commission (FRC) with a one-year mandate to allocate frequencies to individual stations. The act divided the nation into five zones, with one radio commissioner appointed from each zone to ensure geographic fairness in the allocation of stations.[80] Because of a lack of funding (Congress never passed an appropriations bill for the FRC activities) and the death of several FRC appointees, the commission accomplished little in 1927. A bill extending the FRC's term for another year was therefore introduced early in 1928.[81] Debate centered on an amendment proposed by Rep. Edwin Davis of Texas, mandating equal distribution of stations (broadcast licenses, wavelengths, and frequencies) among the five zones, and the allocation of stations among the states within each zone in proportion to population and area. Proponents of the Davis amendment feared a monopoly if the "radio trust" owned the only, or even the biggest, stations.

The mostly Southern and rural advocates for the amendment resented the fact that urban areas had more and higher powered radio stations than did their own regions. An Oklahoma representative recognized "that while many of the programs coming from the big city stations are of general interest, they have no inherent value, either in merit or in the universality of their appeal, over the programs broadcast from the smaller, independent stations." He contended that the Davis amendment would give listeners the "privilege of choosing their entertainment, break the bonds of the monopoly which bind the industry, and secure for the public the essential freedom of the air!"[82] A New York delegate replied that "the cities are willing to spend the money necessary to provide the highest type of amusement and instruction. . . . The radio has a great future. Do not attempt to circumscribe its usefulness by provincial legislation."[83] Characteristically, Fiorello La Guardia was one of the few urban representatives to side with the rural antimonopolists. At one point he exclaimed, "Mr. Chairman, it would be a calamity if the broadcasting power were to be concentrated in one or two points in this country."[84]

Members of Congress remained as interested in the location of transmitters as in the quality and quantity of programs. Congressional debate made a distinction between "equity of transmission" and "equity of service."[85] Many believed that the source of the signal was important because the location of the station would influence its programming. If all programs came from a central source, the regional diversity many listeners enjoyed would disappear. Rural listeners, having experienced local radio service, or just able to imagine it, felt that centralized broadcasting in itself represented not only a business monopoly but a form of urban cultural imperialism.

The Davis amendment, with its support for local stations with access to national events, clearly rejected a system of regulated super-power stations and moved to strengthen rural and small-town stations by enabling them, through the zone system, to compete with city stations for licenses. Neither the Davis amendment nor the Radio Act of 1927 challenged the wired network system already in place and controlled by the receiver manufacturers, even though the wired system centralized programming in much the same way that super-power stations would have done. The network system did not provide the variety of programming that Representative Davis sought, but the congressional insistence that nonurban stations remain strong gave political approval to the radio patent agreement, which set up a structure for national radio based on a wide distribution of stations.[86] The resulting national radio system avoided the possibility that government might take over broadcasting.

A federal takeover had been considered just after World War I, but the strong position of the radio companies, the government's disposition to influence rather than directly regulate, and the geography of the United States all worked against the form of centralized broadcasting so widespread in other parts of the world. The privately controlled and financed wired network system resulted in part from the United States' size and its large, evenly distributed, and linguistically relatively homogeneous population. Most countries with early radio stations, including England and Germany, covered the entire nation with just a few stations owned by the government.[87] One larger country, Australia, which featured a mixed system of government and private stations, had a geographically concentrated population with about 80 percent of listeners living within fifty miles of six cities, so that most of the population could be reached through a few stations.[88] The Soviet Union, another large country, programmed in sixty-two languages over sixty-four stations and thus had little need for nationwide broadcasts.[89] Government ownership of a few radio stations that could reach the entire population made economic and political sense, but government ownership of many smaller stations seemed difficult in a capitalist society that preferred to view itself as decentralized.

Canada, the nation whose geographic and cultural situation most closely resembled that of the United States, had no large radio manufacturing firms pushing to retain private control of broadcasting; it also had the United States as its neighbor. The United States claimed eighty-nine of the ninety-five wavelengths allotted to North America and provided most of the ready-made radio receivers used in Canada.[90] Despite this scarcity of wavelengths, and the proximity and technical superiority of American stations, radio in Canada flourished. National radio service was pioneered by the Canadian National Railroad using government telegraph lines. The Sixtieth Anniversary of Confederation celebration in 1927 was a memorable coast-to-coast broadcast accomplished in "a typical Canadian way, a mixture of public activity, public policy, and private facility." Formation of the Canadian Radio Broadcasting Commission (the forerunner of the Canadian Broadcasting Commission) in 1930 ended this makeshift period.[91] The national system of radio broadcasting that evolved in Canada relied on the same technology as in the United States, but with fewer local stations because of the unavailability of frequencies, and all under the control of the central government.

The relatively unrestricted American system of national radio service proved appealing to business leaders. Wired networks' many local units, rationally joined together, not only gave the appearance of competition and diversity, but fit well with familiar entrepreneurial practices. The network system resembled other national distribution systems set up in the 1920s, such as dealerships, franchises, and chains. Wired network service was often referred to as "chain" broadcasting and featured locally owned companies receiving goods (radio programs) and services from a central organization. The network system seemed familiar and understandable to radio station investors and to advertisers. The fledgling NBC desperately needed to appeal to advertisers in order to defray the expensive wire line charges paid to AT&T. Advertisers, finding much unfamiliar about broadcasting, took comfort in the network structure. Thus, the technological feasibility of a wired network system was reinforced by other factors. Americans' fear of monopoly, the political appeal of decentralized radio transmitting stations, the geographic size of the nation, the relative linguistic homogeneity of the population, and the familiarity of the business community with a "chain" organizational structure all paved the way for the networks.

After a slow start, NBC became quite profitable. Initially it encountered difficulty attracting advertisers and affiliated stations; *Fortune* magazine reported that NBC made no money at all in 1929, in spite of having sold $11,000,000 worth of airtime.[92] Two years later, however, NBC reported a profit of $2,325,229 and boasted seventy-six affiliated stations.[93] Shortly after the founding of NBC, a group of investors led by entrepreneur Arthur Judson launched a second network based on the same principles as NBC and designed as a direct competitor. Lack of operating capital initially plagued the new company, which entered a partnership with Columbia Phonograph Record Company long enough to retain the name Columbia Broadcasting System (CBS). Investments by the Paley family of Philadelphia saved CBS, and young William Paley soon moved to New York to manage his family's money and the company's future. In 1931 CBS claimed a few more affiliated stations than did NBC (ninety-five) and a slightly bigger profit ($2,346,766), although its programming probably reached fewer listeners.[94]

The concept of national radio service preceded the idea of radio as a commercial medium. Direct advertising on radio—companies purchasing time to sell products—had first emerged in a limited way in 1923 with the founding of WEAF, AT&T's station. Characteristically, AT&T believed that the 1919 radio patent agreement gave it the exclusive right to sell radio time, and refused to allow other stations to sell time without its permission. The RCA, GE, and Westinghouse experiments in national radio service therefore occurred before these companies thought seriously of using advertising to subsidize broadcasting expenses. Even on those few stations selling time in the early 1920s, most advertisers were reluctant to take a chance on the new medium. Only after the network system became a reality did broadcast advertising become profitable or necessary.

The technological and economic form that national radio service took soon influenced the content of broadcasting. The huge expense of renting AT&T's wires to send signals from station to station meant that programming had to be centralized both to save money and to attract advertisers needing a national audience. Regional needs and desires went by the boards as broadcasters sought to deliver the largest possible audiences for advertisers interested in national markets. Ethnic and racial diversity, active participation by listeners, and the airing of minority or dissident points of view were sacrificed for a system that provided the same programs to every radio receiver.[95] These changes did not occur overnight, but they increased in momentum as the networks consolidated their power. The wired network system, with centralized programming financed through advertising revenue, shaped what Americans heard when they turned on their radios, and later their televisions.

ARGUMENTS OVER BROADCAST ADVERTISING

Eight hundred people entered *Radio Broadcast*'s 1925 contest, "Who Is To Pay for Broadcasting and How?" offering "ingenious" plans to charge for program listings, schemes for voluntary listener contributions, and even a call for government licensing. As the editors wrote, "suggestions there were of all kinds, and the problem of deciding which one of all the group was the best was not found at all easy." The winning entry sought a tax on vacuum tubes, as an "index of broadcast consumption," to be administered by a federal Bureau of Broadcasting. Despite the award, neither the *Radio Broadcast* editors nor the judges of the contest found much to praise in the winning entry, and they were especially critical of the large government role proposed for distributing the tax revenue. All agreed that "the last word has not been said on this subject."[1] Although radio broadcasting had existed for five years, a single idea of how it should be financed had not yet taken hold. The contest suggested a wealth of options, as broadcasters, listeners, and advertisers vied for control of the airwaves.

EARLY STATIONS

While receiver manufacturers financed some of the earliest radio stations simply to boost their sales, other businesses founded stations to gain publicity or goodwill. Secretary of Commerce Herbert Hoover initially hoped that more businesses might be persuaded to finance radio stations, even though radio gave only an "intangible return" on investment.[2] In his history of early radio, Erik Barnouw lists stations owned by a stockyard, a marble company, a laundry, and a poultry farm.[3] Such stations could be called commercial insofar as some of their programming related to the owner's products, yet they did not sell advertising time to other manufacturers.

While these stations provided models for how business could profit from radio, some financing proposals did not aim to profit the business world. Voluntary contributions to stations from philanthropists or listeners, some observers believed, might keep broadcasting out of the clutches of business. "A powerful station could be put up and operated at a cost less than that required for a reasonable sized library," declared an editorial in the first issue of *Radio Broadcast* magazine, adding that "a properly conducted radio broadcasting station can do at least as great an educational work as does the average library." The editorial predicted "that many such stations will be operating in the next twenty-five years."[4]

Public schools and universities seemed logical sources of financial backing for stations operating in the public interest. Many colleges and school districts did establish radio stations, often as part of their science departments, enlisting teachers and students as performers. By 1925 ninety educational institutions held licenses to broadcast.[5]

A few city governments founded and supported radio stations to be "operated for direct public benefit."[6] Promoters hoped that the first municipal station, WNYC in New York, would provide an alternative to privately owned stations that had begun accepting paid advertisements. Programming on WNYC, however, resembled that heard over other New York stations. The police department broadcast alarms for wanted criminals, and various city agencies presented talks, but WNYC filled most of its broadcast hours with musical selections.[7] In 1926 a newspaper article described WNYC's offerings as "not the most attractive in the metropolitan district by the furthest stretch of the imagination." The station's problems included taxpayers who "would resent any lavish expenditure of talent" and "city officials" who "are not elected for the purpose of giving nightly musical entertainment." One promoter of radio advertising noted that, after broadcasting a year, WNYC could "make a group picture of its usual audience on the City Hall steps."[8] Despite its undistinguished programming, small audiences, poor funding, and attacks by citizens' groups, WNYC survived (until the late 1980s), but it failed to provide much inspiration for other municipal stations. It remained an interesting experiment rather than a genuine alternative.

Despite the fact that the American government never levied taxes specifically to pay for broadcasting, the federal government went on the air early and stayed on. The U.S. Department of Agriculture, for example, produced programs ranging from weather and market reports to household hints, broadcast by private and college stations in rural areas. But the radio corporations lobbied heavily against any extension of the federal role in broadcasting, always fearing a government takeover. Some radio magazines promoted the funding of broadcasting through taxes, highlighting the successful British system, but most listeners seemed reluctant to begin paying for a service they already received free of charge.[9]

Stations approached ordinary listeners for financial support several times during the early 1920s. "The Radio Music Fund Committee" sought gifts to engage the best musical talent, artists "hopelessly beyond the appeal of gratuitous performances," to perform over WEAF in New York.[10] In a widely reported effort, Kansas City station WHB (owned by the Sweeney Auto School) sold tickets for an "invisible theater." Listeners received tickets and a program book for contributions of between one and ten dollars. "We are more than willing to spend money to operate the station," the manager noted, "but with musicians demanding $4 an hour and stage artists one-eighth their weekly salary . . . we believe it is only fair for those sharing the pleasure to pay a portion of the expenses."[11] Advocates of this strategy hoped that the financial support of listeners would keep broadcasting from being exploited by businesses whose aims were "not wholly compatible with the public interest."[12] The problem, one critic wrote, was that if all stations began soliciting funds, "their tin cups would have glistened before our eyes at every street-corner; they would have stood panting at our back doors like hungry dogs."[13]

None of the early experiments in financing radio stations, including commercial sponsorship, worked very well. Yet, as the *Radio Broadcast* contest showed, before 1925 broadcast advertising was considered just one of the options that seemed unsatisfactory. Observers could imagine broadcasting financed in a variety of ways, or even a mixed system with different stations funded in different ways. Before the advent of the networks, advertising stood out among the financing options only because it elicited the loudest protests and had the fewest supporters. The network system's need for large amounts of cash in order to rent wire lines suddenly gave broadcast advertising a privileged position. The networks had the money and energy to push for their choice among the financing plans, and push they did.

OPPONENTS

In 1925 the editors of *Radio Age* noted that "the broadcasters who succumbed to the commercial influence are building up a monster who, like Frankenstein, will slay his creator."[14] Such anti-advertising rhetoric came from every group involved in early radio: listeners, critics, legislators, regulators, and broadcasters. Many critics adopted a hysterical tone when writing of radio advertising, using metaphors out of horror stories to describe the new mutant. Another radio magazine warned that advertising might "become an Old Man Of The Sea—practically impossible to shake off once he got a good grasp" and concluded with a call for "a country-wide movement" with "definite, speedy action" against it.[15] Despite these concerns about listener control and the affect on programs, however, no "country-wide movement" against radio advertising took hold in the early 1920s.

Many broadcasters wanted to dismiss advertising quickly and continue the search for a more practical solution to their economic problem. They believed that "advertising by radio does not offer a solution to the problem of making broadcasting self-supporting" and that advertising presented "dangers to broadcasting" that might cause both radio and advertising to fail.[16] Radio professionals worried that listeners would grow disenchanted with the medium as its novelty faded. One article noted that "bombastic advertising . . . cuts into the vitals of broadcast advertising—its circulation—by creating an apathetic public, impairing listener interest and curtailing the sale of receiver sets." This writer named the worst fear of both the radio and advertising industries: once a method for financing radio had been established, listeners might dislike the solution and turn off their sets without allowing the industry sufficient time to reorganize. Fears that broadcast radio was a fad, and that listeners would be easily alienated, remained widespread in the industry until late in the 1920s and caused many professionals to distrust broadcast advertising.[17]

Early on, the advertising industry became concerned that listeners might resent radio sponsorship and by extension reject all types of advertising. *Printer's Ink*, an advertising trade publication, argued that radio advertising (along with "sky writing," "press agent dope," or any "disguised publicity") was against "good public policy," and that radio was an "objectionable advertising medium." The magazine warned that "an audience . . . wheedled into listening to a selfish message will naturally be offended," and "its ill-will would be directed not only against the company that delivered the story, but also against the advertiser who chooses to talk shop at such an inopportune time."[18] To a certain extent, print advertisers and the advertising industry in general (represented by *Printer's Ink*) saw broadcast advertising as unwanted competition. But beyond that, the often repeated comment that radio advertising, if unwanted, would "probably die by itself in a short time" made advertisers worry that if broadcast advertising failed, all advertising might suffer.[19]

Public attitudes toward broadcast advertising remained difficult to discern, but several groups purporting to speak for listeners reinforced the fears of broadcasters and advertisers. In 1924 the executive secretary of the American Radio Association (ARA), an organization of listeners, explained that "numerous complaints are being received from the radio public which is objecting in increasing numbers to having its news, music, and entertainment interspersed with advertising." The ARA believed that "pure and unadulterated advertising on radio" would be "disastrous to the trade itself."[20] Participants in the Fourth National Radio Conference agreed that the "listening public" found radio advertising "objectionable" and added that "advertising could be made detrimental to the interests of both the public and the broadcasting stations."[21]

Opponents claimed that listeners would be overlooked in programming decisions if advertising supported radio. The first editorial in *Radio Broadcast* magazine called on listeners "to exert their influence in such a way that the entertainment offered them is determined by themselves." At present, the 1922 editorial told listeners, they were "helpless" with regard to radio programming because "you have nothing to say about it, you pay nothing for it, and still more to the point, you have no rights in the matter at all."[22] These critics found inherent problems with any financial solution not based on listener support. "It is plain that the public must meet the cost of broadcasting if the benefit of broadcasting is to be public," warned *Outlook* magazine.[23] Other commentators pointed out that listeners lacked even the last refuge of the consumer, because broadcast advertising was harder to ignore than newspaper and magazine advertising.[24]

Emmanuel Celler, a New York congressman, parodied radio abuses in 1924 as he introduced a bill to control broadcast advertising:

> This is BLAA, broadcasting station of the Jumbo Peanut Company at Newark, New Jersey. You will now have the pleasure of listening to the "Walk Up One Flight Clothing Company's" orchestra. Their first number will be "You Don't Wear Them Out If You Don't Sit Down."

Celler found such gimmicks more than annoying. "Radio is of tremendous value for educational and amusement purposes," he believed, but "unless suitable measures are passed to steer it into proper channels we will, indeed, run amuck." Broadcast advertising, he argued, would damage radio programming by its very presence; it was "worthless stuff which interferes with instructive and informative broadcasting."[25]

Even Secretary Hoover, a believer in private control of most businesses, initially opposed broadcast advertising. At the First National Radio Conference in 1922, Hoover had found it inconceivable that "we should allow so great a possibility for service, for news, for entertainment, for education, and for vital commercial purposes, to be drowned in advertising chatter, or used for commercial purposes."[26] Two years later, he still maintained that the solution to the "problem of remuneration for broadcasting stations" was "the hardest nut in the bowl" to crack.[27]

The notion of "indirect advertising" helped Hoover and others overcome their distaste for pitching products over the air. Difficult to define, indirect advertising permitted the airing of the sponsor's name, but no "direct" selling. How such definitions translated into practice remained even more puzzling. A *New York Times* reporter asked, "what is the distinction between announcing an orchestra under the name of a well-known brand of tea or coffee and actually talking about the tea or coffee?"[28] By October 1924, during the Third National Radio Conference, Hoover had moved cautiously toward support of indirect advertising, maintaining that "the listeners will finally decide in any event."[29] A year later, during the Fourth National Radio Conference, he spoke more positively still of indirect advertising and approved of "unobtrusive publicity" that would be "accompanied by a direct service and engaging entertainment" rather than "unobtrusive advertising."[30] Indirect advertising, Hoover now believed, could strengthen small stations without bothering listeners, involving the federal government, or hurting the large corporations involved in radio.[31]

Hoover's shift in opinion reflected the general indecision about how to finance and regulate broadcasting, but his actions also sprang from his free-market economic principles. The quintessential "scientific" business leader of the 1920s, Hoover approved of government involvement in broadcasting principally to help radio companies rationalize their young industry. He attacked the problems of radio as he did those of the aviation and the electrical power industries: by working for the kind of cooperation between government and business that would benefit both sides and might also stimulate a lagging economy.[32] Hoover believed that the radio industry should resolve the controversy regarding advertising with the approval of its listeners and without government interference. Such beliefs kept Hoover from acting aggressively to contain the growth of broadcast advertising.

General public acceptance of broadcast advertising came only as a result of the radio industry's sustained campaign to promote it. The early promoters of broadcast advertising, aware that it was still considered only one financing option among many, moved to make their strategy look less commercial. Trying to sell the idea to a skeptical advertising industry, they presented radio advertising as a "natural" outgrowth of earlier experiments. The first historians of broadcasting took a similar approach, pointing out that broadcasting in the United States had first prospered because of a patent pool and because of the investments of large receiver manufacturers. In addition, many businesses, including feed and grain merchants, newspapers, department stores, and radio set retailers, had founded radio stations primarily to generate publicity for themselves. Such a view presented broadcast advertising as simply a logical extension of the other early means of financing radio.[33] Later, historians and the radio industry alike preferred to overlook the hard work that had been necessary to sell radio as an advertising medium.

71

THE CAMPAIGN FOR BROADCAST ADVERTISING

If all American broadcasting was, and had always been, essentially commercial, why the opposing outcry against broadcast advertising? Proponents of broadcast advertising tried to paper over the differences between the early "commercial" stations supported by private enterprises and the financing of all operations through the sale of airtime. They sought to convince skeptical listeners and advertisers that broadcast advertising could bring them all the benefits of radio without any costs. This view ignored the difference between one sponsor and hundreds. Programs on stations supported through the sale of time soon became selling vehicles only, while the advertisements took up more and more broadcast time. Many of those involved in early radio saw this difference quite clearly and remained outspoken in their dislike of broadcast advertising. Yet with the founding of the networks, the radio industry had to finance expensive wire rentals in order to provide national service. Advertising was the only financing alternative that had the potential to be hugely profitable. NBC therefore spearheaded a publicity and educational campaign to promote broadcast advertising, a campaign that further influenced radio's shape and content.

According to historian Susan Strasser, advertising professionals had used the military term "campaign" to refer to a coordinated series of promotional activities since the turn of the century.[34] The push to sell broadcast advertising looked exactly like any other early twentieth-century advertising campaign: advertising professionals drew on well-known promotional methods to create acceptance and demand for broadcast advertising. I have deliberately labeled this "the campaign for broadcast advertising" to describe the character and techniques of their efforts.

In addition to promoting radio advertising, the campaign aimed to convince advertisers that radio programs should be treated as products and marketed as such to listeners. In the process, it developed the concept that time, as well as space, could be bought and sold for commercial purposes. Radio advertising ended up reinforcing the advertising industry's theories about how advertising worked, and came to function exactly like advertising in other media. The changes in radio brought about by the selling of broadcast advertising culminated in the promotion of daytime programming. As part of their attempt to make broadcasting fit into preconceived notions about advertising, the promoters presented women in the home as a key audience for radio. Networks worked to sell daytime hours to sponsors by preparing special programs, and the entire broadcast day became commercialized.

PROMOTERS

Most of those involved in advertising in the 1920s had little interest in radio at first. Yet the field of advertising, by then well established and carefully professionalized, included a few salesmen with a mixture of advertising, radio, and journalism or academic experience that made them suitable for promoting broadcast advertising. Their skills enabled them to present the network view of broadcast advertising to their fellow advertising professionals, the public, and potential advertisers.

Between 1927 and 1932 five advertising professionals produced books, and others a new magazine, designed to promote broadcast advertising.[35] The books and magazine articles outlined the theory and methods of successful radio sponsorship. Writing for a varied audience about a little-known subject, the promoters of broadcast advertising found the textbook approach convenient and powerful. This concentrated production of materials reflected both the continued resistance to broadcast advertising and the radio industry's determination to break down that resistance.

NBC kicked off the campaign with the appointment of Frank Arnold as director of development in 1926. The best-known proponent of broadcast advertising, Arnold had worked in merchandising, retailing, magazines, and as an advertising executive before he entered radio. Owen D. Young, chairman of NBC's board, believed Arnold could sell the "present and future opportunities of radio" to "the national advertiser and to the advertising agencies with whom he has been intimately connected for more than 20 years."[36] As "time salesman on an ambassadorial level," Arnold talked to NBC officials about advertising, delivered speeches to business groups about radio's potential (to avoid "arousing suspicion that what they were listening to was propaganda ... my general procedure was to tell the story and let the advertising use follow as an aftermath"), spoke about radio to the general public, organized the NBC promotion department, and even helped with audience mail.[37] In the fall of 1930 Arnold gave a series of thirteen lectures on "Radio Broadcast Advertising" to sixty-two students, each of whom paid $12.50, at City College of New York; he later published these lectures as a book, *Broadcast Advertising: The Fourth Dimension*. Arnold's call for "indirect" advertising, and his belief that "the time will never come when the programs of our great broadcasting systems will be 100% commercial," aimed to reassure those who worried about the increasing commercialization of the air.[38]

Edgar Felix and Orrin Dunlap also published early books advocating the use of radio in advertising. Like many young men during the years before World War I, both had become fascinated with radio, built transmitters and receivers, and "in the period from 1913 to 1915 . . . spent a good deal of time wearing headphones."[39] Both studied electronics and radio more formally as part of their war service and, after completing college and graduate school, looked for jobs in radio. Soon both became professional promoters of radio, first working in advertising agencies and then writing about radio for a variety of publications. Felix edited the radio section of *Advertising and Selling* from 1927 to 1932, while Dunlap served for eighteen years as radio editor of the *New York Times*.[40] In their books, Felix's *Using Radio in Sales Promotion* and Dunlap's *Radio in Advertising*, both admitted that most listeners hated advertising.[41] But if sponsors followed the tips they provided, they maintained, radio advertising could prove successful. Felix's and Dunlap's combination of radio, advertising, and journalism experience made them particularly effective promoters.

Herman Hettinger had a different mix of experience: he trained as an economist and worked as a business school professor before he became a consultant to the radio industry. Hettinger wrote his doctoral dissertation on radio advertising and later alternated between teaching at the University of Pennsylvania's Wharton School of Finance and Commerce and working as the first director of research at the National Association of Broadcasters (a trade lobbying group), where he compiled radio advertising statistics.[42] Despite the use of statistics, charts, and economic analysis, Hettinger's dissertation, later published as *A Decade of Radio Advertising*, followed much the same format, made the same arguments, and reached many of the same conclusions as the previous more anecdotal treatments of radio advertising. Hettinger lacked the practical radio experience of Felix and Dunlap, but his teaching skills and economics background made his arguments persuasive. Like Arnold, Hettinger had worked for the radio industry, particularly that part of it dominated by the networks, and promoted its view of broadcast economics.

The Advertising Agency Looks at Radio, edited by Neville O'Neill, followed the formula of the Arnold, Dunlap, and Felix books, in which advertising professionals justified radio advertising to their colleagues. Seventeen essays, each contributed by a different agency executive, explained how agencies could plan and deliver a radio advertising campaign.[43] O'Neill's book, which advocated vigorous involvement by advertising agencies in radio and favored more direct advertising strategies, illustrated how far the campaign for broadcast advertising had already progressed by 1932.

All these authors and contributors also wrote for *Broadcast Advertising* magazine, which began in April 1929 and continued until absorbed by another journal in December 1932.[44] Based in Chicago, *Broadcast Advertising* maintained strong links with the professional organizations of the radio and advertising industries, publishing speeches delivered at the meetings of the National Association of Broadcasters and the American Association of Advertising Agencies.[45] It continued the promotional work begun in the textbooks by publishing case studies of successful radio advertising and directions for preparing commercial broadcast programs and advertisements.

The early promoters of radio advertising exhibited similar outlooks, career paths, methods of presentation, and concerns. Most had worked in both radio and advertising (or business) at a time when such a combination of experience was rare. They explained the mysteries of broadcasting in terms advertising professionals could understand. Their ties to the networks, and the trade associations dominated by the networks, reinforced their beliefs about the best method to finance radio and fueled their messianic zeal. Drawing on their knowledge of contemporary advertising theory and practice, they presented radio as a familiar, but improved, advertising medium. At the same time, they used a pedagogical approach to reach the public, employing slogans and metaphors to promote radio advertising. The proponents of broadcast advertising shifted their focus as the technology and organization of the radio industry developed, but their persuasive techniques, drawn from the larger advertising industry, remained the same.

CAMPAIGN RHETORIC AND STRATEGIES

In 1925 *Popular Radio* printed a listener's response to the portrayal, by the promoters of broadcast advertising, of radio as magical:

There is one thing I hate to be called,
Against it I boldly protest;
It gives me a shiver
A chill on the liver,
To be hailed as "invisible guest."

It's hard to imagine the ether,
As crawling with bodiless hosts,
But it gives me the creeps,
When a voice from the deeps,
Seeks to claim me as one of the ghosts.

When you call me "dear friend" or "dear fan,"
I'll tune in with fervor and zest,
But somehow I quiver,
And cannot but shiver,
When hailed as "invisible guest."[46]

This poem reveals that the promoters of broadcast advertising had adopted the language of 1920s print advertising, including the use of "magic," to present their case. They also invoked slogans and the appeal of "sincerity" to sell radio advertising, as if it were a product taken on by one of the agencies in which they had worked. Broadcast advertising's proponents also portrayed radio as a desirable sales medium by using words and concepts prevalent in theoretical writing about advertising in the 1920s.[47] Boosters bragged that radio could fulfill advertisers' needs by appealing to consumers' senses, providing control over the surrounding material, becoming an integral part of the advertising campaign, improving brand-name awareness, and involving dealers with the products.

From the beginning, the supporters of broadcast advertising used slogans that mirrored the "indirect" form of advertising they advocated for radio. Felix addressed the need for subtlety in writing slogans (because the "radio audience . . . resents the slightest attempt at direct advertising") and described the case of the Happiness Candy Company, which in its announcement "got over the idea that their stores are conveniently located throughout New York, without resorting to a direct advertising statement, by working in the phrase that 'happiness is just around the corner from you.'" An announcement "to the effect that 'there is a Happiness Candy Store near you' would be neither so subtle nor so favorably remembered," according to Felix.[48] Slogans for radio advertising used the indirect approach both because promoters believed indirect selling worked better and because they sought to remind listeners of the proper form of radio advertising.

Many observers described the new financial arrangement represented by radio advertising as the "American System" of broadcasting, which provided "a rich variety of entertainment at the expense of the advertiser, instead of an anemic flow as in England at the expense of the set owner."[49] Support of broadcast advertising was treated almost as a matter of patriotic pride, while broadcast advertising itself was made to appear as a natural extension of a capitalist economy. By calling attention to radio's conventional and "American" financial structure, promoters aimed to defuse objections to the new system.[50]

Arnold claimed that he invented another slogan, "The Fourth Dimension of Advertising," to describe broadcast advertising, bragging that his slogan had "since become a classic." Advertisers, according to Arnold, had previously depended on the three advertising dimensions of newspapers, magazines, and billboards, and the addition of radio appealed to the sense of sound as well as sight. Arnold's phrase aligned radio with traditional advertising media and, at the same time, presented broadcast advertising as something out of science fiction.[51]

Such slogans joined a long list of metaphors used to describe radio, including many that emphasized its ability to make everyday objects special. Observers often described broadcasting as "traffic through the highways of the sky," for one example, with much ensuing discussion of policemen, local roads, and turnpikes.[52] In the promoters' rhetoric, radio advertising was American, but also fabulous; part of advertising, but also supernatural. Case studies detailing the success of broadcast advertising portrayed radio as fantastic, just as early print advertising copy had commonly portrayed new products as magical.[53] *Broadcast Advertising* magazine featured articles entitled "Radio's Magic Carpet: Extensive Printed Advertising Re-enforces Broadcast Campaign" (the article described advertising by a Persian rug manufacturer); "Putting Aladdin Lamps on the Air Puts Them into Farmers' Homes" and "The Cinderella of Broadcasting, Continuity, Is Paging the Fairy Prince."[54] Promoters also talked about radio's "invisible" audience; how radio magically allowed the advertiser to become a guest in a consumer's home; and the ability of radio advertising to "create an atmosphere" of "fashion and luxury and of Paris itself" for a perfume company. Radio became an "open sesame" to new prospects and broadcasting a "modern miracle."[55]

A continuing tension among competing appeals led advertising professionals to attribute fantastic and magical qualities to a product while at other times depending on "sincerity" or "naturalness" to sell the same object. During the early twentieth century, advertising trade journals often discussed "sincerity," as advertising theorists strove to legitimize their profession to the public, to the government, to other business leaders, and to themselves.[56] Sincerity also became an important trait of individual advertisements. Historian T. J. Jackson Lears noted that "sincerity had become at once a moral stance and a tactic of persuasion" and that advertisers wanted an individual advertisement to "be seamless, that its artifice be concealed, that it seemed straightforward and truthful."[57]

Proponents of broadcast advertising tried to convince listeners that radio was harmless at the same time as they presented it as magical. Presenting radio as a "sincere" medium enabled the promoters to begin emphasizing the compatibility of radio with the contemporaneous advertising industry. They moved quickly to present radio as a particularly trustworthy form of communication. Dunlap wrote "that in some mysterious manner the air waves register not what the performer tries to convey, but what he actually feels. There must be fundamental sincerity. Artifices are baldly exposed."[58] Promoters thus aimed to place radio in a category with other new technologies, principally photography, that were considered incorruptible. The imposition of a machine was perceived to give the information an additional veracity.[59] Radio, in the argument of the promoters, could protect the listener/consumer by automatically exposing lies; one article asserted that "nation-wide audience response is so sensitive that no intelligent advertiser can long misuse this wonderful medium for mass communication."[60]

In addition to presenting radio as magical and trustworthy, promoters of radio advertising chose other appeals from both contemporaneous and older advertising practice to buttress their campaign. The new emphases in the 1920s on the consumer rather than on the product, and on vignettes that illustrated the benefits of product use, did not lend themselves to the kind of indirect advertising then considered proper for radio. As radio advertising became more direct, it focused on putting the advertiser "side by side with the consumer" selling "consumer satisfactions," as Roland Marchand has written.[61] Radio's promoters found more useful material, however, in advertising theories and practices from the decades before 1920. Old advertising concepts tended to be layered on top of each other rather than discarded; advertising professionals used, and seemingly believed, even contradictory theories.[62]

Principles of psychology and appeals to nonrational impulses had entered advertising at the turn of the century. Concepts of association and suggestion, which emphasized sense memory, especially influenced early advertisers. Rather than describing a product, advertisements tried to "control the action of the consumer at the time of purchase" by associating a consumer need with an advertised product.[63] Advertisers, according to Merle Curti, soon accepted the "non-rationality of human nature" and emphasized texts and images that operated by "suggestion, the use of forceful concrete details and pictures, by attention-arresting stimuli, by playing on human sympathy, and by appeals to the senses."[64]

Because descriptive advertising did not work well on radio, broadcasting's proponents embraced the concept of suggestive selling. They presented radio as particularly well-suited to sensory appeals and suggestive advertising, with music replacing the visual stimuli of newspapers, magazines, and billboards. Case studies described successful radio programs that reminded listeners of the sponsor's product—the "tinkling" and "refreshing" music of the Clicquot Club Eskimos to suggest Clicquot Club soda, for example.[65] Radio advertisers held the consumer's attention for an entire half hour and so could more strongly influence buying decisions than advertisers in other media. Hettinger compared the radio program, which was constructed by the advertiser, to magazine pages conceived and written by the magazine staff, and concluded that radio advertising was more effective because "it enables the advertiser to select the type of entertainment most certain to appeal to that part of the public which he is most interested in reaching and to place it next to his own advertising message."[66] Through control of the material surrounding their sales pitch, radio advertisers tapped into consumers' nonrational impulses. Hettinger placed great importance on the atmosphere in which consumers received the advertisement, and believed radio offered advertisers a chance to influence that atmosphere. For example, the broadcaster should "study his musical program" to ensure that "the correct emotional state has been built up before his sales message is delivered, or whether the type of music and performing group chosen is in keeping with the emotional background or feeling-tone which he wishes his product to possess."[67] Much like other believers in radio's commercial utility, Hettinger advocated indirect advertising because it did not offend audiences, but he also presented indirect advertising positively as a way to influence consumers' emotions.[68]

As advertising grew more professionalized and complex in the 1920s, broadcasting promoters presented radio advertising as an integral part of any carefully planned advertising campaign, identifying specific tasks radio could perform. In particular, radio could help advertisers improve brand name consciousness. By the 1920s a reliance on branded products was an important part of American mass marketing. Thus, promoters appealed to brand-name advertisers by emphasizing radio's ability to build a "name-consciousness." The sponsor's name could be used many times during a half-hour broadcast. Dunlap reported that one tire manufacturer told him "that the mention of the company's name twenty-four times in the continuity is possible in so unobtrusive a manner that he believes the audience is scarcely conscious of the repetition."[69] Arnold wrote that testing proved the "value of broadcast advertising as a means of obtaining trade-mark publicity," and speculated that radio succeeded because the trademark "seems more human and more real . . . through the radio message" than it did in cold print.[70] National advertising worked best for low-cost items to which a brand name could be affixed, and the manufacturers of these so-called "convenience goods" needed to be wooed to advertise on radio.[71]

Seeking to attract manufacturers of brand-name products led proponents of radio advertising to become interested in marketing strategies, since nationally marketed goods often faced distribution problems.[72] Broadcasting propaganda repeatedly assured manufacturers that radio programs pleased dealers and helped ensure their cooperation. Arnold devoted a chapter, "Broadcasting Aids Distribution," to the subject, claiming that "broadcast advertising gives the distributor something to talk about in addition to the merchandise itself."[73]

NBC emphasized the usefulness of radio advertising in stimulating dealer goodwill in a series of pamphlets for potential sponsors. One account noted that "radio listeners, prospective customers, and dealers are quite likely to be one and the same," and another that dealers "appreciate the Broadcast Advertising."[74] Another booklet, *Improving the Smiles of a Nation! How Broadcast Advertising Has Worked for Ipana Tooth Paste*, looked closely at "dealer cooperation." A manufacturer making a low-cost, low-margin, easily replicated product (such as toothpaste), "had to persuade consumers to buy his brand at the same time he convinced dealers that they could profit by stocking it."[75] Radio, NBC declared, could help such an advertiser meet both objectives with a single advertisement—a sponsored radio program. The brochure began: "Radio has achieved the apparently impossible, by giving real personality to a toothpaste! . . . Ipana programs have secured . . . the willing support and cooperation of dealers . . .

far beyond that obtained through any other medium."[76] Quotations from dealers' letters were included to support NBC's claim, with one dealer exclaiming, "We appreciate both the music of your Troubadours and also the increased sale of Ipana Tooth Paste. Your last program prompted us to give you one of our windows for display." "Broadcast advertising did this job for Ipana," the brochure continued, because "dealers are keenly interested in the programs themselves. Aside from the entertainment which they personally enjoy in common with other listeners, they realize sales are going to benefit."[77] NBC hoped to convince advertisers that radio could double the advertising dollar by improving both marketing and sales.

CHANGES IN BROADCASTING

Promoters of broadcast advertising had boldly presented radio as a perfect advertising medium—exciting, natural, inherently "American," and sincere—which could improve brand-name consciousness and keep dealers happy. In order to increase radio time sales even further, promoters gradually sought to change radio programming to conform more closely to prevailing theories and practices of advertising. Broadcasters, especially those who had long participated in radio, still rarely thought of broadcasting in commercial terms. But radio needed to become fully commercialized before most advertisers would willingly use it to sell goods. During the late 1920s and early 1930s, therefore, promoters pushed broadcasters toward the use of advertising agencies to sell every broadcast hour as a product in and of itself; toward the standardization and professionalization of operations; and toward daytime programming targeted to women listeners.

The entrance of advertising agencies into radio program production resulted from a combination of propaganda and profit maximization. During the 1920s agencies had resisted radio as an advertising medium, and broadcasters tended to view them as competitors rather than potential allies. As late as 1933, Hettinger described agencies as "newcomers in the field of broadcast advertising," while an early historian of advertising, Ralph Hower, concluded that "the advent of radio gave the agencies much trouble and expense, without any considerable amount of gain in revenue to offset the new burden."[78] But the promoters of radio advertising believed agencies and broadcasters needed each other, particularly since agencies controlled most of the national advertising accounts. An advertising agency must give "this lusty new member [radio] a recognition fully commensurate with its present importance and future potentialities," as one *Broadcast Advertising* writer put it.[79] Although radio stations had, of necessity, initially served as their own producers, conceiving of programs and procuring talent, promoters recognized that programs designed by advertising agencies would be more effective as commercial vehicles than the shows developed by broadcasters.

In the introduction to his book, *The Advertising Agency Looks at Radio*, O'Neill remembered a National Association of Broadcasters convention where broadcasters asked, without a "blush, gulp, or stammer," what advertising agencies did. O'Neill wrote his book as an answer to that question.[80] *Broadcast Advertising* magazine published several sets of paired articles in which station managers and advertising agency executives patiently explained their points of view on broadcast advertising.[81] In addition to the promoters' efforts, networks also worked directly to involve advertising agencies. For example, NBC paid commissions whenever an agency client sponsored a radio show, whether or not the agency participated in the planning. NBC also loaned its employees to help establish radio departments within advertising agencies. These departments served as "propagandists" for the use of radio, especially since no other medium had its own dedicated sections.[82]

As long as the issue of commissions was unresolved, however, a stumbling block to agency participation in radio remained. Hard-won tradition permitted agencies to collect a 15 percent commission from the medium in which the agency placed an ad. Radio stations and networks paid commissions on the time purchases made by agencies, but often refused to pay a commission on the fees for performers. *Broadcast Advertising* explained that if an agency spent $1,000 to place ads in a magazine, its commission was $150. But "the same amount spent with a radio station may very possibly be split $500 for the time and $500 for the talent. In such cases the agency usually receives a commission on time only, or $75."[83] Station managers argued that agencies did little or nothing to deserve a commission on the talent used by a radio station and that agency-produced programs often failed to meet a station's highest standards.[84]

The issue of agency commissions on talent masked a larger question. Agencies believed that if they were to profit in radio, they needed to move into program production, hire performers, receive full commissions on advertising placed on the radio, and charge their clients higher fees for these extra services. The growing complexity of commercialized broadcasting—including the need to publicize radio programs, the increasing expense of more sophisticated programming, and the greater technical demands on station managers—added to the pressure on broadcasters to turn over programming to agencies. By the early 1930s "virtually all sponsored network programs were developed and produced by advertising agencies."[85] Local and independent stations continued to produce some programs, but agencies took over production of national sponsored programs. The effort by the promoters of broadcast advertising to involve advertising agencies in the business of radio was reinforced by the Depression era's economics—agencies wanted to protect their fragile profit margins, and stations needed to reduce their expenses.

The change in who produced radio programs brought changes in how broadcasters and advertisers thought about the programs and, eventually, changes in the programs themselves. Broadcasters considered programs as something for listeners to hear when they turned on the radio, while advertising professionals needed to think about what programs might make listeners *want* to turn on the radio.

Agencies had to assure their clients that large numbers of people heard particular radio programs. The appeal of a program could no longer be left to chance. One advertiser believed that "simply to broadcast and let it go at that . . . would be like hiring a theater and putting on a splendid show without telling anybody about it."[86] Promoters called for radio advertisers to publicize their programs, and warned broadcasters, "don't confuse product advertising with program advertising . . . when you advertise the program, talk about it, not the product." A radio sponsor needed to promote its program "within the advertiser's own organization, within his sales organization, within the ranks of his dealers and finally, among the consumers and potential consumers of his product."[87] Most writers agreed that if a program was to reach more than the "average number" of listeners, an advertiser needed to sell the show to its audience.

Merchandising suggestions included the use of newspaper and magazine advertisements and publicity; notices in trade papers; proper follow-up to listener letters; contests and special offers; window, counter, automobile, and outdoor displays; sales representatives' portfolios; broadsides; and booklets and leaflets. Case histories of successful merchandising abounded.[88] Such merchandising was aimed equally at the radio audience (the consumers) and at the advertisers' dealers and sales force. One company sent its sales representatives bulletins about their radio programs because "it was hard for you fellows to hear the program regularly," and the company wanted its sales force to point out the popularity of the program to dealers.[89]

According to these merchandising theories, a radio program was a product to be sold, and the ultimate aim was the commercialization of every aspect of radio. Dunlap wrote that a program "leads the horse to water," but it was merchandising that "makes it drink." A few promoters believed that attention should be paid first to the program because unless the program was good, "all other broadcast merchandising ideas might just as well have never been."[90] But the majority of those writing on the subject ignored program content in favor of merely listing merchandising methods. The merchandising of radio programs helped fuel a growing public perception of radio as commercialized, despite the large proportion of unsponsored programs still paid for by the networks and local stations throughout the early 1930s.

Radio's emerging commercialization made different demands on the broadcasting industry, especially with regard to the selling of time. The two networks quickly standardized both their arrangements with affiliated stations and the rates they charged advertisers. NBC and CBS paid their affiliates for broadcasting commercial programs sent over the network. NBC paid a flat rate that included production costs and line charges, but the CBS arrangement was more complicated and varied from station to station based on a complex formula and on negotiation. NBC charged affiliated stations for providing unsponsored programs, while CBS gave the programs free but asked the stations to pay line charges.[91] By the early 1930s both networks provided potential advertisers with elaborate printed rate cards outlining charges for combinations of affiliated stations at various times.[92]

Standardization of time selling by local stations came more slowly. A 1931 *Broadcast Advertising* article bemoaned the confusion in local stations' rates by describing a "practical example":

Mr. Jones wishes to learn the cost of one minute announcements daily for one month over a certain group of stations. Referring to present rate schedules, this is what he finds: Station A gives only fifty-word announcements;

Station B gives only 200-word announcements; Station C gives only two-minute announcements; Station D, no quotation; Station E quotes by the word; Station F, "rates on application"; Station G quotes minimum of thirty-nine announcements; Station H quotes minimum of seventy-five announcements.[93]

At its 1932 convention the National Association of Broadcasters approved a standard radio advertising contract for use by member stations. The contract covered issues such as program cancellation by either broadcaster or advertiser, interruptions, use of announcers, and deadlines for program material.[94]

Despite variations among local station practices, affiliation with a network and the commercialization of operations brought a new way of thinking about time. One observer wrote that "a statue of radio Thespis would assuredly be blind and with a stopwatch in one hand, or perhaps in each."[95] Unlike the first radio performers, who were urged to fill as much time as they could, a singer on an early network show remembered that "timing was the sword of Damocles hanging over our heads. We could not be ten seconds overtime without infringing on another sponsor's territory."[96] To the promoters of broadcast advertising, the new importance of time in radio must have suggested a growing acceptance of broadcasting's commercialization.

The development of radio advertising recapitulated aspects of the growth and professionalization of the larger advertising industry. The first national print advertisers had not known the circulations of the widely scattered newspapers in which they advertised. Daniel Pope noted that "until well into the new century, agents and advertisers bought literally billions of dollars of advertising space—worrying all the while—without a reliable idea of how many copies of the publications they were using actually were printed or reached customers." Uncertainty about the size and composition of the audience increased the participation of advertising agencies in the advertising process, as uneasy clients turned to professionals with specialized knowledge. The movement of advertising agencies from space brokers to advertisement producers to marketing advisers had been completed by the 1920s, when the process reoccurred in broadcast advertising.[97] Early radio advertisers also lacked information about audience size and were therefore reluctant to use the medium. Contests and premiums designed to attract mail helped gauge the number of listeners. But the growing participation of advertising agencies in broadcasting also helped rationalize the process and calm the fears of advertisers.

RADIO ADVERTISING TO WOMEN

One of the principal arguments for radio advertising was that it enabled advertisers to reach consumers with messages of home and family at the moments when they were enjoying both. An executive announced that "American businessmen, because of radio, are provided with a latchkey to nearly every home in the United States."[98] To take the final step in the commercialization of broadcasting, promoters worked to build a loyal female radio audience that would regularly listen to radio at home during the day. Promoters had to make daytime broadcasting attractive to advertisers in order for radio to turn a profit and in order to fit broadcasting into advertising objectives that posited a day-long audience. With increased sales of time over the networks in the early 1930s, promoters could foresee a moment when they would run out of evening time to sell. The effort to develop radio advertising directed toward women shows how the campaign to promote broadcast advertising ultimately affected both programming content and broadcasting practice.

Promoters faced several cultural and technological barriers in their efforts to convince advertisers to sponsor radio programs aimed at women. Some advertisers resisted using the home—seen both as a women's workplace and as a space set apart from the harsh economic realities of the marketplace—as a site for consumption. Radio's existence in real time—listeners could not put a radio program aside, like a magazine, for a moment when it would not intrude on housework or the family circle—added to advertisers' reluctance to invade the home with this new medium. Radio also maintained, in the minds of many broadcasters and listeners, the image of a boy's toy and a male-controlled entertainment medium.

The first radio schedules did not include daytime programming at all. Radio reception was better at night, and distant signals came in clearly only after sunset. As late as 1924, "successful broadcasting during the daylight hours" remained a "question which is occupying . . . the attention of radio engineers," as they struggled with unexplained static and fading.[99]

Station managers scrambled to fill the few evening hours with amateur performers and happily ignored daytime programming.

Men had monopolized early radio listening. One needed some technical skill to assemble a radio in the early 1920s and to tune the set properly once it was assembled—skills many American men had learned as hobbyists before World War I and in the armed forces during the war, and then had passed on to their sons.[100] Of course some women did learn about radio and constantly amazed their male counterparts with their abilities. For example, *Radio World* magazine published an early column, "Radio and the Woman," written by Crystal D. Tector, and students at Wellesley College studied radio technology in physics class and had their photographs published in a radio magazine to prove it.[101] As transmitters became more powerful and receivers more sensitive, daylight broadcasting became easier, but the idea persisted of radio as an evening, family, and father-controlled entertainment.

The promoters of broadcast advertising took particular interest in radio's role in the home and family, which had become dominant advertising themes. In print advertising, manufacturers presented their products as contributors to domestic bliss and strongly related family happiness and well-being to intelligent consumption. Historian Otis Pease notes that American advertisers aimed to sell "an entire pattern of consumption" centered on the home, and "advertisers increasingly invaded that allegedly private sphere, the family." The emerging consumer culture would be based on what T. J. Jackson Lears has called a new "domestic ideal."[102]

To remind the advertising industry that broadcasting provided a rich opportunity for those interested in home- and family-based appeals, promoters constantly described radio and radio advertisers as "guests in the home." Frank Arnold (using a rather alarming image of radio as an invasive rather than invited medium) went so far as to write:

Then came radio broadcasting, utilizing the very air we breathe, and with electricity as its vehicle entering the homes of the nation through doors and windows, no matter how tightly barred, and delivering its message audibly through the loud speaker wherever placed. For the first time in the history of mankind, this dream of the centuries found its realization. In the midst of the family circle, in moments of relaxation, the voice of radio brings to the audience its program of entertainment or its message of advertising.[103]

Women's roles as wives and mothers made them pivotal figures in the new advertising theories. Marchand notes that, by the 1920s, male advertising professionals believed they were "engaged primarily in talking to women."[104] Prospective advertisers, however, tended to believe that radio drew a smaller audience during the day because women working in the home were too busy to sit down and listen. As late as 1932, several women wrote of turning on the radio only after their housework was done, and then listening only while they did their sewing.[105] Network programmers therefore aimed to devise formats that would appeal to reluctant advertisers and draw female listeners.

The first daytime radio programs aimed at women—produced for local and regional stations before the networks were established—presented short sponsored talks by representatives of companies that produced goods or services women purchased. Broadcasters saw the programs as an integral part of women's "working day," a time when they could introduce housewives to products "whose chief appeal is to women and which need some interpretation."[106] The programs were instructional, so that women would not feel they were taking time from their busy schedules merely to enjoy light entertainment; instead they would listen to become better wives and mothers. For example, Anna J. Peterson, "our radio mother," broadcast menus and recipes in 1925 for the People's Gas Light and Coke Company over KYW, Chicago. In 1926 Buttericks presented a talk over WJZ, New York, on the "making of winter attire."[107]

After the networks made regular national radio programming possible, broadcasters continued to look for programs that could be presented to advertisers as directly related to women's work in the home. Rather than taking a homemaker away from her chores, educational programs could instruct women in the use of a sponsor's product, and could allow the sponsor to advertise in both the commercials and the program for the same price. Advertisers and broadcasters found a willing ally in the home economics profession, which gladly took up the challenge of using radio to teach women how to shop and do housework more efficiently.[108] The radio home economists also fit well with the contemporary view of using advertising to educate consumers. The advertising industry in the 1920s had found the use of "experts" particularly useful; consumers were made to feel insecure and then were offered advice about what products would bring them a feeling of security.[109] Besides "expertise," radio instructors could provide "warmth," an attribute broadcasters hoped would overcome advertisers' fears about barging into listeners' homes uninvited. One such "authority," broadcasting over WOR in New York City, wrote that women consumers could find the answers to their questions in many places but preferred the "human contact and little more personal touch which they receive when we of the air talk to them."[110]

Identifying an expert as a real person proved an important element of fostering this "personal touch." Three of the best-known experts who went on the air to instruct and sell to American women were Aunt Sammy (Uncle Sam's wife), Betty Crocker, and Ida Bailey Allen. Their programs pioneered formats designed to overcome advertisers' objections to selling to women over the radio. On October 4, 1926, fifty women in fifty radio stations across the country first became "Aunt Sammy" by reading identical scripts prepared by U.S. Department of Agriculture home economists. In that initial fifteen-minute broadcast, Aunt Sammy:

> recited a stanza of doggerel verse, told several jokes, explained how to select and care for linoleum for the kitchen floor, directed how to roast wienies the "modern" way, how to use vinegar left over from a jar of pickles, and how to put up a cucumber relish, defined what a vitamin was, enumerated the five foods essential to the daily diet, listed "what foods should be taken from dishes with fingers," and ended by offering the menu for the day—meat loaf with brown gravy, scalloped potatoes, carrots or beets, fresh sliced tomatoes and lemon jelly dessert.[111]

Aunt Sammy became a hit and remained popular. During the Depression, her cookbook helped listeners get through what she called "these days of thrift."[112]

Broadcasters loved USDA programs such as "The Housekeeper's Chat," which featured Aunt Sammy. They cost little, filled hours unpopular with sponsors, and at the same time helped prove to potential advertisers that similar programs could draw an audience. The large number of listener requests for Aunt Sammy's printed recipes proved that women were listening to her program, and thus encouraged those trying to convince sponsors to invest in daytime programs. While her programs discussed no brand-name products, Aunt Sammy, like the home economist she was, explained and introduced "modern" and "improved" consumer goods of particular use to rural women.[113] She showed how a familiar and friendly "individual" could appeal to women listeners while instructing them in their household duties.

Another fictional character, Betty Crocker, had a more particular message for her listeners: to buy General Mills products. The company invented Crocker to answer questions for consumers by mail, and it soon launched regional cooking schools in which Crocker clones demonstrated the full range of General Mills products. The company founded one of the first radio stations, WCCO in Minneapolis, and the home economists who portrayed Crocker eagerly took to the airwaves to spread their ideas to a larger audience. At first, different Betty Crockers broadcast from various stations, but after the advent of network radio one woman speaking from the Minneapolis studio could be heard in many cities. General Mills remained convinced that its instructional radio program helped sell its products, and Betty Crocker long provided a model for other sponsors in combining instruction with the promotion of particular products.[114]

Trained as a dietician and working as a cooking school instructor and cookbook author, Ida Bailey Allen was one of the first nonfictional experts approached by broadcasters to give morning radio talks. After the formation of CBS, when radio time became more expensive, Allen wondered "how in the world I could finance broadcasts to the entire country." An executive at the company that published Allen's cookbooks suggested that she handle the problem like a magazine by selling segments of the program to interested sponsors.[115] CBS agreed to air Allen's program, "The National Homemaker's Club," and by 1930 she had her own radio studio, test kitchen, beauty boudoir, living room, and elaborately decorated executive offices with daily fresh flowers, all intended to serve as models for her listeners.[116] Allen's magazine-style radio format lured advertisers by giving them a chance to sponsor portions of programs without a major commitment of time or money. Companies that made products with low unit costs could afford to buy small blocks of radio time without the expense of sponsoring an entire program.

Aunt Sammy, Betty Crocker, and Ida Bailey Allen all showed that broadcasters could design programs to overcome advertisers' objections to daytime radio. Moreover, these models illustrated programming forms the networks would adopt and market to completely commercialize the broadcast day. One approach was to gather various short sponsored talks together in a magazine program, like Ida Bailey Allen's. The networks would then sell airtime for commercials and assure advertisers that a network home economist would provide a relevant talk to appear directly preceding their message.[117] This may well have been the first attempt to sell "spot advertisements." The networks thus developed these early daytime shows to appeal specifically to advertisers, presaging the later form taken by all commercial broadcasting.

As late as 1932, however, broadcasters were still encountering problems selling their daytime hours. Although the commercialized broadcasting system dominated by the networks was in place, only one-third of network programming was commercially sponsored. Mornings came close to the evening level, with 29.5 percent of the hours paid for by advertisers, but in the afternoons only 11.8 percent of the broadcast hours were sold.[118] An NBC internal memo from 1933 called daytime broadcasting a "hodge-podge arrangement" and recommended greater thought and structure for the daytime schedule.[119] For the next five years, NBC made a special attempt to encourage advertisers to buy daytime hours, publishing pamphlets entitled "Wake Up to Daytime Possibilities"; "Sell the Housewife and You Sell All"; "At Least 72.9% of the Women Are at Home at Any Given DAYTIME Hour. Tell Them . . . You'll Sell Them!"; and "28.9% of All NBC Sponsored Programs Are DAYTIME Programs: Daytime Is Sales Time."[120]

Having made a beginning at selling morning hours for instructional programs, the networks strove to convince more sponsors to buy time in the afternoons. "Soap operas"—serial melodramas sponsored by detergent manufacturers—quickly came to dominate the afternoon hours. One inspiration for the soaps were the skits presented during the morning instructional shows. Characters such as Uncle Ebenezer and nephew Billy sometimes joined Aunt Sammy, as did Finicky Florine and Percy DeWallington Waffle, fussy eaters who drove their mothers crazy.[121] Soap operas followed the criteria proven successful in the morning instructional shows: they featured recurring characters using products, lasted fifteen minutes rather than the evening's usual half-hour, and were sold to companies that manufactured something women bought routinely without consultation. Other factors, notably the soap companies' advertising needs during the Depression and the success of continuing evening dramas such as "Amos 'n' Andy" and "The Rise of the Goldbergs," also influenced the emergence of the afternoon soaps.[122] But networks based the soap operas on a marketing concept—that women, a perfect audience for advertisers, were best reached in their homes by radio—that had, over the previous ten years, been tested and sold to advertisers by those who had a stake in fully commercialized broadcasting. Expenditures for daytime radio advertising more than doubled between 1935 and 1939, and daytime radio finally began to be profitable.[123]

Radio advertising to women was a tough sell, but one that the broadcast industry had to make so that radio conformed to other ideas about advertising prevalent in the 1920s, when many advertising professionals came to think of women as the chief consumers.[124] The eventual acceptance, by broadcasters and advertisers, of daytime radio programs directed at women marked the conclusion of the campaign to promote broadcast advertising. The promoters had succeeded both in convincing advertisers that radio was a useful advertising medium able to reach consumers in their homes, and in convincing broadcasters that all programming should be available for sponsorship. In the process, the form and content of radio programming changed. The promoters presented all such changes as improvements, just as they presented broadcast advertising as "natural." In truth, the evolutionary adaptations in radio programming—such as the movement from local amateur musicians to nationally celebrated vaudeville performers—brought both gains and losses to radio listeners.

How to Build a Two-Stage Radio-Frequency Amplifier

THE MARCH OF RADIO

A New Method of Transmitting Pictures by Wire or Radio

DOUBLEDAY, PAGE & COMPANY   GARDEN CITY, NEW YORK

Radio Broadcast's cover of May 1925 illustrated a familiar scene. Young men and boys were the first to learn about radio, and they often introduced their families to the wonders of long-distance listening. (*Radio Broadcast* 2, May 1923)

How Far Did You Hear Last Night?

The lure of distant stations grips the radio fan. Even the seasoned old timer gets a thrill when he brings in a station'way across the continent, or sits, in awe, as a clear Spanish message comes thru the ether from Cuba or Mexico.

Michigan "Senior" Regenerative Radio Receiving Set

Its power over distance marks the *Michigan "Senior" Regenerative Radio Receiving Set* as an instrument almost in a class by itself.

Its Michigan Split-Hair Vernier Dial Adjuster—exclusive with us—permits a finer, more accurate tuning than is possible with ordinary dial controls.

A wonderfully simple set to operate. A ten-year old girl in Michigan brings in New York, Denver, Atlanta, Dallas, and other distant stations.

It is the ideal *Home* set; beautiful in its Grand Rapids wood-craftsmanship and finish—a real ornament to the cultured home. The family possessing it never lacks for entertainment or instruction—and is the envy of its neighbors.

Manufactured under the Armstrong License (U.S. Patent No. 1,113,149, and pending letters of patent No. 807,388; for amateur and experimental use only). This protects dealers and users against possible legal complications and insures a set that conforms with the latest thought in advanced Radio engineering. We manufacture complete line of condensers, Rheostats, Amplifiers, Variometers, Varicouplers. Write for catalog.

Send for free *Descriptive Circular*, giving name and address of local dealer you'd prefer to have do the installation if you conclude to buy.

MICHIGAN RADIO CORPORATION

GRAND RAPIDS, MICHIGAN

Because listeners sought programs from far away, early advertisements for radio receivers touted the long distances they could span. (*Radio Broadcast* 2, January 1923)

Sponsors sent 50,000 copies of the "Clicquot Fox Trot March" to radio listeners to promote their program. The banjo orchestra took the name of the product's mascot (pictured at the left) to remind listeners of the cold, clear taste of Clicquot Club ginger ale. (Archives Center, National Museum of American History, Smithsonian Institution)

Farmers became regular radio listeners, either in their homes or as here, in a bank, to obtain market and weather reports from commercial centers. (Thomas C. Knight Collection, Series A, Box 8, Archives Center, National Museum of American History, Smithsonian Institution)

Broadcasters worked to convince advertisers that women listened to the radio during the day as they did housework. As shown here, recipes (followed by commercials for food and appliances) could reach women as they canned in their kitchens. (Thomas C. Knight Collection, Series A, Box 6, Archives Center, National Museum of American History, Smithsonian Institution)

When leaky batteries gave way to household current and headsets to loudspeakers, radio receivers moved from Americans' garages into their living rooms, and advertisers began to think of radio as a good way to reach consumers—principally men—in their homes. This photograph of an RCA Radiola probably dates from 1926. (Thomas C. Knight Collection, Series A, Box 8, Archives Center, National Museum of American History, Smithsonian Institution)

KFKX, Westinghouse's repeating station in Hastings, Nebraska, was housed in a wooden shack. Its disarray and small scale point toward the failure of shortwave rebroadcasting as a way of providing national radio service. (H. D. Roess Collection, National Museum of American History, Smithsonian Institution)

This photograph of an early broadcast studio (WDY in New Jersey) shows that acoustical design in 1921 included household drapes and a towel tied around the microphone for sound absorption. (Thomas C. Knight Collection, Series A, Box 3, Archives Center, National Museum of American History, Smithsonian Institution)

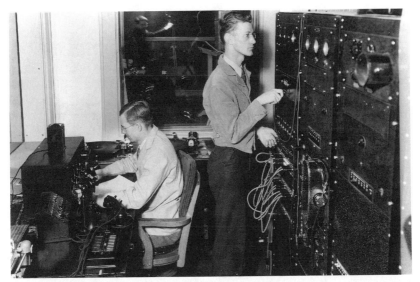

Purchasing the proper equipment to comply with FRC regulations proved expensive for many radio stations funded by colleges. Shown here is the control room of WHA, founded by the University of Wisconsin. (University of Wisconsin-Madison Archives)

The Wagner-Hatfield amendment would have reserved a certain percentage of frequencies for nonprofit stations such as WHA, one of the first college radio stations, run by students at the University of Wisconsin. (University of Wisconsin-Madison Archives)

Leaders of business and government attending the Third National Radio Confer-
ence in 1924 objected to David Sarnoff's super-power proposal because of the po-
tential for an RCA monopoly on national radio service. Left to right: C. Francis
Jenkins, radio inventor; David Sarnoff, vice-president and general manager of
RCA; Maj. Gen. George Owen Squier, former chief of the U.S. Army Signal
Corps; and Secretary of Commerce Herbert Hoover. (Prints and Photographs
Division, Library of Congress)

David Sarnoff, eventually chairman of RCA, was a shrewd infighter who managed to keep himself and his corporation in key positions as the broadcasting industry evolved. (Thomas C. Knight Collection, Series A, Box 13, Archives Center, National Museum of American History, Smithsonian Institution)

By the late 1920s manufacturers were renting downtown auditoriums to display receivers in "living-room" settings, decorated in a variety of styles. This radio exhibit took place in Syracuse, New York, in 1927. (George H. Clark Collection, Archives Center, National Museum of American History, Smithsonian Institution)

The first radio stores, like this one in Peekskill, New York, displayed ready-made radios as expensive products requiring considerable consumer instruction. (Thomas C. Knight Collection, Series A, Box 8, Archives Center, National Museum of American History, Smithsonian Institution)

In response to the Depression, advertisers often presented products in luxurious settings, using what historian Roland Marchand has labeled the "democracy of goods" appeal. The text accompanying this publicity photo proclaimed that ordinary consumers could buy the same radio receiver and hear the same broadcasts as these rich people. (Thomas C. Knight Collection, Series A, Box 8, Archives Center, National Museum of American History, Smithsonian Institution)

Wendell Hall, star of the "Eveready Hour," got married on November 5, 1924, over the airwaves. Shown here with his bride, Hall managed to become personally famous but remained identified with Eveready batteries. (George C. Clark Collection, Series B, Box 13, Archives Center, National Museum of American History, Smithsonian Institution)

Billy Jones and Ernie Hare enjoyed their biggest success as the "Happiness Boys," advertising a candy company, and then found it difficult to switch sponsors. Here they sing as the "Interwoven Pair" for a sock manufacturer. (From Alfred N. Goldsmith and Austin C. Lescarboura, *This Thing Called Broadcasting*, New York: Henry Holt, 1930)

Rudy Vallee, shown here at the opening of the Shoreham Hotel in Washington, D.C., October 1930, hosted the "Fleischmann Hour." Already a movie star before moving to radio, Vallee kept his own name and identity while introducing many vaudevillians to broadcast audiences. (Prints and Photographs Division, Library of Congress)

Eddie Cantor made his first broadcast over WJZ–Newark about 1922 (as shown here) and then left the airwaves until 1931. Driven from the stage by the Depression and lured by high salaries in broadcasting, many vaudeville stars turned to radio in the early 1930s. (George C. Clark Collection, Series B, Box 13, Archives Center, National Museum of American History, Smithsonian Institution)

This 1923 photograph, probably a publicity stunt, shows the importance to farmers of up-to-date information. (Prints and Photographs Division, Library of Congress)

Early radio broadcasters, desperate for programs, lured many vocalists from the worlds of opera and Broadway into the studio. Here Olga Petrova sings the theme song of the Broadway comedy *The White Peacock*, in full costume. (Thomas C. Knight Collection, Series A, Box 14, Archives Center, National Museum of American History, Smithsonian Institution)

The Whittall Rug Company staged this 1928 photograph featuring its radio dance band, the Whittall Anglo-Persians, seated on one of its products. Despite the fact that radio shows in the 1920s had no studio audiences, performers often appeared in costume for both broadcasts and publicity shots. (George C. Clark Collection, Series B, Box 13, Archives Center, National Museum of American History, Smithsonian Institution)

In 1928 the musicians who portrayed "The Michelin Men" took anonymity to extremes, adopting both the name and form of the product they promoted. (George C. Clark Collection, Series B, Box 9, Archives Center, National Museum of American History, Smithsonian Institution)

The increasing commercialization of the airwaves drove many listeners wild, as suggested in this 1928 H. T. Webster cartoon, which appeared in the *New York World*. (H. T. Webster Collection, State Historical Society of Wisconsin, Madison)

Here the cartoonist ridicules advertisers' view of radio listeners. (H. T. Webster Collection, State Historical Society of Wisconsin, Madison)

As illustrated in this H. T. Webster cartoon from the *New York Herald Tribune*, even the most conventional listener sought to avoid radio advertising. (H. T. Webster Collection, State Historical Society of Wisconsin, Madison)

"THEN TWENTY IRATE LISTENERS WRITE A LETTER TO SECRETARY HOOVER."

This cartoon from a 1926 issue of *Radio Broadcast* magazine shows a variety of listeners seated on a receiver while writing angry letters about broadcasting to the Secretary of Commerce. (*Radio Broadcast* 8, March 1926)

TWISTING THE DIALS

Changes in Radio Programming

How do you do, everybody, how do you do?
How do you do, everybody, how are you?
Don't forget your Friday date,
Seven-thirty until eight.
How do you doodle doodle doodle doodle do?

Billy Jones and Ernie Hare, known as the "Happiness Boys," opened and closed their weekly, half-hour radio show for five and a half years in the early 1920s with their theme song, "How Do You Do?" Their program was different in several respects from other radio shows of the early 1920s: few early radio shows had sponsors, like Happiness Candy, or featured professional performers, like Jones and Hare. From 1923 to 1933 Jones and Hare enjoyed a huge success, but then had to scramble for radio jobs as the industry changed dramatically with the introduction of networks and fully commercialized national broadcasting. They remained on the air until Hare's death in 1939, but their popularity had peaked.

The rise and decline of the Happiness Boys illustrates the influence on broadcasting both of the network system and the advertising industry. Programming, performers, advertising, advertisers, and audience surveying all changed dramatically over the first twelve years of broadcasting. Some programming and personnel changes stemmed from social and cultural factors—among others, changing tastes, the Depression, and increased nationwide acceptance of the urban experience. But the push for national radio, the establishment of the wired network system, and the campaign to promote broadcasting to advertisers had even more immediate effects.

Relatively unknown recording artists such as the Happiness Boys, with their small-town humor, gave way to already celebrated urban vaudevillians; regional sponsors were replaced by national sponsors; listeners' letters ceded influence to the new art of audience surveys. These differences came about as a decentralized regional system, with small advertisers afraid of offending listeners, evolved into a centralized national system, with corporate sponsors largely in control of programming. As the promoters of broadcast advertising worked to make radio more closely match prior advertising media, station managers and performers simultaneously sought models for new programs and advertisements in their own short history.

EARLY RADIO PROGRAMMING

In 1925 one observer called radio stations (carefully excepting the big city stations) "cheap hangouts for jobless small-time vaudeville performers, industrious song pushers, parlor boobs, hopeless pupils of honorless music teachers, nutty reformers, quack health doctors and Kiwanis Club lecturers."[1] The Happiness Boys competed against all these performers, a mixture of the best and worst of American entertainment. Most stations in the 1920s were desperate to fill the few hours a day they stayed on the air. Early radio listeners thus heard a somewhat chaotic jumble of different kinds of music, talks, poetry, children's stories, plays, and sports. Music predominated, performed by local amateurs with an occasional traveling professional or hotel dance band coaxed before the microphone by the lure of free publicity. Soloists such as singers, violinists, and pianists were most common. Many radio musicians showed little skill in their performances

94

of traditional sentimental ballads or light classics, yet touring dance bands brought the best in popular music, brilliantly performed, to the airwaves. According to *Radio Broadcast*, Chicago's first station, KYW (built by Westinghouse), presented the entire 1921 season of the Chicago Opera Company. When the season ended, KYW scrambled for other programming to fill its schedule.[2]

The very first broadcast radio stations had experimented with phonograph records—placing the microphone next to the phonograph's horn—but the poor quality of the transmission discouraged listeners. As a matter of prestige, therefore, early stations boasted that they used only live musicians. The U.S. Department of Commerce institutionalized the prejudice against recordings in 1922 by relegating stations transmitting recordings to less desirable frequencies. Even when improved technology permitted the electrical broadcast of recordings, regulations still favored live programming and thus the wealthier stations that could afford to pay performers.[3]

The emphasis on live programming, and disappointment over the uneven quality of the performers available, led many station managers to regular broadcasts of community events. In the early 1920s radio stations frequently "picked up" religious services by sending engineers with microphones to local churches. The engineers transmitted the services over telephone or telegraph lines to the stations for broadcast. Relayed in the same manner, banquet and political speeches formed another programming mainstay, followed quickly by the hotel dance bands who performed in the same rooms in which the speeches had been given. Sporting events also proved logical candidates for "pickup."[4]

Most early radio stations lost money, partly because the station management had no clear purpose in broadcasting. Entertaining listeners was not always the top priority, with some stations programming for "uplift" or education. Controversies over programming seldom emerged, for it was difficult to determine what listeners wanted to hear, management was unsure what it wanted to broadcast, and performers were so scarce that stations put anyone willing on the air immediately. Station managers (who also usually acted as announcers) made the programming decisions. Often young men with some wartime radio experience, these early managers had little knowledge of the entertainment business, and expediency dictated the content of most programs. The manager of a Kentucky radio station wrote that "it was necessary to have a long string of volunteers on call and for them to be dependable enough to cross our threshold promptly thirty minutes before starting time." He reported that he left the choice of material to the artist, but that "half an hour was none too long in which to orientate their introductions, think up a few words about each musical selection, and, if possible some interesting fact concerning the life of its composer."[5] Despite the half-hour allotted for preparation, things often went wrong, so that the timing of early radio programs was informal and imprecise.

Announcers often asked listeners to mail in letters, so they could find out who was in the audience. (The very first stations—broadcasting code rather than words or music—had requested that those who received the signal send postcards, so that the stations could calculate their range.) This practice continued into the 1930s, with letters providing a rough measure of program popularity. Writing to radio stations became part of the fun of listening, with notes from distance fiends bragging about how "far" they could hear fading into letters from faithful listeners complaining about a particular announcer. One station manager commented that listeners could help radio stations "now maintained at large expense to the operating company and giving programmes entirely free of charge" by sending "a card acknowledging receipt of the broadcast." Later, program sponsors encouraged letters by offering gifts or premiums to listeners who wrote. Listeners' letters contained suggestions about every aspect of broadcasting, from programming to hours on the air.[6]

As listeners tired of pursuing distant radio signals and sought better programming, radio magazines and stations became more interested in what programs listeners liked. Even before radio had much advertising, or stations thought of turning a profit, more systematic studies of listener preferences were attempted. In a 1926 article, "Meet Mr. Average Radio Enthusiast," *Radio Broadcast* reported on seven hundred responses to a questionnaire asking about preferences in radio sets and parts. Only one paragraph mentioned programming, noting that "ten and five tenths percent made suggestions for better broadcasting, asking for the encouragement of better programs, less prolific announcing, better pronunciation in announcing, less jazz, and better quality in transmission."[7]

Many of the early surveys focused on the jazz-versus-classical-music debate. Atwater Kent, a receiving set manufacturer and sponsor of a program featuring classical music, undertook a poll described in the April 1926 *Radio Broadcast*. Listeners wanted "high-class entertainment," more variety in programming, and better announcing, the magazine reported. The majority thought there was too much jazz, but 2,400 out of 2,600 respondents said there was just enough classical music.[8] *Radio Age* noted that in a Chicago listener survey "only 1.7% of the listeners want grand opera"; "two-thirds . . . who mailed in their votes were men"; and "almost one-fourth wanted classical music." The magazine failed to mention that the accompanying figures showed that while 24.7% desired classical music, 29% sought popular music.[9]

Proponents of classical music and jazz fought throughout the early 1920s.[10] Their battle was part of a larger struggle over control of programming and the nature of broadcasting. At first, station owners and managers preferred classical music because they saw programming as a form of listener education and uplift, while listeners often sought jazz. Commercialization made listener preferences, within limits, more important, and weakened the argument that programs served any purpose other than entertainment. While classical music continued to hold a place in radio programming, gone were the days when operatic selections could constitute a major part of a station's offerings. Each station had to draw the biggest audience it could to make its time attractive to sponsors, and so programming aimed to lure the largest possible number of listeners.

In addition to chronicling the classical-versus-jazz controversy, early radio audience surveys reported that listeners enjoyed sponsored programs, largely because they featured consistent and professional performers. In January and February of 1927, *Radio Broadcast* asked readers to "Tell Us What You Like in Radio Programs." The editors concluded, based on a thousand responses, that "under present radio conditions, the city listener, especially in the large city, relies on his local stations for the most part, while those living some distance from the so-called 'key stations'" relied on strategic tuning to locate faraway stations. By 1927, in other words, long-distance listening remained popular only for those without access to high-quality local programming. Listeners enjoyed the sponsored programs best—this several months before the founding of NBC. Respondents mentioned the Happiness Boys as well as the "Eveready Hour," Atwater Kent, A & P Gypsies, Clicquot Club Eskimos, Ipana Troubadours, "Maxwell Hour," and Goldy and Dusty.[11]

Harried station managers were finding that sponsorship could fill radio time with little station effort and improve program quality by featuring professional performers. Sponsors were spending money on broadcasting, something most stations could not do, at a time when listeners were clamoring increasingly for better programs.[12] *Popular Radio* explained that commercial broadcasters "are interested in results rather than in philanthropy," and "they are making every effort to entertain as many listeners as possible," a goal not necessarily shared by the first broadcasters.[13] It was not surprising that listeners enjoyed the shows designed by sponsors to please them. While never in a majority, the pre-network sponsored shows of the mid-1920s became important models for later programming.

PRE-NETWORK SPONSORED SHOWS

In August 1923 Billy Jones and Ernie Hare first appeared on radio as the Happiness Boys to promote the Happiness Candy Company at a time when radio industry leaders and observers were heatedly debating the question, "who pays for broadcasting?" Jones and Hare presented a program different from almost anything else heard in 1923. The Happiness Candy Company's purchase of time on New York's WEAF could have happened only on a station owned, or licensed, by AT&T, as it then maintained the sole right to sell time over the air. Yet most companies remained reluctant to buy time on WEAF, making the candy company's sponsorship a daring move. Happiness Candy Company was thus one of the first American corporations to consider radio a regional selling tool; it approached WEAF because the station's advanced technology promised a strong signal to a large audience.

The Happiness Boys were also unusual in their regular weekly time slot: "your Friday date, seven-thirty until eight." Most radio programs of the early 1920s, sponsored or unsponsored, were one-time events. Because amateur performers, usually unreliable, could not be persuaded to appear regularly, a weekly entertainment program had never been tried before. As late as 1926, *Radio Broadcast* magazine debated the virtues of recurring programming and concluded that "weekly features . . . constitute the best that radio has to offer" since the programs were aired at a "fixed hour," were "easy to locate," and provided "a more or less uniform type of program, so the listener knows what to expect."[14]

The use of a theme song to identify the "Happiness Boys" show was also innovative and notable.[15] Jones and Hare had worked in vaudeville but were earning their living as recording artists when Happiness Candy hired them. Their extensive experience in the entertainment industry, including specialized practice before a microphone, made them a rarity in early radio. On the show and on their records (which they continued to produce at a prodigious rate) they performed "song and patter," a mixture of comic songs and jokes commonly used by two-man minstrel and vaudeville acts.[16] Besides introducing comedy to radio, the Happiness Boys brought to the airwaves their polished renditions of sentimental ballads, skillful harmonies, and an appealing manner.

Radio Broadcast reported that, while a statement that Happiness Candy was providing the hour's entertainment did not hurt listeners, "a bit more music and a correspondingly decreased period of self-approbation would be more conducive to candy buying."[17] Listener dislike of early radio advertising influenced the shape and form of the Happiness Candy Company's program, which followed the techniques of indirect advertising, including naming the performers after the product (hence the "Happiness Boys") as an inoffensive way of repeating the sponsor's name several times during a program. Other advertisements, however brief, usually brought complaints from listeners unused to any sales pitches over the air. The Happiness Boys also sang cheerful songs, since their employer believed that geniality reminded the audience of the product's name.

Sponsorship such as the Happiness Candy Company's had emerged shortly after the birth of broadcast radio. Small-town and rural stations presented a few sponsored shows, but the most popular originated from the urban stations. These programs went out to several stations on one of the pre-network chains, or were transmitted with a strong signal sent by the latest equipment. *Radio Broadcast*, reporting on its 1927 audience survey, noted that the programs broadcast over several stations naturally received the most votes, "but the comparative popularity of broadcasts such as that of the Happiness Boys [WEAF, New York] or Sam 'n' Henry [WMAQ, Chicago, later "Amos 'n' Andy"] is remarkable, for each feature is broadcast over but one station."[18] This popularity was by design: broadcasters and sponsors were tailoring these programs to appeal to a large regional, rather than local, audience.

Before the founding of the networks, the New York stations owned by the feuding members of the radio trust led in presenting regional sponsored shows, at least partly because a large number of skilled performers and national corporations made their headquarters in New York. Financed as showplaces by the radio trust, these stations (WEAF, WJZ, and WJY) had the best equipment and participated in most of the early chain experiments, easily linking up with stations in other cities owned by the same parent company.

As the first station to accept paid advertisements, AT&T's WEAF had the edge in sponsorship. Before the telephone company founded WEAF, no one considered selling time on the air; any business that wanted its name mentioned on the radio had to buy a station. The telephone company, building on its tradition that the sender of messages pays for the privilege, launched WEAF with the idea that "the American Telephone and Telegraph Company will provide no programs of its own," but would instead "provide the channels through which anyone . . . can send out their own programs." AT&T moved quickly to create a monopoly on sponsored broadcasting by announcing that the radio patent agreement gave AT&T the exclusive right to sell radio time, and by refusing other stations the use of telephone lines to link up and provide the larger audiences sought by advertisers.[19] The other patent pool members disputed AT&T's exclusive right to sell time, but rarely challenged the company directly on this issue, preferring to seek other ways to profit from radio.

Because it sold time, WEAF had the greatest number of sponsored hours, but other New York stations also featured programs that carried the names of local and regional companies. Beginning in 1923, RCA operated two stations in the New York area: WJY and WJZ (founded by Westinghouse). In an unusual move, the RCA stations specialized; WJZ broadcast lighter entertainment, while WJY listeners heard classical music and lectures.[20] Handwritten WJY and WJZ program logs show that, at first, the stations broadcast only from 4 to 11 p.m. and relied on remote pickups from hotels for dance orchestras or banquet speeches.

Filling broadcast time remained a problem for WJY and WJZ until the discovery that sponsoring companies, given an hour on the radio, were willing to produce and fund programming themselves. As early as the spring and summer of 1923, the logs listed the "National Biscuit Co. Band"; "R. H. Macy presents, 'Once Upon a Time' by the Employees of R. H. Macy and Co., Inc."; and the "Wanamaker Organ Recital," programs which apparently featured company workers as performers.[21] Over the next three years, the number of sponsored hours grew, with more log entries that read "music free" (meaning that the station did not pay the performers). Sponsors increasingly recruited professional performers and paid them if they insisted on remuneration. Some of the logs had continuities (announcer's scripts) scrawled on them; at this stage, station announcers still said nothing about products, but rather told the name of the program and, with a few rhetorical flourishes, introduced the musical selections.[22] Sponsored shows included "50 Questions" by *Time*, the weekly newsmagazine; "Buescher Saxophone Hour," courtesy of New York Band Instrument Company; "Royal Typewriter Salon Orchestra"; "New York Edison Hour"; "Victor Hour"; "Breyer Hour"; "Bakelite Hour"; "Butterick Fashion Talk"; and "The Ray-O-Vac Twins."[23] Most of these programs were musical, most were heard more than once (sometimes at irregular intervals), and most were broadcast over WJZ.

WJZ and WJY also increased the number and improved the quality of their broadcasts through participation in small chains. By 1925 WJY either sent one program a night to other cities or picked up one show from outside New York. Most often, WJY took plays from WGY (owned by General Electric) in Schenectady and sent hotel dance band concerts to WGY and WRC (owned by RCA) in Washington, D.C. The chain provided these extra programs cheaply and enabled each station to specialize while still giving local listeners some variety. WGY, for example, became expert in radio drama, as Schenectady lacked hotels with first-rate musical entertainment.[24] The chain also carried sponsored shows such as the "Brunswick Hour of Music," originating on April 7, 1925, and sent to WGY, WRC, and Westinghouse stations KYW, Chicago; KDKA, Pittsburgh; and WBZ, Springfield, Massachusetts. The program featured John Charles Thomas, baritone, Elisabeth Rethberg, soprano, and the Brunswick Symphony Orchestra.[25] According to the patent pool agreement before the founding of NBC, sponsored shows and the use of chains belonged exclusively to AT&T and WEAF, and yet both chains and sponsorship played important roles in the programming of WJY and WJZ.

WEAF had cause for worry about the competition from the RCA stations, since its concept of broadcasting-for-hire did not achieve overnight success. An early WEAF employee recalled "it used to disturb us greatly" that the staff of WJZ went to advertisers and said "we'll give you the time for nothing if you will put your program on WJZ." The "rough competition" over potential sponsors continued until NBC was formed.[26] One observer noted of WEAF that "after two months' operation a total of only three hours of air time had been bought and the station's revenues had amounted to only $550."[27] When one of WEAF's sales representatives "succeeded in bringing in an account, it was almost like a Christmas holiday. . . . that was how few and far between these commercial accounts were at the onset of the business."[28] If AT&T wanted programs on WEAF, it looked like the telephone company itself would have to provide them—a wholly unforseen circumstance. Only after programs were first developed by telephone company employees did advertisers begin to pay for sponsorship at WEAF; Billy Jones and Ernie Hare started with a "sustaining program" before being sponsored by Happiness Candy.[29] While 1923 brought a slight improvement in business, WEAF continued to operate at a loss until 1924, when it first showed a small profit.[30]

WEAF established strict standards regarding program and advertising content. AT&T forbade price references, package descriptions, sales arguments, or the offering of samples, and worried about the personal or offensive nature of some products such as toothpaste and cigarettes. No advertising was permitted on Sunday.[31] Gradually advertising became more accepted and AT&T relaxed many of the rules, but the earliest WEAF programs closely resembled those broadcast by their competitors, WJZ and WJY.

Unlike WJY and WJZ, however, WEAF aimed to make money, not simply to cover its costs. When NBC formed, WEAF became the leading station of its more commercial and popular chain (the red network), and many of its programs were adopted by the network. WJZ and WJY became the anchor stations of the blue network, which featured unsponsored public-service programming and classical music.[32]

The new era of program sponsorship had a rapid impact on the content of radio shows. The earliest sponsors in the 1920s were middle-sized firms that manufactured relatively inexpensive products consumers bought regularly and frequently, including candy (Happiness Candy Company, Smith Brothers cough drops), toothpaste (Ipana), groceries (A & P), soft drinks (Clicquot Club ginger ale), tires (B. F. Goodrich), and batteries (Eveready). Because many Americans still thought of radio as frivolous, and because of uncertainty about the size and composition of the radio audience, broadcast advertisers seldom tried to influence consumers to make expensive purchases. Radio-set manufacturers, as the exception to this rule, did advertise over their own medium.

Most early radio sponsors shared one other trait—they were experiencing some difficulty in maintaining their market share. Some companies believed they needed daring strategies, including radio advertising, to remain competitive. Primed for new survival strategies, such firms found radio advertising just another aspect of necessary business modification. Until the mid-1930s, only risk-taking businesses advertised on the radio.

Radio sponsors of the 1920s usually produced their programs themselves, with some help from station personnel. Performers often came from the recording industry, because they had experience before the microphone and because they believed broadcast work might help publicize their recordings. Recording companies warned that radio would cut into the sales of records and diminish the popularity of some artists, but the musicians themselves, including Jones and Hare, disagreed.[33] Most vaudeville performers, on the other hand, ignored radio in the 1920s because it paid little or nothing and had microphones instead of live audiences; vaudeville traveling schedules also permitted little time for outside engagements.[34]

Recording artists possessed another attribute that early radio advertisers looked for: anonymity. The type of advertising used on radio called for performers who could submerge their own identities to promote a product. Vaudeville stars would not and, as well-known figures, could not take a role that obliterated their personae. Jones and Hare, on the other hand, *were* the Happiness Boys, and while listeners knew their personal names, the sponsor's name remained far more important. Many radio performers remained completely unknown. The identity of the Goodrich Silver Masked Tenor was a closely guarded secret, as were the identities of Paul Oliver and Olive Palmer, who sang for the Palmolive Company, and Goldy and Dusty, the Gold Dust twins hired by a cleanser manufacturer.[35] Announcers never mentioned the individual names of the Ipana Troubadours, the A & P Gypsies, or the Clicquot Club Eskimos.[36] Advertisers in the 1920s and early 1930s wanted the emphasis placed on their brand names and looked to the performers not for prestige (as they would later), but for entertainment that would remind listeners of the product.

Three programs—the "Eveready Hour," the "Clicquot Club Eskimos," and the "Happiness Boys"—illustrate the various forms and contexts of early sponsored radio. In each case, the sponsoring corporation faced marketing problems that could be addressed by radio. Each of the products advertised was purchased often and distributed regionally. The performers on each show remained anonymous, and most came from the recording industry. Listeners heard the beginnings of more commercialized broadcasting in these programs, which provided models for the network shows that began several years later.

The National Carbon Company chairman's fascination with broadcasting, as well as the company's dependence on the radio industry (many of its Eveready batteries were manufactured for radio sets), led it to begin broadcasting in December 1923. George C. Furness, representing the company, negotiated directly with George McClelland of WEAF.[37] McClelland suggested that National Carbon choose a program format then underrepresented on radio—either a minstrel show, a drama, or an instrumental ensemble playing the "more familiar classics." Furness reported that "we shall never forget McClelland's expression when it was announced to him that the Eveready folks had decided to utilize all" the programs he suggested, "alternating" over a year. McClelland's shock may also have stemmed from the fact that the deal represented "WEAF's first long term contract."[38] The first Eveready show presented an orchestra, a jazz band, and a one-act play.[39]

The content and form of the program evolved slowly. Until September 1924 the programs remained a mixture of miscellaneous readings, plays, and music (including the Flonzaley String Quartet and Yap's Hawaiian Ensemble) performed by freelance professionals.[40] Those involved with the show then decided to try something different: "to engage a permanent group of . . . artists . . . whose combined talents would permit the building of a more uniform program from week to week."[41] In addition to the new performers, the "Eveready Hour" (the name itself was new in September) experimented with "theme" programs, during which every song and reading related to a central concept. The earliest experiments included an Armistice Day presentation and a "Golden Wedding" program featuring the songs of Stephen Foster. Theme programs called for special skills on the part of Graham McNamee, the assigned announcer, who "had to impersonate everything from a bo's'un's mate to a voice as impersonalized as a Roman oracle" although "frequently our scripts would reach him only a few hours prior to going on the air."[42] Because of their popularity, the theme programs came to dominate the "Eveready Hour."

Other Eveready performers proved as flexible and talented as McNamee. Martin "Red" Christiansen, a New York cabdriver, became Eveready's most unusual performer in 1925 when he described his adventures on Galapagos following a shipwreck. Eveready invited Christiansen back every year to repeat his recital.[43] Wendell Hall, best known of the troupe, began his career on a Chicago radio station before becoming Eveready's "Red-Headed Music Maker." A man with a flair for self-promotion, he capped his 1924 tour for Eveready by getting married on the radio. Both the tour and the marriage brought a flood of listener mail.[44] The correspondents made the comparisons between performer and product that the National Carbon Company hoped for: comments included, "would like to say if your Ever Ready batteries are as good as your brand of entertainment, why me for the Ever Ready Battery"; "he was . . . as good as the Ever-ready battery that brought him to me"; "if the Battery Service Company which you represent are half as good as you, they must be high powered"; "he is like the Eveready battery he represents, 100% Good"; and "the Eveready Batteries ought to give a good spark with a live wire like you with them."[45] Hall walked a fine line, becoming personally well-known through his own efforts but maintaining his identification with Eveready.

Before the establishment of the networks, Eveready artists often traveled to present their show over different stations. The National Carbon Company clearly stated that "the growth of chains was too slow" for its purposes. Realizing that "large sections of the country still could not be reached by the regular Eveready Hour," the company arranged tours "to cover those areas without hooked up stations."[46] Because performers did so much touring, the Eveready shows hired minor vaudevillians, accustomed to traveling. WEAF encouraged such tours as a means of keeping the precious Eveready account. The National Carbon Company was essentially trying to advertise to national audiences, even before the technology and administrative structures of the networks were in place.

Radio sponsorship solved several marketing problems for the National Carbon Company. Consumers bought batteries often, yet understood little about them. Competing battery firms made extravagant claims for their products, leaving buyers confused and the industry in turmoil.[47] National Carbon Company's use of radio set itself apart, directly reaching an audience of active consumers, since all radios were then powered by batteries. The "Eveready Hour" even made some listeners use up their batteries faster as they regularly tuned in the program, and gave valuable exposure to a company seeking a national reputation for quality and dependability.[48]

When the Clicquot Club Eskimos went on the air two years later, they found a larger radio audience than the one initially available to the National Carbon Company. Broadcasting technology had changed by December 13, 1925, when Clicquot Club Ginger Ale sponsored its first show.

As a result, that program went out over WEAF and eleven other stations connected by telephone lines in Boston; Providence, Rhode Island; Washington, D.C.; Philadelphia; Pittsburgh; Cincinnati; Buffalo; Detroit; Davenport, Iowa; Minneapolis; and St. Louis.[49] Unlike the "Eveready Hour," the new program already had a chain of stations willing and able to broadcast the sponsor's music and message to regional audiences.

Because of distribution limitations, Clicquot Club was not, in 1925, interested in advertising to a national market. Instead, radio addressed a different marketing problem—the brand's French name was hard for Americans to pronounce and therefore to request. Earl Kimball, the company's president and founder, strongly believed in advertising and simultaneously used different forms of advertising throughout the 1920s.[50] But, as later broadcast advertising textbooks maintained, radio had a special role to play in Clicquot Club advertising: "radio has taught listeners how to pronounce Clicquot," making "it easy to ask . . . for the product." The announcer served as the teacher, "week in and week out," intoning that "Klee-ko is spelled C-L-I-C-Q-U-O-T."[51] As brand names became increasingly important, radio made Clicquot Club part of everyday language.

Clicquot Club also found itself in an expanding market during the 1920s. Demand increased for bottled soft drinks as alternatives to liquor banned during Prohibition and as mixers for bootleg liquor. At the same time, tastes had changed and more people consumed cold drinks all year.[52] Clicquot Club expanded with the demand, changing from a local bottler into a regional Northeast business.

When Kimball first became interested in radio advertising, he worked directly with Dan Tuthill and George Podeyn of WEAF because, as Kimball told the WEAF representatives, "my advertising agency doesn't believe in radio, so we'll go ahead without consulting it." (After the program began, the agency representing Clicquot Club rebated part of its commission, because it had not worked on the radio program.)[53] Tuthill arranged an audition so Kimball could listen to a banjo orchestra led by Harry Reser and announced by Graham McNamee. Kimball loved the show and named the orchestra after his product's symbol, an Eskimo.

The program devised by Clicquot Club and WEAF swiftly became a prime model of the indirect advertising the radio industry then thought proper. A later NBC publication noted that "it was obvious that ginger, pep, sparkle and snap were qualities that form the very essence of the product" and so "manifestly, peppy musical numbers of lively tempo were in order. The banjo, an instrument of brightness and animation, was deemed most suitable in typifying the snap of Clicquot Club personality." The booklet continued that "the idea of Clicquot Club's refreshing and exhilarating tang is 'put over' in every line of this concern's continuities."[54] WEAF and the Clicquot Club Company worked hard to link the program's content with the product. Frank Arnold portrayed the Clicquot Club Eskimos as "the ideal in the field of audible advertising" because "the program personifies the product." His textbook pointed out that the program produced "the effect of an effervescent beverage together with clinking ice in a crystal goblet," with the program's music chosen "to conform with this idea of personification until the Eskimos and their tinkling music program became synonymous with Clicquot Club Ginger Ale."[55]

A surviving show continuity from November 7, 1930, is surprisingly short. The announcer mentioned Clicquot Club Ginger Ale only three times during the half-hour program. The program began, as always, with the "Clicquot March" (composed by chief Eskimo Harry Reser), which featured sleigh bells, a snapping whip, and the bark of an Eskimo husky. (Copies of the march, wrapped in Clicquot Club advertising, were sent to 50,000 listeners, a move that pleased those broadcast advertising promoters who advocated "merchandising.")[56] After the march, the announcer declared:

> The Clicquot Club Eskimos! Summoned for your entertainment from
> their igloos in the frozen Northland by the makers of Clicquot Club Ginger Ale. Clicquot is spelled C-L-I-C-Q-U-O-T. It is the famous mellow,
> old ginger ale made in three very different blends—Pale Dry, Golden and
> Sec—to suit different tastes or moods or occasions.
>
> And now the Eskimos' spirits bubble over into zestful melody as they
> bring you a medley of tunes from *Whoopee*—"My Baby Cares for Me" and
> "A Girl Friend of a Boy Friend of Mine."[57]

The Eskimos played three more numbers, "Constantinople and Chilly Pom Pom Pee," "A Peach of a Pair," and Victor Herbert's "Badinage," before the next mention of the product. The announcer described the varieties of ginger ale and assured listeners that Clicquot Club used new bottles ("no bottle is ever used twice"). This middle commercial announcement was probably added to program scripts only late in the 1920s. The Eskimos played four more musical selections, including a solo by Harry Reser, before the closing announcement:

As the shadows of night close in behind the departing Eskimos, they call a merry "Good-Night." Don't forget to tune in for them again next Friday evening at the same hour. And don't forget to choose *your* favorite from the three Clicquot Club Ginger Ales—Pale Dry, Golden and Sec.

The Clicquot Club Eskimos have come to you from the New York studios of the National Broadcasting Company.[58]

Announcements in earlier broadcasts were fewer and shorter, so that a script from a 1926 program probably contained less advertising than this 1930 version.

The only Eskimo ever named on the program, Harry Reser (himself a banjo player), had previously directed small group recording sessions for Brunswick and Columbia records. Originally the Eskimos all played banjos, but later the group became a full dance band. It was known for novelty tunes like "Thanks for the Buggy Ride," "Barney Google," "Yes, We Have No Bananas," and "Ain't She Sweet," but occasionally broadcast such light classics as Franz von Suppé's *Poet and Peasant* Overture.[59] The Eskimos made records and toured to give live performances. Even before studio audiences became common, members of the band dressed in Eskimo costumes for broadcasts. They continued the custom when on tour and later in front of studio audiences.

Clicquot Club ended the program on July 17, 1933. Both the repeal of Prohibition and the Depression had decreased Clicquot Club sales. Internal NBC memos noted that a decline in revenues forced the company to cut expenditures and prices. Other memos suggested that product pricing cuts (because they varied over the nation) and new packaging (because it needed visual introduction) influenced the company's decision.[60] But changes in the radio industry also contributed to Clicquot Club's financial problems. By 1933 the many sponsors seeking to get on the air had driven up the price for radio time. In 1932 NBC's New England representative and Clicquot's new advertising agency recommended that Clicquot Club increase its program budget from $1,000 to $2,500 per week.[61] Faced with the Depression, the repeal of Prohibition, and growing program and time costs, the company dropped radio advertising.

Like the Clicquot Club Eskimos, the Happiness Boys thrived on early radio. The popularity of the team in the 1920s was reflected in the many articles written about them, mentions made of their act by other artists, their mail (often reported as 700 letters a week), and their large salaries

(Hare claimed to be "working on my second million" at the time of the stock market crash). Fifty years later, a Canadian listener "especially" remembered Jones and Hare as "really good."[62]

Happiness Candy had entered radio to solidify its position in the changing candy industry. In the 1920s candy bought from barrels gave way to boxed and branded confections. Changes in technology also contributed to changes in promotion, advertising, and distribution. The market featured new products, new companies, and new ways to merchandise, and sometimes competing firms even advertised jointly to increase consumption.[63] Launched as a regional concern (Feurst and Kraemer, New Orleans), Happiness Candy purchased Baltimore and New York factories in the early 1920s. By 1927 sixty-eight Happiness Candy stores and restaurants in New York, Washington, D.C., and other northeastern cities sold its products.[64] The company was willing to take a chance on the new medium of radio because, although broadcast advertising might be risky, so was doing nothing in a changing market.

The first continuity for the "Happiness Boys" listed seven songs—three duets and four solos—with a "gag" following each song. A warning began the script: "Don't forget to mention after every song that it is the Happiness Boys from station WEAF entertaining." While later programs became more elaborate, the basic format probably varied only slightly. Jones and Hare began with a simple piano accompaniment, which was later replaced by a small orchestra; programs occasionally featured guests.[65]

Those who enjoyed Jones and Hare noted that their style mattered as much as the content of their programs. One textbook author thought the Happiness Boys stood "head and shoulders above most of their rivals," but noted "they can hardly be said to get over because of the material they select." They succeeded because "they can make you laugh at a veteran joke. They laugh at each other and their hearty laughter is contagious. They never permit a deadly silence after they have sprung one of their 'gags,' nor do they laugh too loud and long." The boys knew how to turn failure to their advantage: "when one tells a story that does not go over, his teammate taunts him and carries the radio audience along." Finally, Jones and Hare remembered the listeners: "never for an instant do they miss the radio audience's reactions, either consciously or subconsciously."[66] The performers' consciousness of an audience remained important for radio performers, whether the consciousness had been honed in recording studios or on vaudeville circuits. Heywood Broun, an accomplished critic, thought theaters should delay Friday night openings so he could hear the Happiness Boys, "the indisputable leaders of radio entertaining." He continued:

> Many of the jokes broadcast by these two are entirely familiar to me. If, upon a printed page I saw: "What's worse than raining cats and dogs?— Hailing taxicabs," I would not laugh inordinately. I could even contain myself if I heard it in the theater. But it does seem to me a wholly captivating joke to come sliding out of thin air. . . . Above all others, Hare and Jones have mastered radio ease. They seem near at hand and are wholly casual in every vocal inflection.[67]

Clearly, Jones and Hare relied on their likable personalities, their ease in front of the microphone, and their musical talent rather than on original material.

Audiences saw Jones and Hare as slightly old-fashioned, a result of both their style and their use of well-worn material. Historians have often classified them (as well as most other early radio performers) as vaudevillians transplanted to radio.[68] Yet Jones and Hare, like other early radio stars, were recording artists. Not only did they lack vaudeville experience, but the content of their programs did not truly derive from vaudeville. Jones and Hare performed as a two-act, a form that grew out of the interchanges between end men in minstrel shows. Part of the humor in a two-act lay in the supposed differences between the two performers: Ernie Hare, a "settled family man," versus Billy Jones, a "swinging bachelor." The word play and stock ethnic humor basic to the team's repertoire also came from minstrel shows.[69] Listeners in the 1920s found Jones and Hare appealing and familiar at least in part because they harked back to earlier entertainments from which vaudeville had evolved. By the 1920s vaudeville was dominated by a generation of Jewish comedians and their urbanized "New Humor"—performers and a style that did not appear on radio until a decade later.[70]

Jones and Hare also looked to the past for subjects, often singing nostalgic songs about rural folks. Their first hit, even before they went on the radio, was "Down at the Swimming Hole," recorded for several labels in 1921.[71] The song outlined a carefree country life to which the singers longed to return. Many other songs contained similar sentiments, including "In the Little Red Schoolhouse," "Down by the Old Apple Tree," "Just a Little Old Schoolhouse," and "Shout Hallelujah! Cause I'm Home."[72]

Some of these songs reflected a highly romanticized view of the Old South as warm, carefree, and rural.[73] The Happiness Boys had personal reasons for singing about the South (Hare had been born and raised in Virginia and returned often to visit), yet the songs also referred back to the minstrel tradition and reflected the 1920s concern with rural life and its values.[74]

Many of Jones and Hare's songs commented on issues of the day from the viewpoint of rural skeptics. They sang of flappers ("Don't Bring Lulu"); divorce ("No One Knows What It's All About"); ethnic diversity ("Hooray for the Irish!"; "Me No a Speak Good English"); and the migration from country to city ("In the Little Red School House"; "From De Ol Home Town").[75] In their comic songs they mentioned specific events, such as Prohibition ("Pardon Me While I Laugh"); the opening of King Tut's tomb ("King Tut"); the introduction of the Model A ("Henry's Made a Lady out of Lizzie"); Lindbergh's flight ("When Lindy Comes Home"); and the 1928 election ("Mr. Hoover—Mr. Smith").[76]

The Happiness Boys did not shrink from commenting on another 1920s phenomenon, broadcast radio. In one of their cleverest recordings, "Twisting the Dials," they made fun of radio programming by recreating an evening's entertainment over stations "OUCH," "BUNK," and "ITCH." They parodied orchestras ("the first number on the program tonight will be rendered—'to be rendered' meaning 'to be torn apart'—by the Silent Dozen Orchestra"); station breaks ("when you hear the beautiful chimes it will be exactly six and seven-eighths split seconds past eight o'clock Eastern Daylight Standard Railroad Western Mountain Central Time"); operatic sopranos (Miss Loud-and-Screeching in an aria from *La Bum*); and homemaker hints (famous recipes sponsored by the "Bicarbonate Soda Association," given by "Professor Don't Eater").[77] The homegrown radio programs that Jones and Hare lampooned in 1928 were already being replaced by slicker, more professional, and more commercialized forms. Indeed the Happiness Boys themselves were among the first casualties of that change.

TRANSITIONAL PROGRAMMING, 1927–31

Many of the changes in radio programming, which seemed to happen suddenly in the 1930s, had their roots in the programs of the late 1920s. These transitional shows shared characteristics with both earlier and later radio

111

programs. The new variety shows relied heavily on music and presented a mixture of acts reminiscent of early radio's haphazard programming. The first comic dramas featured actors submerging their identities much as the early sponsored performers had done. Yet the emergence of individual radio stars, coupled with the introduction of ethnicity to the airwaves, presaged the more elaborate programs of the 1930s. Audience surveying also became more sophisticated, with an increasing use of social scientific methods.

Early radio stars faced declining opportunities in the late 1920s, and many later disappeared altogether from the airwaves. A 1932 *Radio Guide* article, "Branded Men and Women: Pioneers Who Paved the Way and Paid with Personal Oblivion," explained that while many listeners remembered "Olive Palmer" and "Paul Oliver," they knew little of the actual performers, Virginia Rea and Frank Munn, who had been "both well paid, widely talked of individuals under their radio names" but were today "off the air, unheard of."[78] The article also mentioned Joe White, the "Silver Masked Tenor"; the Whitall Anglo-Persians; the Edison Ensemble on WJZ; the "Gold Dust Twins"; and the "Royal Typewriter Hour" with its "Royal Hero" and "Royal Heroine" as examples of "branded" personalities who found it difficult obtaining additional radio work because fans did not know their names.

Radio's popularity had lasted long enough that many entertainers wanted and needed to change sponsors. But as a result of performing as trademark characters, artists often could not capitalize on their past successes. Employers hesitated hiring an artist closely identified with another product. As the *Radio Guide* article asked, "how much does the second or third sponsor pay for the radio advertising of the original sponsor, and does he lose on his campaign when he uses an individual or group widely known as the 'radio trade-mark' of the first advertiser?"[79]

After about five years as the Happiness Boys, Jones and Hare began broadcasting late in 1928 as the "Interwoven Pair" for the Interwoven Sock Company. The show continued into the 1931 season with moderate success. Jones and Hare were next briefly heard as the "Flit Soldiers" before signing with Best Foods in March 1932 to become the "Best Food Boys."[80] "Branding" remained a problem for the duo. As *Radio Guide* remarked, "Jones and Hare are still generally remembered, by those radio listeners who remember advertising at all, as the good will ambassadors of candy, not of insecticides or hosiery."[81] A 1932 NBC memo transmitted an advertising agency request "that in all of our releases concerning Billy

Jones and Ernie Hare we refrain from any mention of their former titles, such as 'Happiness Boys' and the 'Interwoven Pair.'"[82] Along with the difficulties presented by sponsorship changes, stylistic changes in popular radio programs also contributed to the decline of early radio performers. While Jones and Hare continued to use much the same format and material, radio programming was changing around them.

During this transitional period, variety programs differed only slightly from what had come before. Two of the most popular offerings of the late 1920s, the "Cities Service Concerts" (featuring Jessica Dragonette) and the "Fleischmann Hour" (hosted by Rudy Vallee), maintained familiar formats but starred established performers who used their real names. Although still young when they became radio stars, both Dragonette and Vallee had already made reputations as performers in other entertainment forms.

Dragonette soon faced her own "branding" problem. Before Cities Service hired her, Dragonette had studied music, appeared on the stage, and sung on the radio for Philco, a radio manufacturer. The "Cities Service Concerts" began in February 1927, but not until December 1929 did the winning combination of Rosario Bourdon, conductor, and Jessica Dragonette, soprano, appear before the microphone.[83] Dragonette later wrote that when she joined the Cities Service program, "the audience was continually wondering why I was not presented in dramatic scenes where I could speak as well as sing." The producers informed her that "we don't want you to speak at all on the program. Why should we remind the audience of your former sponsor?"[84] Each Cities Service hour presented a rigid sequence of semiclassical and romantic popular songs, with Dragonette singing exactly eight solos and duets. In addition to Dragonette and Bourdon, the lavishly produced programs featured large orchestras and Metropolitan Opera stars. Continuing programming disputes eventually led to Dragonette's much-publicized departure from the program.[85]

Rudy Vallee headed a variety program, the "Fleischmann Hour," that began in 1929, ran for almost ten years, and pioneered innovations that were widely copied. As the "Vagabond Lover," Vallee had already won a reputation as a band singer popular with young women. Many well-known vaudevillians, later hosts of their own programs, made their first radio appearances with Vallee. These guests, who included Eddie Cantor, George Burns and Gracie Allen, and Ed Wynn, acted in comic and dramatic sketches written especially for their talents.[86]

The "Fleischmann Hour" also highlighted how the increased size and wealth of sponsors influenced the choice of radio performers and programming. In the 1920s Fleischmann's Yeast had used print advertising to transform the image of its product from merely a baking aid into a multipurpose health product. Fleischmann's wanted to continue grabbing consumer attention to keep demand high, and it saw radio as the right vehicle for further promotion.[87] Unlike earlier radio sponsors, both Fleischmann's and Cities Service had long advertised to a national market, and Fleischmann's search for nationally famous performers for its radio show foreshadowed the later actions of other large corporations.

The introduction of nonmusical, dramatic shows brought the biggest change in radio program form and content. During the early 1920s, plays written especially for the medium had been the only dramas on radio. A weekly, plotted program with repeating characters did not exist until Freeman Gosden and Charles Correll started work on the precursor to "Amos 'n' Andy" in 1926. Gosden and Correll, along with Gertrude Berg (who wrote and starred in "The Rise of the Goldbergs"), invented a new form, which also brought ethnicity to the previously homogenized airwaves.

Listeners and radio professionals liked "Amos 'n' Andy"'s experimental form, but the subject—the lives of urban black taxicab drivers and their friends—proved problematic. Gosden and Correll (both white) wrote, produced, and played most of the characters. Begun as "Sam 'n' Henry" over WMAQ in Chicago, the show quickly succeeded, and Gosden and Correll sought to reach a larger audience through the sale of recordings to other stations. WMAQ, however, refused permission for this "chainless chain." In March 1928, therefore, Gosden and Correll moved to WGN, changed the program's name to "Amos 'n' Andy," and began sending electrical transcription recordings to other stations. In May 1929 a Lord and Thomas advertising agency executive wrote to the president of his agency, Albert Lasker, proposing that they seek sponsorship to present "Amos 'n' Andy" over a network. Lasker found a sponsor, Pepsodent, and a network, NBC, and suggested they team up on the new program. Lasker had to convince NBC president Merlin Aylesworth that "a mass audience would accept groups of characters in situation comedies who were not predominately White, Anglo-Saxon and Protestant."[88] "Amos 'n' Andy" debuted on the NBC blue network in August 1929.

The national popularity of "Amos 'n' Andy" became legendary. The show captured 60 percent of all listeners—sometimes more than 40 million people. Sales of radio sets increased 23 percent between 1928 and

1929, a rise often attributed in large part to this single program. White audiences, despite the initial concern of radio professionals, loved the show. African American audiences had mixed reactions, just as they had had to earlier black-faced minstrels. While some black publications supported the program for presenting African Americans as human and lovable, many found the programs to be demeaning and stereotyped. Beginning in April 1931 the *Pittsburgh Courier,* a black weekly newspaper, gathered 740,000 signatures in a petition campaign to have the program removed from the air.[89] This crusade had little effect on the network, the sponsor, or the performers (Gosden and Correll always insisted they respected the characters they portrayed), but it showed that the changing content of radio programs might make them more controversial than the less ambitious programming of the past.

Some aspects of "Amos 'n' Andy" were similar to earlier programs. As with the Happiness Boys, minstrel shows influenced Gosden and Correll more than did vaudeville. One historian wrote that the black dialect and stupidity of Amos and Andy showed "that they were modeled rather directly on the 'Tambo and Bones' figures of minstrelsy."[90] Gosden and Correll also perpetuated the tradition of performers' anonymity. They spent their careers known only by their stage names, playing the first characters they had created.

"The Rise of the Goldbergs" shared many characteristics with "Amos 'n' Andy." It too began as an unsponsored show, featured a continuing group of characters, placed artistic control in the hands of those who acted in and wrote the program, and focused attention on a group of Americans who had not been heard before on the radio. Unlike Gosden and Correll, however, Gertrude Berg, the writer, producer, and star of "The Rise of the Goldbergs," was a member of the group about whom she wrote. Berg had begun her scriptwriting and performing career entertaining guests at her father's Catskill resort hotel. Her radio program presented the everyday life of a Jewish immigrant family living on New York City's Lower East Side, and much of the material came from her observations at her family's hotel and in New York's Jewish neighborhoods.[91]

NBC worried constantly about the appeal of the program. Begun in November 1929 as a weekly fifteen-minute show, "The Goldbergs" expanded to a daily program in July 1931, when Pepsodent assumed sponsorship. A 1932 report on "The Goldbergs," prepared by the NBC statistical department, reassured network executives "that there is a large audience for good programs of 'a Jewish type'"; that "the success of this program should make a telling argument for Jewish programs"; and that "an analysis of their mail receipts indicates that this popularity is not restricted to any geographic region." It quoted Pepsodent's advertising manager that "although the program concerns a Jewish family, the vast majority . . . of appeals to keep it on the air came from Gentiles."[92] The popularity of "The Rise of the Goldbergs" calmed NBC's fears about how listeners would respond to Jews on the radio, although public relations executives still hesitated about releasing pictures of the largely Jewish cast.[93] Such a concern was pressing, since many of the vaudeville stars about to enter radio were Jewish. Along with "Amos 'n' Andy," "The Rise of the Goldbergs" prepared both broadcasters and listeners for the ethnic vaudeville performers who answered the call for fresh radio talent in the early 1930s.

At least in part because of its worries over the subject matter, NBC carefully reviewed the mail it received about "The Goldbergs." In the early 1930s Pepsodent offered listeners a drinking glass in return for an empty Pepsodent carton and a vote on the program's future. The *New York Times* reported that the response numbered 842,000 letters. The NBC statistics department computed the percentage of Goldberg mail each station received compared with the station's "total NBC mail" and concluded that "the popularity of this feature is not limited to any one section or to the audience of several stations."[94]

While the new networks still relied heavily on such listener mail, they also sought more scientific surveys as part of the campaign to promote broadcast advertising. They hoped that more sophisticated audience profiles would help convince sponsors that loyal radio audiences existed and that broadcast advertising worked. Daniel Starch, director of research for the American Association of Advertising Agencies and a business research consultant, undertook "A Study of Radio Broadcasting Based Exclusively on Personal Interviews with Families in the United States East of the Rocky Mountains" for NBC in 1928, updating and expanding the report by including the Pacific Coast in 1930. Starch, with a Ph.D. in psychology from the University of Iowa, spent most of his career measuring advertising effectiveness.[95] Between March 15 and April 15, 1928, he questioned 17,099 families, of whom 5,608 owned radios and 11,491 did not. The survey asked who listened to the radio and when, information NBC hoped to use to plan programs and lure sponsors.

Starch also attempted to find out, in general terms, what kinds of programs listeners liked. One question asked, "Do you prefer radio programs like Eveready, Damrosch, General Motors, Colliers, Maxwell, Goodrich, and Ipana?" and reported that four-fifths of the families did prefer such programs.[96] In his 1930 revised study, Starch made the purpose of the question clearer by beginning it "Do you like sponsored programs such as . . ." and added a note that "this question was asked for the purpose of obtaining direct expression of opinion relating to advertised programs on the air." The addition of the Pacific Coast listeners in 1930 and the changing of the wording did not significantly affect the response to this question.[97]

In many respects the Starch surveys resembled earlier efforts by radio magazines, individual stations, and private companies that had used questionnaires to gauge audience interest and composition. The difference lay in the elaborate social scientific rationale for Starch's survey and his concentration on the issues most important to advertisers. As advertising revenues grew in importance and as the Depression set in, broadcasters sought to interest larger and more stable corporations in sponsorship. Such businesses wanted proof that their message would reach and please the public. Yet neither the Starch surveys nor their predecessors provided detailed information about particular programs, and as yet there were no comparisons among programs.

VAUDEVILLE COMES TO RADIO

According to Carroll Carroll, an advertising executive, "the real gut power of radio surfaced around 1931 when advertisers began to abandon such obvious broadcast nomenclature as the A & P Gypsies, Paul Oliver and Olive Palmer in the Palmolive Hour, the Gold Dust Twins, the Happiness Boys (later the Interwoven Pair—a sock act), the Clicquot Club Eskimos and [replace them] with the use of star talent."

Radio programs did begin to sound different in the 1930s. Gone now were the anonymous musicians playing nostalgic or semiclassical songs. Gone too were diffident advertisers favoring indirect appeals. Carroll (using tasteless sexual stereotyping) explained the appeal of such a change: "the people—the advertising people—during the eighteen years or so of radio's rise and decline were like children turned loose in a candy store.

117

Not only had they found a new way of advertising that paid off like a nympho in a frat house, they found it was fun."[98]

The technology of the network system, dependent (like vaudeville) on local outlets, helped bring established vaudeville stars to radio. That step helped convince many listeners that radio existed as an entertainment, rather than an educational, medium and therefore could be commercial. The relaxed, old-fashioned, small-town humor of the Happiness Boys gave way to the frenzy of Eddie Cantor. Cantor's national prominence and proven attraction made him a logical choice to star over a network system that now closely resembled a vaudeville circuit. By the early 1930s broadcast advertising had become accepted, national audiences were available, and small businesses, hit hard by the Depression, had stopped advertising and been replaced over the airwaves by large corporations and their advertising agencies.

In 1932 NBC had fewer advertisers than in 1931, but each spent more on radio.[99] For example, Standard Brands (makers of Chase and Sanborn coffee, Fleischmann's yeast, and Royal Jell-o, among other products) sponsored three programs. Such large companies spent more on radio programs and often sought well-known performers for prestige. Radio's now comparatively generous salaries—combined with diminishing vaudeville opportunities—lured stars such as Cantor to network shows.

Broadcast advertisers, for their part, believed that radio audiences were now listening to specific favorite programs, and sponsors hoped that well-known entertainers would sustain interest. NBC's director of advertising sales wrote that in the "old days" an advertiser remained "satisfied to be named as the sponsor of a musical program," but that as time went on "he found it possible to obtain fuller value from his broadcast advertising by making a more pointed sales talk about his product."[100] Broadcast advertising thus became more direct, and unabashed commercials began asking consumers outright to buy products.

These changes in broadcast advertising convinced sponsors of the usefulness of advertising agencies. Carroll wrote that "because everybody was ad-libbing his way through the air-waves," the J. Walter Thompson agency decided that "to get radio shows that would work as advertising" it would have to write and produce them. The Thompson agency established a radio department that scripted and produced shows and commercials for clients, "right from an opening like 'Heigh-ho, everybody, this is Rudy Vallee' through to such closings as Eddie Cantor singing, 'I love to spend this hour with you / As friend to friend I'm sorry it's through.'"[101] Throughout the 1930s it was the agencies, with the assistance of the performers involved, that produced most network radio programs.

The new emphasis on advertising meant that programming became more rigid. As the cost of radio time rose, each program carefully allocated its precious minutes among commercial breaks and program content. Scripts became ever more elaborate and choreographed, so that advertisers could be assured of a professional rendition of their message and so that agencies could justify their high fees. By 1934 sponsored radio programs already differed considerably in form, content, and style from the "Happiness Boys" program of ten years earlier.

Many of these changes date from 1931, when Eddie Cantor became the host of the "Chase and Sanborn Hour," although the biggest transformation occurred during the 1932 radio season, when a host of new radio shows debuted featuring Ed Wynn, George Burns and Gracie Allen, Jack Benny, George Jessel, Jack Pearl, and Fred Allen.[102] These new programs followed the form of the previous radio variety shows, drawing from the "Eveready Hour," the "Clicquot Club Eskimos," the "Fleischmann Hour," and the "Cities Service Concerts." Now, however, the star and host was often a comedian, and the shows emphasized comic sketches.

Cantor, born poor and Jewish on New York's East Side, had quit school early to play vaudeville (often as a black-faced juggler), work in the Ziegfeld Follies, and perform in nightclubs.[103] He lost a great deal of money in the stock-market crash and, after having earlier decided to retire in 1929, instead found himself seeking work to support his family. Between 1929 and 1931 Cantor worked sporadically on Broadway and in films, and wrote a book before finding a well-paying radio job.[104] Unlike earlier radio performers, Cantor had no formal musical training; but he did have an understanding, honed by years of touring, of the national audience.[105] Already well-known when hired by Chase and Sanborn, he became enormously popular as a result of his radio show.

Earlier, Cantor had participated in the "New Humor" brought by immigrants to the vaudeville stage. Albert McLean has described vaudeville's urban and ethnic (mostly Jewish) humor as based on verbal misunderstandings, rooted in stories of family life and of the underdog, and with a compressed and frantic form built around the joke (a modern invention that flourished in vaudeville). The compression and verbal basis of this humor made it natural for radio. The radio performers of the 1920s had relied on music and on what McLean calls the "relaxed whimsy of the minstrel show."[106] Cantor's programs, by contrast, featured jokes, skits, and stories about Ida Cantor and the couple's five daughters. Cantor's scripts, written by David Freedman (many of radio's new writers, as well as performers, now came from vaudeville), depended on a "joke factory" where young writers reworked old jokes to fit the week's subject.[107]

The vaudevillians also chose subjects new to radio. McLean describes vaudeville humor as "more excited, more aggressive, and less sympathetic than that to which the middle classes of the nineteenth century had been accustomed," and notes that while vaudeville managers watched for forbidden language and subjects, comics sometimes used hokum, "jasbo," and "gravy" (different levels of vulgarity) to get laughs.[108] Performers coming to radio from vaudeville therefore lacked experience with the restrictions imposed on home entertainment—experience that earlier radio performers had usually gained in the recording industry. A 1932 NBC memo explained that "the entrance of the theatre writer and theatre comedian" has "put a new phase in radio material," noting that "it is imperative that from this date on no remarks of questionable nature be permitted in our continuities" because "radio got its great start by giving clean, wholesome entertainment . . . and we must stop material in bad taste."[109] A later memo attributed this problem to the ethnicity of the new radio performers and their previous careers. The memo writer (John Royal), contending that "there is a lot of material in regular theater routines of comedians that we cannot use on the radio, and the fact that one of the Jewish race does something, does not excuse him with the rest of the Jewish race," concluded that "we must be very careful about this."[110] Broadcasters worried that while theater audiences might be willing to listen to vulgarity and ethnic humor in vaudeville houses, radio listeners would not want such subjects, language, or performing styles in their living rooms.

Vaudeville entertainers and broadcasters had to make other adjustments to each other. Although many radio shows had studio audiences, audience participation was not encouraged until vaudeville performers came to radio. Some programs even separated the audience from the performers with a glass curtain. Cantor later remembered the weekly speech that was made to his show's first audiences:

> Ladies and gentlemen, you are here as guests of Chase and Sanborn. We
> ask you to co-operate with us in not applauding, not laughing, so that our

listening audience can have the illusion of hearing a show without distraction.[111]

Radio's coldness shocked vaudevillians such as Cantor, who were accustomed to interaction between audience and performer.

Several radio stars later claimed to have been the first to invite on-air audience reactions, but it was Cantor's particular way of playing to the audience that made his program such a success. Cantor wrote that "what brought my first radio show to life and took it to the top was the participation, for the first time, of a studio audience."[112] His first experiment in audience participation occurred when he couldn't resist donning a woman's hat and fur scarf to enliven a routine. Cantor based many of his comic radio sketches on outrageous costumes, which the announcer would describe to the radio listeners. Vaudeville's reliance on such visual clowning posed problems when performers moved to radio. The response of the studio audience provided some justification for visual gags, but the performers who relied on word play and situation comedy lasted longer on radio than those who appeared in funny hats.[113]

Cantor's show highlights other differences between the older, largely anonymous radio performers and the new breed of radio stars. Carroll remembered Cantor's tantrums at having to cut his program scripts to fit into an hour, and noted that "Eddie had power. At one time 50 percent of the radios tuned in between 8:00 and 9:00 p.m. EST on any Sunday evening were turned to Eddie Cantor."[114] Cantor derived part of this power from new methods of audience surveying that provided more detailed information on the popularity of specific programs. These new audience surveys (forerunners of the postwar rating services) began in 1930 with a report prepared by Crossley, Inc. (a research organization owned by Archibald Crossley) for the Association of National Advertisers (ANA). The report, *The Advertiser Looks at Radio*, summarized the radio research done up to that time. Crossley concluded that the information then available (including Starch's radio listener profiles) was "totally inadequate" and that broadcasting needed "more information on an authoritative, organized basis."[115] The ANA Radio Committee decided to cooperate with other interested parties in financing a system of audience surveys to be undertaken by Crossley, Inc. The original subscribers to what was called the Cooperative Analysis of Broadcasting (CAB) project were radio sponsors, but within the first year advertising agencies began to participate as well.[116]

121

After four months Crossley, Inc., reported on its first surveys to the forty-four CAB participants. The surveys answered three questions: what proportion of listeners tuned in at a particular day and hour, who the listeners were, and what programs and stations listeners chose.[117] This first report included essays on research methodology, operating plan, and "what makes a program popular," as well as listings of programs and the percentage of the audience listening to each. Crossley, Inc., submitted yearly summaries to CAB members, as well as quarterly updates, station area studies, and program reports. The reports became increasingly elaborate, with charts and essays providing information gleaned from phone calls made four times daily. The CAB surveys, financed as they were by national advertisers, focused on national programs but, as the competition between NBC and CBS for affiliates heated up, station area surveys also began to measure the relative popularity of local radio stations.[118]

Crossley, Inc., believed that "each dollar spent on radio should be subjected to searching inquiry regarding the return on investment."[119] The casual and unscientific methods of surveying used by earlier broadcasters now seemed, by the early 1930s, inadequate. Advertisers soon found even the Crossley "recall" method (phoning several hours after a program ended) wanting. In 1934 C. F. Hooper began a service of "co-incidental" telephone interviews (conducted while a program was still in progress).[120] The search for greater reliability and the continued application of the latest social science techniques to radio audience surveys reflected the increasing amounts of money being spent by advertisers on radio programming.

ELECTRICAL TRANSCRIPTIONS VERSUS NETWORKS

Even as the networks and advertising agencies consolidated their control over radio, alternative means of delivering programming remained. Electrical transcriptions briefly brought prerecorded programming back to radio in the 1930s, providing small, regional businesses with access to radio listeners. Because early experiments with presenting recordings over the air had been disappointing, most early radio featured live performers. Although the technology for directly broadcasting recorded programs may have existed earlier, the radio industry first became aware of the potential of electrical transcriptions in 1929.[121] During the transcription process, engineers recorded performances on wax discs, duplicated the recordings, and then sent them to stations equipped to broadcast them. As one observer noted, "no microphone picks up the sound waves. . . . the transcription is immediately translated into the form of electrical impulses, amplified and broadcast, thus insuring a faithful reproduction of what originally was recorded."[122] Transcriptions sounded much better on the air than had ordinary recordings, and they offered some advantages over the expensive and elaborate network system. Mailing transcriptions of entire programs to selected local stations gave a sponsor total control over both the content of advertisements and their placement, and achieved substantial savings for both advertisers and stations.[123]

In fact, transcriptions favored exactly the type of radio advertisers, performers, and programs that the wired networks were moving away from. After Clicquot Club canceled its Eskimos program in 1933, citing distribution problems and rising network costs, the Eskimos returned on transcriptions during World War II and again in 1948, over a regional network.[124] Their renewed popularity in these later incarnations suggests that the Eskimos might have enjoyed longer success if the technology for supplying national radio had been different.

But the networks saw transcriptions as competitive and worked to undermine them. In 1933 NBC banned the use of electrical transcriptions on all stations it owned and operated.[125] The Federal Radio Commission entered the fray by requiring an announcement, in varying forms, whenever a radio station played an electrical transcription. The announcement was prohibitive in its effects, because listeners tended to turn off any program they knew to be "canned," but the regulatory agency characteristically supported the already powerful networks.[126] By the time the Clicquot Eskimos turned to them, electrical transcriptions survived only as supplements to the established network system.

The inability of recordings to provide simultaneous broadcasting of events, plus a certain amount of organizational confusion involved in the business of electrical transcription, enabled the networks to maintain a superior position. A mixed system, with wired networks providing live out-of-studio programming and electrical transcriptions providing additional entertainment, might have succeeded in providing greater programming diversity. But as the networks gained strength, they turned from seeking support through public relations and persuasion (as in the campaign to promote broadcast advertising) to crushing opposition through governmental influence and economic power.

Meanwhile, the forerunners of the sponsored system of radio programming receded into history. Experiments using radio as an advertising medium had deprived early performers of their names, and the money spent to ensure the success of those who came after reinforced the anonymity of the radio stars of the 1920s. Throughout the period programs continued to be produced in a variety of ways and for a variety of reasons, any of which might have served as a model radio system. But the triumph of sponsorship overshadowed other possibilities in the same way that the fame of radio stars of the 1930s eclipsed that of their predecessors.

DRUNK AND DISORDERLY

The Backlash against
Broadcast Advertising

As the networks established themselves and commercialized programming took over the airwaves, a diverse group of educators, publishers, and reformers voiced clear opposition to broadcast advertising. James Rorty summarized these protests against the growing commercialism of radio when he wrote that "in its essence, the charge levelled against the 'American System' of advertising-subsidized radio broadcasting is that it is drunk and disorderly."[1] Rorty's phrase implied that commercialized broadcasting was socially unacceptable, morally bankrupt, and, in those waning days of Prohibition, subject to government regulation. The dissatisfaction grew out of the earlier resistance to commercial broadcasting and responded to the success of the campaign to promote broadcast advertising. The protesters and the radio industry fought over federal regulation of broadcasting, each side seeking to have its vision of radio written into law.

Many observers of early broadcast radio had worried about the influence of commercialism. The protests in the early 1930s complained as well of the power of the networks to force competitors out of business. The opposition included educational and religious groups, political reformers, and newspaper publishers worried about competition from radio advertising. While the promoters of broadcast advertising had used their knowledge of advertising appeals to sell a commercialized radio system, their opponents relied on less flamboyant and, in the end, less persuasive techniques, including educational radio stations run by universities, the publication of scholarly articles and books, and lobbying on Capitol Hill. This small and underfinanced group (especially when compared to the radio networks) nevertheless managed to call public attention to the problems inherent in a commercialized radio system, and to renew hope that fundamental change was still possible.

The Depression and the New Deal influenced both these protests and the responses to them. Concerns about competition in a tight business climate as well as a questioning of the efficiency and morality of capitalism underlay much of the criticism. The protesters turned to the federal government, then in an active phase of business regulation, for help in containing the radio monopoly. But the growing importance of broadcasting in politics and the huge profits made by broadcasters during difficult times gave the networks and the radio industry enormous leverage with legislators and federal officials.

Confusion over the best means for protecting the public from unfair or unethical business practices had a long history, and the protections most often had proven favorable to the businesses being regulated. In a manner reminiscent of earlier debates, Congress considered whether to regulate the results of the growing commercialism of radio or to strengthen the alternatives (in the form of local or nonprofit stations) to the networks. The result of these deliberations, the 1934 Communications Act, barely mentioned networks or advertising, and did not include any protections for educational, religious, farm, or labor stations. By ignoring the two most dynamic forces in radio, the Communications Act accepted and reinforced commercial broadcasting. In addition, it placed alternative nonprofit stations in such a weak position that they could never challenge a system financed through the sale of time to advertisers. The Communications Act continues to control American broadcasting today—not only because it serves as the primary legislation outlining the regulatory powers of the Federal Communications Commission, but also because it validated and strengthened the commercialized system of broadcasting that began in radio and then was transferred, almost without change, to television.

TIMING OF THE PROTESTS

A number of factors moved educational, religious, and political leaders to protest the form and content of American broadcasting. As the commercialization of radio grew, as indirect advertising gave way to direct advertising, and as the programs presented on the radio became more formulaic, some listeners found themselves disappointed. The increasing strength of radio networks as competitors with newspapers and nonprofit stations spurred those particular groups into action. In addition, the federal reallocation of radio frequencies, which favored commercial stations at the behest of the industry, angered educational broadcasters. The growing power and influence of leftist political movements, which viewed capitalism skeptically, also contributed to the criticism. Finally, beginning in 1932, the New Deal climate that regarded business as an activity to be regulated in the public interest, meant that the conflict between the radio industry and its detractors would be played out in the congressional battle over the 1934 Communications Act.

Historian Susan Douglas points out that "from its first public unveiling and through the next 25 years, the invention [of radio] evoked a range of prophecies—some realistic, some fantastic, and nearly all idealistic—of a world improved through radio."[2] Clayton Koppes describes early listeners' perceptions of broadcasting and notes that "almost every corner of society acclaimed radio as a bright hope for a better world," but "bitter disillusionment . . . set in as radio lost its novelty and idealism."[3] Because of these rosy early expectations, the reality of commercial radio seemed especially discouraging. A group of educators wrote in 1930 that although they had "hailed" radio as a "new opportunity," the "actual result has been disappointing . . . with a large majority of . . . stations surcharging the air with triviality, mediocrity, and syncopated noise, not to mention advertising propaganda, buffoonery, quackery, and sectarianism."[4] Some of the criticism, like the educators' complaints about "syncopated noise," replayed earlier elitist objections to radio jazz, but other critics harbored bigger visions that commercial radio had failed to realize.

The backlash against broadcast advertising occurred during a time of consumer agitation and pressure to reform all kinds of advertising. Franklin Roosevelt's New Deal invited ordinary citizens to be represented in the National Recovery Administration, invigorated the Food and Drug Administration, and helped spark an organized consumer movement. A series of books (including Stuart Chase and F. J. Schlink's *Your Money's Worth: A Study in the Waste of the Consumer's Dollar* and Arthur Kallet and F. J. Schlink's *100,000,000 Guinea Pigs: Dangers in Everyday Foods, Drugs, and Cosmetics*) and the founding of a number of watchdog organizations marked the new consumerism. Two of its main goals—product testing and consumer education—were responses to the untrustworthiness of advertising. Like the earlier critics of advertising who had founded the Truth in Advertising movement during the Progressive era, and the national Better Business Bureau's campaign against paid testimonials in the 1920s, the reformers of the 1930s focused on the misleading content of specific advertisements rather than the fact that all advertisements were essentially designed to mislead. This emphasis allowed the advertising industry to respond with a flurry of self-regulation that disguised the fact that not much had changed.[5]

Those who disliked commercialized radio often focused on the so-called "quacks." The more outrageous uses of the medium reminded listeners that all advertisers intruded on radio programming to sell products. Dr. John R. Brinkley, who broadcast over his own station KFKB from his home in Milford, Kansas, was the most celebrated fraud on the airwaves. In 1928 he expanded his original sales pitch—for goat gland transplants that presumably restored the virility of elderly men—to cover children's diseases, a "Medical Question Box of the Air," and the distribution of his own dubious medicines through affiliated pharmacies nationwide. Both the American Medical Association and the Federal Radio Commission acted against Brinkley and, by 1930, his medical and broadcasting licenses had been revoked.[6] Brinkley was particularly flagrant, but not unique. Many other pitch artists rushed to sell worthless wares over the airwaves.[7] To reformers, the commercial network stations seemed little better than co-conspirators of the quacks and just as much in need of correction.

Broadcasters had argued in the 1920s that indirect advertising—the mere mention of a sponsor's name—would not interfere with listening pleasure. In 1925 the Fourth National Radio Conference had resolved that programming which "limits itself to the building of good will for the sponsor of the program" served the best interests of the public, the radio industry, and the broadcaster.[8] One writer asked, "How long do you think an audience would listen to the A & P Gypsies if every number were followed by a dissertation on the quality and price of their beans and pickles? A single, dignified announcement is quite sufficient."[9] The belief that listeners would hear only "dignified announcements" had helped make advertising acceptable as a solution to broadcasting's financial problems. But the radio industry had broken its promise that broadcast advertising would be indirect and instead had moved to more direct "spots" and more advertising-supported sponsored shows. By 1929 one magazine article, "Radio: A Blessing or a Curse?" referred to radio as "just another medium—like the newspapers, the magazines, the billboards, and the mail box—for advertisers to use in pestering us."[10]

Broadcasters had portrayed listeners as the controlling force, able to reject any advertising or programming they disliked. Bruce Bliven, writing in 1924 for *Century* magazine, had argued that while advertising on radio was "undesirable" and should be prohibited, "incidental advertising . . . if unwanted by the listening public will probably die of itself in a short time."[11] The editor of *Radio Broadcast* had reassured listeners that, although "one frequently hears the fear expressed that broadcast programs will eventually turn into nothing but constant and very insidious advertising," the "natural adjustment of things will prevent the overloading of the air with advertising that is objectionable."[12] According to this line of reasoning, actions by listeners—other than changing the channel or not buying the product advertised—were unnecessary because the form broadcasting took would be a "natural" and proper one.

Yet when listeners tuned out one station because it carried too much advertising, they found few less-commercialized alternatives. By the early 1930s commercialized broadcasting was in a dominant position as a result of government support, the organization of commercial stations into wired networks, and the accompanying vigor of the network affiliates. The resulting oligopoly precluded listener "control" of either broadcast advertising or programming.

The networks, for example, routinely ignored listener requests for educational programs, either for information or for personal improvement. Most sponsors had no interest in paying for programs that would attract only a small audience. The networks listed only about one-third of their broadcasting hours as commercial in 1932, but many of the noncommercial (what the networks called "sustaining") programs resembled commercial shows in form and content. The networks typically used sustaining programs as tryouts for commercial shows. In addition, the networks relegated the few educational programs that they did still present, including

Walter Damrosch's music appreciation lectures, the "National Farm and Home Hour," and the Metropolitan Opera broadcasts, to morning and weekend hours when many people found it inconvenient to listen.[13]

Complaints about the lack of educational programs increased as pressures mounted on the nonprofit stations originally founded to air educational programming. In the early 1930s the Federal Radio Commission (FRC) began a reallocation that required many stations to change frequencies and broadcast hours. The FRC, established under the 1927 Radio Act, got off to a slow start owing to lack of funding, the deaths of several of the first commissioners, and the need to have its charter reapproved yearly by Congress.[14] Both the original Radio Act and its 1928 extension, however, called for a reallocation of the radio spectrum, and the FRC's implementation of the reallocation favored commercial stations at the expense of nonprofit stations.[15]

The reallocation process left nonprofit stations feeling that they were running "on flat tires. . . . the air is free all right, but try to get some of it."[16] Educational stations especially objected when their assignments changed several times and always for the worse. The manager of a college radio station wrote to a colleague in 1931 that "many college and school owned stations have been assigned poor and noisy channels. Quite a number have been put on Canadian shared channels where they cannot use the full power of their transmitters."[17] The college stations argued that "the commercial stations have the advantage in hearings before the Radio Commission in that they have the money to back up their demands, and also they have a thorough organization that is looking after their interests."[18]

By every account, educational stations were struggling to survive in the late 1920s and early 1930s. The number of licenses issued to educational stations dropped precipitously during the period: the government issued 177 licenses to educational institutions between 1921 and 1926, and only 12 between 1927 and 1933. Adding to the decline, the number of licenses lost by educational stations stayed more constant: 94 stations gave up licenses between 1921 and 1926, while 64 stations stopped operating in the next five years. Of the 202 licenses granted to educational institutions between 1921 and 1936, only 38 were still held by them in January 1936.[19]

Even the most innocuous FRC rulings had adverse financial repercussions for nonprofit stations. When the commission ordered all broadcasters to stay on their assigned frequencies, the stations had to "purchase expensive frequency control equipment that is made by only a few companies and is sold only at a very high price."[20] The desperate financial problems brought by the Depression were exacerbated by the expenses involved in complying with such new federal regulations. The educators began to join other nonprofit broadcasters in seeking legislative protection against "a negligent and commercially minded Federal Radio Commission."[21] One educational broadcaster wrote that "broadcasting stations in colleges and universities have . . . rights on the air on a par with those . . . so anxious to entertain the public in order to increase their profits," but increasingly the federal government did not share this point of view.[22] Like most agencies, the FRC tended to regulate competition in ways that favored the largest companies.

Not only educational stations, but other commercial enterprises began to see the networks as competition. The growing success, in spite of hard times, of sponsored programs and of the networks themselves aroused jealousy among competing media then struggling to remain solvent. *Fortune* magazine noted that network advertising income rose significantly between 1930 and 1931, with NBC going from earnings of $20,000,000 to $25,900,000 and CBS from $8,586,000 to $11,621,000.[23] Especially during these first years of the Depression, many observers believed that broadcast advertising diverted revenue directly from newspapers and magazines. Long ambivalent toward radio, newspapers found the competition increasingly uncomfortable, as radio's share of gross advertising spending rose from 1.4 percent in 1928 to 6.6 percent in 1931 and to 12.3 percent in 1935.[24]

Political issues of the day raised additional questions about radio's commercialization. The repeal of Prohibition forced the networks to consider the question of liquor advertising and, for the first time, to examine their commercial standards. Even before the New Deal, Congress had considered consolidating the regulation of wired and wireless communication. That effort, which gathered momentum during the Hundred Days, raised questions about commercialism and monopoly control in radio, and gave dissidents a chance to be heard.[25] The New Deal also gave a new impetus to the consumer movement, with its suspicion of all forms of advertising.[26] The climate created by the Depression encouraged anticommercialism to flourish. James Rorty wrote that the problem of controlling and administering radio broadcasting was "approximately coextensive with the problem of controlling and administering the modern world in the economic and cultural interests of the people who inhabit it." He asked,

"Could a more or less mythical political democracy, holding the bag of an unplanned, traditionally exploitative capitalist economy . . . pull radio out of that bag and make it approximately functional?"[27]

Today, with commercialized broadcasting hegemonic, alternatives are difficult to envision. In the early 1930s, however, critics such as Rorty proposed and experimented with other possibilities.

THE PROTESTERS AND THEIR AGENDAS

The resistance to commercial radio in the early 1930s brought together a diverse group of people with a wide range of complaints. Educators led the fight but formed different alliances using a variety of tactics, from lobbying Congress to conducting research. Leftist critics joined educators in worrying about the effects of commercialization on American culture, criticizing the lack of choices available to listeners, and bemoaning the fact that radio had not lived up to its potential. Newspapers joined nonprofit educational stations in decrying the increasing dominance of the networks, even if they failed to share concerns about educational programming.

Educational radio stations had the most at stake in the battle against broadcasting commercialism, and they appeared to be losing. There had been 121 educational stations in the mid-1920s; 77 in 1929; and only 53—occupying just one-sixteenth of the available frequencies—by 1931.[28] In 1925 a group of educational broadcasters attending the Fourth National Radio Conference organized the Association of College and University Broadcasting Stations (ACUBS) because they knew that "the[ir] broadcasting interests . . . would not be given proper consideration by the . . . large commercial broadcasting stations."[29] ACUBS members, located at midwestern, state-supported universities, focused at first on survival. Neither the organization nor its members had much money. The ACUBS financial statement for 1929 reported a small surplus as a result of only $46.97 in expenditures, $69 raised as dues, and a previous balance of $80.[30] Individual member stations and their representatives were experiencing even more difficulty. The secretary of ACUBS wrote, regarding the 1930 annual meeting, that "since I will have to go entirely at my own expense, I am anxious to know about any special provisions for economical rooming and eating while there."[31] As the Depression deepened, stations dropped out because they lacked funds to send personnel to annual meetings or to pay dues.

Despite its limited resources, ACUBS moved on several fronts to challenge the supremacy of the networks. Its members worked to influence radio legislation, maintaining a detailed correspondence with congressional leaders about provisions of the 1927 Radio Act.[32] ACUBS proposed that a reconfigured radio commission, including representatives of education, regulate broadcasting rather than the Secretary of Commerce. ACUBS members voiced disappointment that the 1927 Act did not guarantee "due regard to the requests of educational institutions for opportunities to broadcast educational programs."[33]

After its first annual meeting in 1930, the organization became even more active. With mixed success, it pressured state governments to support educational broadcasting, campaigned for the appointment of sympathetic candidates to the FRC, testified before the FRC, and worked for a reallocation of the radio spectrum that would protect its members.[34] As one supportive observer noted, however, "the Association had little money, and it had given members scarcely more comfort in the difficult days they faced than men without shelter on a winter night might get from huddling together."[35] Its regional focus and membership, plus its limited funding, hampered its effectiveness.

A related group, the National Committee on Education by Radio (NCER), had a national membership, more funding than ACUBS, and a somewhat more focused agenda. NCER sought the reservation of 15 percent of all radio frequencies for educational stations and the "uplift" of American culture through the improvement of radio broadcasting.[36] Founded as a federation of other groups in December 1930, NCER grew out of a conference called by the U.S. Commissioner of Education that had included representatives of various educational organizations, among them ACUBS. NCER received moneys primarily from the Payne Fund, a charitable foundation supporting research into the effects of contemporary institutions on young people.[37] NCER provided a Washington service bureau to help educational stations with federal paperwork and lobbied, provided public information, and sponsored research and experimentation. In addition, it published a weekly bulletin, *Education by Radio*, and financed the preparation and publication of a study, *An Appraisal of Radio Broadcasting in the Land Grant Colleges and State Universities*.[38]

NCER called a national meeting in the spring of 1932 to discuss "The

Use of Radio as a Cultural Agency in a Democracy." Representatives from education, government, and nonprofit stations were invited, but the networks and commercial stations were excluded.[39] Cooperation with the networks, NCER activists believed, might "result in further surrenders of power and privilege to the profit-making stations."[40]

Colleges and other nonprofit broadcasters (including labor, municipal, religious, and agricultural stations) had provided alternative programming since the beginning of broadcast radio. In the early 1930s they were joined by other experimenters. The Ohio School of the Air began in January 1929 and broadcast "short periods of instruction which fit into existing courses" in public schools. By April 1929 100,000 students in twenty-two states listened to these programs broadcast over WEAO (the Ohio State University station) and WLW (the powerful and far-reaching Cincinnati station founded by radio manufacturer Powel Crosley), featuring prominent speakers on current events, health, art appreciation, and science, as well as dramatizations of history, literary masterpieces, and travelogues. The Ohio School continued broadcasting well into the 1930s.[41]

Another unusual proposal for educational programming originated in California with the planning of the Pacific-Western Broadcasting Federation. Begun by "educators, representatives of civic organizations, business men and ministers," the federation sought to build "one genuine UNIVERSITY OF THE AIR." This radio "university" would provide extensive airtime to "learned societies, colleges and universities, civic, social, artistic, and religious bodies," in order to present and popularize the "best in the humanities, social sciences and recreations." It would also provide entertainment—"because the Federation berates banality and bally-hoo in broadcasting, it should not be supposed that there is any lack whatever of realization of the need for relaxation under the terrific pressure of modern life." Programs were to include music, plays, a children's hour, sports, information (especially concerning mental hygiene and public health), discussions of controversial public issues, religious presentations, and charitable appeals. The federation estimated the cost of building its radio station at $1,100,000 and of running it at $530,000 per year. Plans called for obtaining funds from private donors, from cooperating institutions that would subsidize individual programs, and from the sale of time to businesses that sought "indirect publicity."[42] The federation's proposals—apparently never implemented—approached the issues facing radio with unusual creativity, imagining a broadcasting system free from both commercial and governmental control.

While some educators lobbied against radio's growing commercialism and some experimented with noncommercial programming, others favored a form of action more traditional within the academic community: research. The Institute for Education by Radio, part of the Ohio State University Bureau of Educational Research, became the primary research arm of the 1930s protests against commercial radio. Its fifth yearbook noted that the institute "does not shelter present practices; it does not advocate changes," but rather "it specializes in problems where the practical solution seems more immediate." Supported by the Payne Fund, the institute sponsored yearly meetings beginning in 1930 and published the proceedings. ACUBS members were frequent speakers (the ACUBS annual meeting took place in conjunction with the institute's sessions), as were representatives from other nations. In its emphasis on practicality, the institute aligned itself with its cosponsor, the Ohio State Board of Education. Ohio had been a leader in the use of radio in its classrooms, and institute members often heard descriptions of Ohio experiments.[43]

Others approached radio research more theoretically than did the institute. Advertising had turned broadcasting into a search for audiences, and the question of audience lent itself to research and academic debate. In *The Control of Radio*, published in 1934, Jerome Kerwin, a professor of political science at the University of Chicago, criticized radio's uncontrolled monopoly, the organization and personnel of the FRC, the high cost of AT&T's charges for wire lines (which forced the networks to seek too much advertising revenue), and, more generally, the now rampant commercialism.[44] He believed that the search for large audiences and the presentation of educational programming could not be reconciled with broadcasters' search for profits, because "in order to secure the large audiences which the advertisers want and will pay for, it is necessary to stage the least elevating types of program during the best listening hours." Kerwin concluded that "practically every program . . . suggests a surrender to current standards of taste."[45]

Advocating a chain of government radio stations supported by the federal government, Kerwin, like some other detractors of the networks, cited the British system as a partial model.[46] Many American educators interested in broadcasting sought changes in radio so that the new medium would elevate public taste, as the British Broadcasting Corporation had set out to do. Kerwin presented a somewhat more complex view. On one hand, he found public taste appalling. "If education is to be the aim of radio broadcasting," Kerwin wrote, "it is absurd to talk at the same time

... of giving the public what it wants," because "education must come from above at all times." Yet he also attacked as "callous, indifferent, and irresponsible" the common refrain of broadcasters that "we give the public what it wants." Maintaining that "all the evidence that the people of the country are getting what they want is not in," Kerwin noted that many listeners believed programming complaints were "futile as long as commercialism lies at the base of the broadcasting structure."[47] Kerwin thus articulated the common academic belief that radio listeners needed both "uplift" and protection from excessive commercialism.

Protests against commercialism also came from the American left. Radical thinking avoided, for the most part, the confusion that simultaneously accused broadcasters of underestimating the public and excoriated the public for bad taste in enjoying the programs presented to them. Leftist analysts focused on the corrupting power of commercialism, the public's right to control the airwaves, and a faith in the ability of people, once free of capitalist monopolies, to create a superior culture.

James Rorty, a one-time advertising copywriter and later a founding editor of *The New Masses*, wrote extensively on the evils of commercial broadcasting in Marxist terms, not as a means of production but as part of the superstructure.[48] Daniel Pope has pointed out that, with regard to advertising in general, Rorty contradicted himself by at once reducing advertising to "merely a facet of the conspicuous consumption and conspicuous waste that a business society demanded" and then focusing on the "centrality of advertising in modern America."[49] Rorty treated radio in much the same dualistic way. Radio was a "new instrument of social communication" that contributed "nothing qualitative to the culture" but merely communicated "the pseudo-culture that we had evolved." It was simply "a great mirror in which the social and cultural anomalies of our 'ad-man's civilization' are grotesquely magnified."[50] Yet Rorty also contended that "the control of radio means increasingly the control of public opinion."[51]

Rorty attacked commercial radio both because it influenced public opinion and because it symbolized corporate America's dominance. In the end, he advocated government intervention to bring "order on the air," supporting both the reservation of frequencies for nonprofit stations and comprehensive communications legislation.[52] Rorty worked on his own, but freely expressed opinions about other anticommercial advocates. He applauded the NCER for "militant" actions, but doubted the motives of those newspapers that protested broadcast advertising. Rorty maintained that "the interest of the press in 'reforming' the radio was strictly competitive and pecuniary in quality although, of course, the appeal to public opinion was not made in those terms."[53]

Despite Rorty's scorn, the press played a prominent role in the attacks on commercialized radio. Mainstream newspaper publishers worked on two fronts: against radio news, which seemed to compete directly with them, and against newspaper printing of radio schedules. One notable outbreak of hostilities even came to be called the "press-radio war." In April 1933 the Associated Press, followed by other wire services and under pressure from the American Newspaper Publishers Association (ANPA), refused radio networks the use of news it gathered. NBC and CBS retaliated by founding their own news departments, while independent radio stations continued receiving news from the wire services. The newspaper publishers thus failed to keep news off the radio, but continuing threats by newspapers to drop program listings worried radio advertisers. Network representatives sought a meeting with ANPA. An agreement signed in December 1933 created the Press-Radio Bureau, paid for by NBC and CBS and staffed by the wire services. The bureau daily provided two five-minute news summaries, one to be broadcast after 9:30 a.m. and the other after 9 p.m., so as not to compete with the news presented in morning and evening newspapers. The networks agreed to present the bureau's news unsponsored, and to confine their other news reports to "analysis" or "commentary."[54] This compromise between newspaper publishers and broadcasters led to the development of the radio news commentators and analysts so familiar in the late 1930s and 1940s.[55]

One newspaper, the *Ventura Free Press* of Ventura, California, sponsored a more direct attack on commercial radio. H. O. Davis, publisher of the *Free Press*, bombarded newspaper editors with articles deploring broadcast advertising, the lack of educational programs on radio, and the sinister activities of the radio monopoly. The *Free Press* claimed 746 cooperating newspapers, 523 dailies and 223 weeklies, "in every state in the Union pledging their active support."[56] Its most sustained effort came with the distribution of *Empire of the Air*, fifty articles first sent to newspapers nationwide and then privately published as a book in 1932. In this jeremiad Davis wrote that commercialized stations "so crowd the air channels that the rights of education, labor, and agriculture have suffered," and that "we have seen the ether given over to the advertiser and the home invaded by the salesman." Davis advocated a limit to broadcast advertising, the reservation of channels for education, the supervision of programs by the FRC, and the provision of free programs to local stations to enable them to survive without network affiliation.[57]

The motivation behind the *Ventura Free Press* campaign remained murky. In a letter Davis explained that he had bought the *Ventura Free Press* when he suffered a breakdown "after a career in motion pictures, as reorganizer and editor of *Ladies' Home Journal*, and as regional director for W. R. Hearst." The *Press* proved "sadly run down and neglected," and Davis sought a "broad national issue" in order "to regain local prestige in a hurry."[58] At other times, Davis gave a less personal explanation: he wanted to remove advertising from the air to make room "for channels for education, information, the public service," and "to protect the country's publishers against unfair competition."[59]

Most newspaper publishers believed that radio advertising threatened their profits but, like Davis, they cloaked economic self-interest in seemingly unselfish rhetoric. They emphasized the problems of educational broadcasters and the menace to programming of both radio advertisements and the radio monopoly. Davis urged publishers to attack the radio monopoly in their columns with the *Free Press*'s material.[60] He sent a "Dear Publisher" letter explaining his purpose along with one early release:

> Radio advertising is giving you sharp competition. Radio advertising is a
> nuisance resented by your radio-owning readers. Radio advertising is the
> basis on which a dangerous monopoly is being built. The Ventura Free
> Press, in co-operation with a thousand other newspapers, is endeavoring to
> arouse public sentiment for the support of legislation that will defeat the
> purpose of the radio monopoly and drive direct advertising from the air.[61]

Davis followed up his press releases with lists of "suggestions for the conduct of local campaigns by individual publishers." Realizing that educators and publishers sought the same ends for different reasons, he claimed to be trying to "coordinate" their efforts.[62]

In fact, however, the educators, radicals, and newspaper publishers who objected to commercial radio rarely worked together in the early 1930s. They failed, at this point, to rally around one solution to the problems of commercialization and instead proposed diverse alternatives ranging from model nonprofit stations to revised federal regulations. The government's regulatory mechanisms, however, were easily manipulated by the industry they had been set up to control.

INDUSTRY RESPONSE TO THE PROTESTS

The networks and the radio industry, always vigilant concerning complaints that might lead to more government regulation or to a mobilization of public opinion against them, reacted quickly to the backlash against commercialism. Those with a stake in commercialized broadcasting moved to address the criticisms without changing the basis on which radio operated. They spoke out in public to promote commercialized broadcasting; spread their message through sympathetic organizations; and pressured the federal government to ensure, through regulation, that the "American system of broadcasting" would become permanent.

Commercialized broadcasters followed the activities of their opponents in great detail, paying attention to the smallest criticism and calling in favors to find out what the reformers planned. NBC executives received copies of numerous *Ventura Free Press* publications, passed along by newspaper publishers who also owned network-affiliated radio stations.[63] In addition, NBC and RCA directly investigated Davis and the *Ventura Free Press* several times. NBC's manager of press relations met with the *Ventura Free Press* public relations staff in Los Angeles during September 1931 and reported back to NBC. In October a representative of RCA met with another *Ventura Free Press* employee and sent a confidential report to RCA president David Sarnoff and NBC president Merlin Aylesworth. NBC vice-president Frank Mason also asked the publisher of the *Norfolk Daily News* to seek personal information from friends in Ventura, California, about Davis himself.[64]

These NBC and RCA efforts consisted of information gathering only, with no action planned against the small but annoying *Ventura Free Press*. Neither NBC nor RCA seriously considered changing the practices criticized by Davis or any other protester. The radio industry remained anxious about any opposition that might attract public attention, but only in order to preempt it before it resulted in greater governmental control or a loss in profits.

The networks also undertook public relations activities that seemed to bolster educational programming over the commercial airwaves.

Shortly after its own founding, NBC formed a National Advisory Council, composed of people prominent in business, politics, and education, to ensure that "the actions of the company were in the public interest."[65] An education subcommittee of the council reported yearly that the network was cooperating fully with educators and presenting many high-caliber educational programs.[66] The National Advisory Council aimed to help NBC forestall the objections of educators both by identifying prominent citizens who supported the educational policies of the network and by emphasizing its public service activities over its profit-making. CBS joined NBC in touting the educational programs it presented, notably the "American School of the Air." Sometimes in collaboration with the National Association of Broadcasters, NBC undertook other public relations activities to bolster the idea that educational programs belonged on commercial rather than nonprofit stations.[67] The objective was to force nonprofit broadcasters out of business by claiming to do the same job they did.

One organization of educators collaborated in advancing the notion that the networks welcomed educational programming. The National Advisory Council on Radio in Education (NACRE), which shared members with the NBC National Advisory Council and the National Association of Broadcasters, believed the networks would willingly turn over time for high-quality educational programming.[68] NACRE thus served as a kind of "company union" for the networks. NBC's National Advisory Council reported that NACRE, founded in May 1930, sought to "devise, develop, and sponsor suitable programs" so that the "Council may be recognized as the mouthpiece of American education in respect to educational broadcasting."[69] Funded by John D. Rockefeller, Jr., and the Carnegie Corporation, NACRE prepared programs for both CBS and NBC on economics, psychology, vocational guidance, civics, and labor, and sold nearly 250,000 listeners' guides in 1931 alone.[70]

Speeches at the NACRE assemblies in 1931, 1932, and 1933 revealed both the organization's identification with commercial radio and its low regard for educational stations. Network executives were honored participants at these assemblies, joining government officials, national education association officers, and network-friendly college professors to discuss the development and regulation of radio advertising, broadcasting in the schools, radio legislation, and commercial broadcasting and education.[71] Members of NACRE believed that commercial stations would always have "more unsold time on their hands than they know what to do with," and would give these unsold hours "to educational institutions in the generally vain hope that they will make sensible use of it."[72] In return for the time, and for the access to a varied audience, the educators would have to "disregard many pedagogical practices which have been developed over many decades" in order to produce programs that would "hold an audience."[73] Like the networks, NACRE members complained that the dullness of educational radio stations drove listeners away and decreased the audience for all broadcasting. NACRE saw no conflict between the commercial basis of radio and its use for education, refusing to consider that selling a product and educating a student might be incompatible goals. Rather, it believed that the need of the networks to reach large numbers of consumers complemented the interest of the schools in reaching large audiences for educational purposes.[74]

Reform-minded critics, especially those involved in educational radio stations, did not share NACRE's trust in the commercial networks or its belief that advertising and education were mutually beneficial. James Rorty attacked NACRE for accepting free radio time and asserted that the networks used radio only "in their own private commercial interest and that of the commercial advertisers," a purpose inimical to "genuine education."[75] Jerome Kerwin held that what the networks gave they could also take away, noting that the ease "with which educational programs are brushed aside for the sponsored programs has created the disconcerting feeling that the place of worthwhile programs is not only secondary, but insecure."[76] An ACUBS member wrote that the networks' educational programs served merely as "bait to a trap": once the "big broadcasters" gained control, they would "offer no programs that are not paid for at the most exorbitant prices" and "certainly none will then be offered unless they can be used to sell cigars, cigarettes, toothpastes, patent medicines, etc."[77]

While commercial broadcasters influenced and used NACRE, they also felt the need for an organization of their own to promote commercial radio. The National Association of Broadcasters (NAB), founded in 1922, became an effective lobbying and public relations agent. Its activities ranged from officials speaking in favor of commercially sponsored educational radio programs to the publication of a 200-page book "presenting arguments in support of the system of broadcasting in the United States" for use by high-school debaters.[78] It adopted a "Code of Ethics" in 1925 and strengthened it in 1929, in an effort to curb criticism through self-regulation of fraudulent advertising and the advertising of harmful products.[79] Its members were kept informed of the alliances and activities of the *Ventura Free Press*, and excerpts from Davis's newspaper stories and letters appeared in the NAB newsletter.[80] The association's most effective work came as it interacted with the federal government on behalf of its members. NAB leaders believed they had "fathered" the 1927 Radio Act by helping shepherd the bill through Congress. One historian noted the "many informal services" the NAB "rendered" to the new Federal Radio Commission during its first months after passage of the act.[81]

The networks found pressure on Congress and the Federal Radio Commission (later the Federal Communications Commission) to be their most effective strategy in resisting the reformers. Even CBS, only rarely visible on the national scene during its early years, presented its side of the ongoing argument to the regulatory agency and to the public. William Paley, founder and president of CBS, testified before the commission in 1934, and CBS published his talk as a pamphlet, *Radio as a Cultural Force*. Paley equated the commercial and educational missions of broadcasting when he described radio as "a new force in the distribution of goods as well as in the dissemination of ideas." Speaking directly to the arguments of the reformers, Paley discussed the importance of audience, asserted that CBS gave the public what it wanted to hear, listed the many "educational, informational, and generally cultural programs" presented by CBS, and denied that the network practiced censorship in any form.[82]

The inquiry at which Paley testified marked the next step in the reform campaign, as the foes of commercial radio proposed that Congress reserve channels for the use of nonprofit stations. The protesters hoped to turn the frequency reallocation process (once used to harass them) against the power of the networks. In this next stage of the war, both sides focused on the federal government as it prepared the 1934 Communications Act. The attempt to set aside certain frequencies for education and religious programming became a crucial battle.

CONGRESSIONAL ATTEMPTS TO REFORM COMMERCIAL RADIO

Congress had first asserted the federal right to regulate radio in the 1912 Radio Act, but the beginning of broadcasting in 1920 brought new problems with which it was ill-equipped to deal.[83] Few members of Congress even knew at that point how radio worked. As late as 1929, during a discussion of the installation of broadcasting equipment in the chamber, one senator asked "if that radio is put back in the corner of the chamber here close to my seat whether it would be possible for one of those anarchists to send something through it and blow us all out of here."[84] Congress thus depended on the radio industry for information on technical matters and on every other subject having to do with broadcasting.

Despite Congress's ignorance, both the detractors and defenders of commercialized broadcasting turned to the federal government for help in their efforts to influence broadcast radio's form and content. Throughout the 1920s and early 1930s Congress considered radio regulation and, while both sides sought to influence that legislation, the forces for commercialization clearly won. Although the Senate commissioned a study of commercial radio, Congress avoided outright regulation of either broadcast advertising or the radio networks. Instead, congressional attempts at reform fell into two categories—efforts to strengthen the ability of local stations to resist network domination, and attempts to guarantee nonprofit groups access to the airwaves—neither of which had much effect. By not pressing for more fundamental changes, the networks' opponents reinforced the congressional inclination to leave the commercialized system intact. Lobbyists for both sides emphasized legislation that regulated the results of the commercial system but left untouched the basis of that system.

During the years between the beginning of broadcasting and 1927, Congress had debated the question of where regulatory power should reside. The establishment of the Federal Radio Commission (FRC) grew out of a conference committee compromise on the 1927 Radio Act. The House bill called for the FRC to act in a purely advisory capacity, but the Senate gave the FRC authority over radio regulation. The compromise empowered the FRC to issue licenses for only one year, after which the Secretary of Commerce would take over that authority with the expert advice of the FRC.[85] Congress supposed that one year would give the FRC time to create a basic license allocation plan that the Secretary of Commerce could implement. Extension in 1928 of the FRC's power for another year seemed sensible, because the commission had made little headway in sorting out the license problem.[86]

The 1928 extension of the Radio Act contained the Davis amendment, which called for a geographic equalization of license grants and was one of Congress's first attempts to support alternatives to network radio.[87] Representatives of rural areas, concerned about a network monopoly of the airwaves, sponsored this and several other legislative initiatives to strengthen local stations. One Oklahoma representative noted that "so much power has been granted to the . . . chain stations, that they are absolutely crowding the small independent stations off the air." The legislation under consideration would keep the commission from doing what "it has done in the past," ignoring "all the rest of the country" and letting "a few stations in New York and Chicago dominate."[88] Members of Congress believed that each listener deserved to hear programs originating from an independent local station, rather than over a network affiliate or a faraway, powerful channel.

Both the House and the Senate debated several provisions in the early 1930s to ease the financial and managerial burdens of smaller stations and thus to improve their competitive position. Station owners, the sponsoring members of Congress argued, should be able to appeal FRC decisions in local courts, in order to promote local autonomy and to save money on travel expenses. One bill even proposed a complex formula for radio cases, with some disputes to be heard in local courts, others in three judge district courts, and the rest in the D.C. Circuit Court of Appeals.[89] Another attempt to allow the conduct of more business locally involved the use of examiners, instead of commissioners, to hold hearings. Proponents believed that this change would permit hearings in different communities with greater ease and speed. The scheme failed to win approval, partly because examiners appointed by the FRC, unlike the commissioners themselves, would not have been responsible to Congress.[90]

Representative Davis and his colleagues sought to preserve alternatives to homogeneous programming from big-city sources. But the Davis amendment forced the FRC to spend its time devising a complex reallocation plan that, in practice, often discriminated against nonprofit and non-network stations.[91] As it worked out, the amendment also helped ensure the survival of the networks by creating a system of widely scattered but strong local outlets, a system the networks found particularly convenient. Local stations not affiliated with a network—primarily those sponsored by colleges and universities—actually faced more difficulties because of the new legislation, while other bills designed to help them failed to pass.

Despite the failure of early congressional radio reform, network opponents who had had little luck attracting support with their underfinanced public relations campaigns continued to turn to the federal government for help. *Broadcast Advertising* magazine scorned such lobbying, as radio critics "unable to make an impression on the public, who seemed well pleased with things as they are . . . changed their tactics and went after the FRC and Congress in whose hands the control of radio lies."[92] The defenders of commercial broadcasting often portrayed their opponents as advocating complete government ownership and operation of the American radio system.[93] In fact, however, the protesters were asking that the government only act to preserve a mixed system of commercial and nonprofit stations.

The protests against commercial radio did help to change the nature of proposed radio legislation. Early congressional efforts at reform of the radio industry had concentrated on structure rather than content. As broadcast advertising grew, and as its critics began to complain, Congress took notice. In 1932 Sen. James Couzens, a businessman with little experience in radio legislation, introduced a resolution "calling for a report from the FRC on the use of radio facilities for commercial advertising purposes." The resolution, directly critical of the commercialism of American broadcasting, noted "there is growing dissatisfaction with the present use of radio facilities for the purposes of commercial advertising."[94] Couzens's original resolution included seven questions about "the feasibility of government ownership and operation of broadcasting facilities"; the extent to which broadcasting stations were "used for commercial advertising purposes"; the power available to commercial stations; possible plans "to reduce, to limit, to control, and perhaps to eliminate the use of radio facilities for advertising purposes"; methods used by other nations to control broadcast advertising; whether announcements of sponsorship alone would be "practicable and satisfactory"; and financial information concerning representative broadcasting stations. Sen. Clarence Dill, sponsor of the 1927 Radio Act and now the object of fierce lobbying, saw a chance to placate educators clamoring for action and added eight questions to those of Senator Couzens, all of which dealt with educational radio stations and with educational programming on commercial stations.[95]

In public, both the radio industry and its detractors welcomed the FRC survey. The president of NBC believed the investigation would highlight "the splendid public service that most broadcasters are performing today" and he awaited "the result of this investigation with the greatest optimism."[96] The National Association of Broadcasters (NAB) adopted a resolution calling the Senate request "an opportunity to demonstrate to the American people the superiority of our system of broadcasting."[97] *Broadcast Advertising* agreed that a report to the Senate would find the "American" system "the only plan possible for a democracy," and called the survey "a showdown, with all the cards on the table. . . . a chance to drive home the fact . . . that too much advertising is not radio's only fault, nor its worst one."[98]

The behind-the-scenes maneuverings of the broadcasting industry, however, belied its public confidence. The NAB began a secret emergency fund-raising program to cover the cost of "providing the broadcasting stations with materials designed to present to the American public the real facts."[99] NBC scrambled to give its affiliates information "with which to answer questions regarding network programs," as it "is to our best advantage" that the answers given to the FRC survey be "uniform."[100]

Reformers saw the survey as a chance to show "the commercial radio monopoly" that "the American people are disgusted with the glaring evils which have been allowed to grow up in American radio by a negligent and commercially-minded Federal Radio Commission."[101] As usual, they relied on volunteers to present their case to the FRC and the public, and never marshaled the same level of pressure as did the commercial broadcasters. One member of the National Committee on Education by Radio (NCER) wrote to another that the matter "will require some pretty clever handling and I do not feel equal to the task." The educators did complain, after the fact, about the unfairness of the survey, noting that the FRC had chosen National Education Week, when networks broadcast more educational programs, as the sample period. Further, they argued that the FRC ignored the NCER and other educational organizations, while it did talk to advertisers' organizations.[102]

The FRC's commitment to commercial radio pervaded its report, *Commercial Radio Advertising*, delivered and printed in 1932.[103] To answer the Senate's questions, the FRC solicited information from stations about their programs and practices, particularly during the week of November 8–14, 1931. It also corresponded with individual advertising agencies, the American Association of Advertising Agencies, the Secretary of State, and with others who had knowledge of broadcasting in foreign countries.[104] The report took the simple form of answers to the previously specified congressional questions, with the FRC presenting itself as a neutral purveyor of information. The responses to the questions about educational

146

broadcasting were extremely detailed and quoted extensively from FRC dockets, but the FRC relied on opinion in its discussion of commercial radio. The commission contended that, at most, one-third of all radio broadcasts were commercial, while other programs, termed "sustaining," were "presented by the station without compensation and at its expense."[105] The FRC explained this apparent altruism by noting that sustaining programs helped stations serve the public interest as mandated by the 1927 Radio Act, enlarging and holding an audience and thereby increasing the value of time available for commercial programs.[106]

The report's concluding statements on the relationship between sustaining and commercial programming observed that "a radio broadcast station can present sustaining programs that are of great educational value and rich in entertainment only in a degree measured by the revenue derived from the sale of time for purposes of commercial advertising." The FRC reminded Congress that if it restricted radio sponsorship to announcements only, advertisers might stop using radio and "such non-use would immediately and inevitably be reflected in a decrease both in quantity and quality of programs made available to the public."[107] The report thus clearly outlined the perils to broadcasting if advertising disappeared, but it never addressed the other contingency: what would happen if sustaining programs vanished, victims to the growing demand by sponsors for airtime?

The report's conclusion emphasized the commission's own competence to regulate broadcasting. "The proper solution," the FRC wrote, "would seem to lie in legislation authorizing the commission to enact certain regulations . . . rather than specific legislation on the subject by Congress."[108] The FRC existed from year to year, dependent on yearly legislation for its continuance. Yet by 1932 it had accumulated a staff and bureaucracy that used the Senate's questions to make a case for their own jobs. Throughout the report, the FRC presented solutions to radio's problems that maintained or increased the commission's power.

Despite the FRC's dislike of "specific legislation," Congress exhibited a growing interest in regulating broadcast advertising, especially during the election year of 1932. Fiorello La Guardia, a progressive Republican from New York City, probably intended to protect political advertisers when he introduced a bill to establish reasonable fees for radio advertising. Another proposal prohibited commercials on Sunday. Both bills died in committee.[109] Organized labor and agricultural groups also sought legislation to change frequency allocations. Early in 1931 Sen. Otis F. Glenn of Illinois introduced an amendment to a House radio bill calling for the assignment of a cleared channel frequency to labor.[110] A year later the Chicago Federation of Labor lobbied for a clear channel for their station WCFL, got bills introduced in the House and Senate, and testified at hearings before the Senate Committee on Interstate Commerce, worrying the NAB.[111] The United Farm Federation of America suggested in 1932 that Congress set aside a clear radio channel for the "exclusive use of radio stations that may be erected by or devoted to the independent farm organizations only" and saw their resolution printed in the *Congressional Record*.[112]

The opponents of commercial radio soon moved from advocating individual channels set aside for particular nonprofit groups, to calling for a percentage of frequencies to be reserved for nonprofit stations. This new strategy rallied and brought together diverse groups. As early as 1931 Sen. Simon D. Fess, a Republican from Ohio, had introduced an amendment to the 1927 Radio Act to reserve 15 percent of all radio licenses for educational broadcasting. Despite the backing of various educators and reformers, Senator Fess had been unable to win congressional support for the proposal. "I never could get any reaction in favor of it," he told *Education by Radio*. "As soon as it was offered, the stations began a propaganda against it; just why I do not know."[113] The commercial radio magazines had raised a hue and cry against the Fess amendment. One editorial in *Radio Digest* had begun, "it seems incredible that so many of our great army of teachers should permit themselves to fall into the hands of schemers." The editor had considered the passage of the Fess bill "one of the most telling blows imaginable to the American Plan" and "the opening wedge to the complete dissolution of the system."[114]

It fell to Father John Harney, the father superior of the Paulist Fathers in New York City, to try to unite the nation's nonprofit groups and their congressional supporters behind a proposal to reserve 25 percent of all frequencies for "human welfare" organizations. A Roman Catholic religious order, the Paulist Fathers had founded a radio station in 1924. After being switched from frequency to frequency, and then forced to share time with other stations over the congested New York airwaves, WLWL found itself, despite appeals to the FRC, allotted only 15½ hours weekly to broadcast. Father Harney decided to "attack on a wider front." In March 1934 educational, labor, and agricultural groups rushed to Harney's support after he presented an amendment to the Senate Committee on Interstate Commerce calling for certain frequencies to be reserved for nonprofit stations. Harney organized Catholic organizations and Catholic members of Congress to support his proposal and enlisted senators Robert Wagner of New York and Henry Hatfield of West Virginia to serve as cosponsors of his amendment.[115]

Consideration of the Wagner-Hatfield amendment became part of the continuing congressional debate that preceded the 1934 Communications Act. Lack of information and imagination about radio's potential power had short-circuited the 1927 congressional attempt at long-lasting, comprehensive radio legislation. In an effort to correct the oversights of the 1927 Radio Act, many representatives and senators had considered consolidating the regulation of all forms of communications.[116] Yet radio's growing political importance, FRC susceptibility to congressional pressure, and industry opposition to most proposed legislation had made Congress reluctant to take action. Amendments to the 1927 Radio Act had enabled the FRC to continue functioning and had given further shape to both the regulatory framework and the radio industry itself.

By early 1933 the lack of a coherent federal radio policy had become woefully apparent, and Congress passed a comprehensive radio bill only to see it blocked by lame-duck President Herbert Hoover's pocket veto. The 1927 Radio Act had essentially been created through the series of national radio conferences called by Hoover as Secretary of Commerce. Proud of his handiwork, Hoover apparently wanted no changes in what he considered "his" act.[117]

In March 1933, however, Franklin D. Roosevelt was sworn in as president, and the obstacles that had plagued earlier legislation receded. Members of Congress felt confident that they now knew how and where to place regulatory power, and which problems to face and which to ignore. (Most members placed both radio advertising and the network system in the category of issues best ignored.) The New Deal added to the push for new legislation. Congressional actions during the first months of Roosevelt's administration established several new administrative agencies, much like the FRC, vested with large discretionary powers and subject only to narrow judicial review. The New Deal Congress also moved away from a concern for small business toward attempts to regulate existing corporate combinations, in the same way earlier Congresses had approached the radio industry. Perhaps most significantly, Roosevelt broadcast six fireside chats in 1933 and 1934, seizing on "radio as a revolutionary new medium of person-to-person communications" and teaching members of Congress an unforgettable lesson about the political importance of broadcasting.[118]

In a 1934 message to Congress, Roosevelt called for a new "communications" bill, proposing a commission charged with regulating all forms of communications. Congress had discussed the possibility of a communications commission as early as 1929, and although many observers expressed surprise when the 1934 Communications Act, with its grant of large discretionary power to the newly created Federal Communications Commission, easily passed Congress, earlier debates, especially in 1933, had paved the way for its approval.[119]

The new bill also resolved several pressing regulatory problems. In 1934 the question of antitrust violations in the radio industry remained a major issue in Congress. The emphasis of the 1934 Communications Act on public service proved a basis for accepting the status quo of both the equipment "trust" (the manufacturers of receivers and transmitters) and the network system of chain broadcasting, thus pleasing both the general public and the radio industry. The act stated its purpose as "regulating interstate and foreign commerce by wire and radio so as to make available . . . a rapid, efficient, nation-wide and world-wide wire and communication service with adequate facilities at reasonable charges."[120] Accepting at long last the necessity for some regulation of radio, Congress now found its models in public utility and railroad legislation. The public utility model had appeared tangentially in the 1927 Radio Act, with the phrase that licenses should be granted to those serving "the public interest, convenience, or necessity"; this phrase had been developed in the public utilities field and was carried over into the 1934 Act.[121] The continuing congressional analogies between radio and railroad were incorporated as well, so that the language of the legislation designed to regulate radio mirrored the language of railroad regulation.[122] Congress thus consciously based its approach to the new technology of radio on those familiar regulatory forms that had earlier—as far as it was concerned—proved successful.

The few restrictions found in the 1927 Radio Act regarding monopoly within the radio industry were repeated in the 1934 Communications Act. With a statement forbidding interlocking directorates—a direct result of experience with the radio industry—Congress augmented provisions applying antitrust statutes to the manufacture of radio equipment and refusing licenses to any group found guilty of monopoly.[123] The 1934 act also continued the policy of the Davis amendment of insuring equal geographic distribution of radio licenses.[124] Proponents of a strong Federal Communications Commission lobbied against proposed provisions that would have strengthened local stations, including opportunities for local review and the use of examiners rather than commissioners. An amendment, introduced by Senator Dill but not part of the final bill, forbade monopoly in local station ownership. Senator Dill accepted consolidation at the national level, putting his efforts into an attempt to preserve competition at the local level.[125] On the whole, Congress in 1934 seemed content to regard radio manufacturing and broadcasting as interwoven parts of a natural monopoly. The networks, which in all their publicity had sought to appear as natural monopolies, thus escaped regulation.

The introduction of the Wagner-Hatfield amendment was the only challenge to congressional unanimity about the 1934 Communications Act. Much of the debate on the bill concerned this amendment, which had been reported out of committee with only its sponsors voting for approval. The original amendment called for the revocation of broadcasting licenses within ninety days and the reallocation of 25 percent of all frequencies to nonprofit groups. The provision that aroused the greatest controversy would have permitted nonprofit stations to sell time to defray their expenses. Senators Wagner and Hatfield spoke at length on the economic hardships of educational radio and on the importance of adult education in the United States. They willingly changed the ninety-day grace period before license reallocation to six months, the length of time for which broadcast licenses traditionally had been granted. But neither Wagner nor Hatfield could deny that the reallocation of all stations would be a huge job, nor were they willing to compromise on allowing nonprofit stations to sell some portion of their airtime. Senator Dill attacked the amendment on the grounds that, given the opportunity to sell time, the newly protected stations would be no different than commercial stations.

Members of Congress eventually defeated the amendment without having to vote on it by requesting that the new Federal Communications Commission make a study of the issue.[126] The reasons for the defeat were many. One historian faults Wagner and Hatfield's "stubborn reluctance" to change the provision that would have allowed educational stations to sell time, believing that they weakened their case by not considering other means of financial support.[127] But the promoters of the amendment had contended that without some means of support, educational stations would be as bad off as ever. Erik Barnouw blames the divisions within the ranks of the educators, as compared with the unity of the commercial broadcasters.[128] As always, the broadcasting industry had drawn together to oppose the amendment, since it represented both a cut in revenue of up to 25 percent and an extension of regulation. The National Association of Broadcasters had objected to the new category of stations as appealing only to special interests, maintaining that "the sole test of fitness for a broadcasting license is service to the public as a whole, as distinguished from service to any particular class, group or denomination."[129]

Congressional attitudes and preconceptions also worked against the amendment, which ran counter in some respects to the New Deal's faith in the delegation of broad powers to strong federal regulatory commissions. Sam Rayburn, a leading Democrat representative from Texas, believed that if Congress were to tell the FRC how to allocate frequencies "we would be in the same position that Congress would be in if, after giving to the Interstate Commerce Commission its function of regulating railroads and fixing the rates, we would then start out to introduce and pass measures to revise the rate structure."[130] In the end, the 1934 Communications Act gave the Federal Communications Commission unrestricted discretionary powers in the matter of license granting.[131] Left to the mercy of the new FCC, educational and other nonprofit stations faced continuing discrimination.

The FRC thus emerged strengthened by its transformation into the FCC. Its own bureaucratic momentum, combined with congressional knowledge of administrative agencies' susceptibility to pressure, made its inclusion in the new regulatory framework practically a foregone conclusion. Additionally, radio's growing use as a political tool and its importance in everyday life made administrative regulation, usually little noticed outside the industry, more appealing to Congress than prescriptive legislation. In its only attempt to influence programming, Congress left intact the 1927 provision mandating equal time for political candidates and forbidding censorship of political broadcasts.[132]

In many ways, Congress's attitude toward commercial broadcasting reflected what Ellis Hawley has called "the New Deal and the problem of monopoly." Hawley outlines two streams of economic thought operating during the New Deal, tracing them back to the New Nationalism and New Freedom first discussed in the 1912 presidential election: antimonopolists who believed in breaking up trusts to improve competition faced off against those who found monopolies inevitable and thus in need of control.[133] Just as in the rest of the New Deal era's legislation, a dialectic between regulation and competition can be found in the federal response to radio. At once concerned about the "radio trust" in manufacturing and the control of broadcasting by only a few companies, all three branches of the federal government also saw the need for a rationalization of the "natural monopoly" enjoyed by the networks. Federal planning and regulation, they hoped, might mitigate the drawbacks of a monopolistic system and increase competition. In the end, however, governmental regulation only strengthened the largest and commercialized broadcasting companies at the expense of the smaller and nonprofit broadcasters, and lessened competition, outcomes that mirrored most other interactions between the New Deal government and the economy.

CONCLUSION

In John Cheever's short story "The Enormous Radio," a young couple named the Westcotts buy a new radio because they enjoy classical music. But the radio brings more than music into their home. The narrator describes the radio as "powerful and ugly," with a "mistaken sensitivity to discord" that enables Irene Westcott to eavesdrop on the arguments and troubles of other families in her apartment building. The Westcotts get the radio repaired so that it again plays classical music, but it is too late to fix the damage done to the family's peaceful facade. Jim accuses Irene of wasting money, stealing from her dying mother, and having a Caribbean abortion. At the end of the story, Irene turns to the radio,

> hoping that the instrument might speak to her kindly. . . . Jim continued to shout at her from the door. The voice on the radio was suave and noncommittal. "An early-morning railroad disaster in Tokyo," the loudspeaker said, "killed twenty-nine people. A fire in a Catholic hospital near Buffalo for the care of blind children was extinguished early this morning by nuns. The temperature is forty-seven. The humidity is eighty-nine."[1]

CHANGES

Cheever describes how the introduction of radio changed American lives for the worse—a change that involved not only specific radio programs, but the relationships among people and between people and the world around them. Even as broadcasting changed its audience, it continued to change itself.

With the introduction of television, the story of radio advertising becomes two stories: the commercialized broadcasting system, developed in radio, moved to television, while radio itself changed dramatically. Television quickly took over from radio the central place in the living room. Commercialized television networks presented news, entertainment, and educational programs appealing to white, middle-class, suburban families watching together in the evening, and programs aimed at women and children in specialized time periods, with all programs financed through the sale of time to sponsors. Radio became a more personal medium, with people listening to news and music (rather than drama or comedy programs) alone in their homes and cars. Radio programmers reached out increasingly to more diverse and particularized audiences, rather than to the white "middle Americans" sought by television advertisers.

Television, in many ways and for a long time, resembled radio in 1934. Not until the late 1980s did the network system begin to weaken. To examine the continuing interaction among networks, technology, commercialization, and programming, we must turn to television, where the issues of advertising and its influence still provoke intense debate. On the other hand, postwar radio looked quite different than it did in 1934. Having successfully reinvented itself, radio today provides a model of how a technology can adapt to meet new circumstances. Broadcast television itself may be replaced by other technologies and join radio as a medium that is more interesting, less expensive to program, and therefore more responsive to specialized audiences.

THE REST OF THE STORY IN RADIO

Radio programs of the late 1930s and 1940s resembled those that had debuted on the new radio networks. Comedy, in a variety of formats, re-

155

mained the most popular radio fare into the 1950s. Comedians smoothly made the transition from gently spoofing the Depression to gently spoofing World War II, always mindful that the federal government was controlling the licensing and frequency allocations and that major corporations were paying the bills. By the 1940s most radio shows featured heavy-hitting advertising, often as part of the program, produced by agencies located in Hollywood. Several novels, including Frederic Wakeman's *The Hucksters* and Herman Wouk's *Inside Outside*, suggest how the increasing commercialization of radio brought new pressures to bear on writers and performers.[2]

At the same time, dramatic shows, during what came to be called radio's "golden age," flourished. These dramas grew out of the continuing comedy serials that had begun with "Amos 'n' Andy" and "The Rise of the Goldbergs" in the late 1920s. By the end of the 1930s network radio featured several dramatic anthology programs whose writers, often drawing upon the left-wing political consciousness of the era, experimented with radio's aural qualities and ability to deliver political messages. The scripts had widely varied formats, and some featured musical montages and poetry. Norman Corwin, a writer for "Columbia Workshop" on CBS, wrote and directed twenty-six radio plays in as many weeks in 1940 in a series called "26 by Corwin."[3] Another Corwin project, an exploration of the Bill of Rights entitled "We Hold These Truths," intensified patriotic themes he had explored before. Broadcast just eight days after the attack on Pearl Harbor, the show demonstrated how radio writers were able to move quite easily, both professionally and intellectually, into wartime programming.

Radio made three contributions to the war effort—news programs supported American intervention, propaganda broadcast over shortwave radio targeted Nazi-occupied Europe, and broadcasts to the troops via the Armed Forces Radio Service boosted morale—and was further changed in the process. In the 1940s, when most Americans thought of the radio, they thought of war news. Yet news had come late to the airwaves. The agreement that concluded the 1933 "press-radio war" allowed radio announcers to "comment" on the news rather than report it; the "commentators," as radio reporters came to be called, did just that until the Munich crisis of 1938, when H. V. Kaltenborn, a former newspaper reporter, made 102 broadcasts in eighteen days. Sleeping at the CBS studio, Kaltenborn, the son of German immigrants, translated the speeches of French and German leaders as they came over the shortwave radio and broadcast them

156

to American listeners. Being connected to events across the United States was suddenly no longer enough. With the help of radio broadcasts, Americans began to seek a connection to other parts of the world.[4]

As the war erupted, the United States rushed to catch up with the Axis powers, who had begun using radio for propaganda in the 1930s. Americans knew the political power of radio, having listened intently to President Roosevelt's fireside chats, but many were wary of the power of propaganda. In 1942 the president authorized the Overseas Branch of the Office of War Information to begin broadcasting over its Voice of America (VOA) frequencies to areas under Axis control. Historian Holly Cowan Shulman has described how the format and content of the VOA broadcasts changed as American foreign policy, domestic politics, and cultural climate shifted during the course of the war.[5] The first VOA broadcasts drew directly from the experimental programs of commercial radio. VOA programmers, including John Houseman, borrowed radio techniques from Norman Corwin to make their broadcasts more compelling. As the war progressed, VOA broadcasts became more factual and detailed, and resembled news broadcasts rather than modernist radio documentaries. In many ways, along with the wartime radio correspondents such as Edward R. Murrow, Eric Sevareid, and William Shirer, the VOA illustrated the division in broadcast programming that took place in the 1940s, partly owing to the war. Entertainment programming and news programming separated, and listeners came to believe that such a division was natural and preferable to the intermingling of fact and fiction that 1930s radio had featured. Today many critics disparage television "docudramas," which resemble Corwin's and Houseman's radio programs, for conflating truth with fantasy. The VOA, at least in part to hide its own propaganda aims, helped construct the broadcasting convention that news programs were both "objective" and distinct in style and substance from entertainment programming.

Another wartime radio activity, that of the Armed Forces Radio Service (AFRS), also influenced commercial programming. Radio was so much a part of mid-twentieth-century American life that during World War II the armed forces arranged for soldiers in both Europe and the Pacific to listen in. Samuel Brylawski notes that by 1945 the AFRS sent fifty hours of radio programming weekly to overseas outlets, producing forty-three programs (fourteen hours) itself and distributing another thirty-six hours of commercial radio (with advertising messages deleted). One series, "Command Performance," which began before the founding of the AFRS, used prerecorded programs to make the performers' lives easier, proving to the radio industry that a reliable technology existed to edit programs and broadcast them from discs. Each week the program featured a "command performance" from some of America's best-known radio and film stars. The producers assembled the best "takes," deleted the off-color jokes and time-sensitive material, and sent the shows out to AFRS stations on records for rebroadcast.[6]

Recorded programs had long been an anathema to the networks, which had touted their live entertainment throughout the 1930s and early 1940s. Recordings, however, which could be cheaper to produce, offered performers additional flexibility and control. Bing Crosby's experience on "Command Performance" may have moved him to demand a transcription clause in his 1946 contract with the American Broadcasting Company (ABC). Crosby recorded his programs in Los Angeles at his convenience and shipped them back to ABC in New York for broadcast. The increasing use of such recorded material paved the way for the rebirth of radio as a musical medium after the introduction of television.

As an alternative programmer in an industry controlled by the networks, the presence of AFRS demonstrated a wider range of possibilities for radio than most people had imagined. While dependent on the networks for many of its most popular programs, the AFRS routinely deleted all commercial references and advertising. It even retitled programs that carried a sponsor's name: the "Camel Caravan" became "Comedy Caravan," the "Maxwell House Program" became "Fanny Brice–Frank Morgan," and the "Chase and Sanborn Hour" became "Charlie McCarthy." Brylawski notes a number of reasons for this "denaturing" of programs, including complaints from service personnel and American agreements with the noncommercial British Broadcasting Corporation (BBC) to use BBC transmitters to broadcast AFRS programs. Most important, the advertisements seemed inappropriate for GIs in the field. Brylawski writes that "troops fighting in the Pacific did not want to hear about 'refreshing Coca-Cola' nor did they appreciate the 'dangers of the common cold.'"[7] The radio industry had worked since the 1920s to make broadcast advertising seem natural and reassuringly "American," but the stark contrast between wartime realities and radio merchandising appeals revealed that advertising was neither wholly accepted yet nor considered particularly patriotic.

After the war, opposition to commercialized broadcasting resurfaced, most notably in Frederic Wakeman's enormously popular comic novel, *The Hucksters*.[8] Wakeman, a former employee of the Lord and Thomas advertising agency, wrote a fictionalized account of his experiences producing radio programs and working for George Washington Hill, president of the American Tobacco Company, a large radio advertiser and a Lord and Thomas client. The book and its 1947 film version describe the travails of a young agency executive coping with an eccentric and demanding client. Wakeman presents amusing instances of the subservience of advertising and broadcasting professionals relative to their corporate clients; in *The Hucksters*, selling Beautee Soap meant bowing to the company president's predilections for laughably simple-minded radio programs and ad campaigns. Wakeman blames the mediocrity of radio programming on sponsorship and clearly states that sponsors controlled radio.

The renewed resistance to commercialized radio represented by Wakeman's book had little effect against the enormous power and influence of the networks. In addition, the transformation of broadcasting as the war ended confused the opponents of commercialism. The introduction of television distracted much of the public, and blinded critics to the fact that the system they had decried in radio was being carried over into television broadcasting.

In response to television's devastating and instant popularity, radio stations adopted a strategy that they had previously rejected: specialization. This path was already illustrated by the small group of urban radio stations aimed at African Americans. Television, taking up where radio had left off, offered programs primarily aimed at white, suburban, middle-class families. Many African Americans in the late 1940s, uninterested in television programming and often not able to afford the new sets, turned to those radio stations that broadcast rhythm-and-blues, jazz, and gospel recordings. The success of "Negro radio" showed that a segmented market approach could work.

Radio stations gradually discovered that they could identify and serve other special interest groups who found little to interest them on television.[9] White teenagers found the music they heard on black-oriented postwar radio stations so compelling in its form and content that they spent more and more time tuned in. Based on musical styles derived directly from African Americans, rock 'n' roll was broadcast in the 1950s over millions of radios, enabling young people to temporarily cross some class and racial lines, and giving postwar radio its most loyal audience.

Teenage interest in radio grew out of a technological change as well as from social and cultural factors. The invention of the transistor in 1947, like the introduction of the audion after World War I, expanded radio's possibilities. The transistor acted like a vacuum tube in conducting, modulating, and amplifying signals, allowing radios to be made cheaper, smaller, and more durable than prewar sets.[10] With transistor radios, broadcast listening became a personal and portable experience for many people. The smaller size and lower cost of the new models enabled teenagers to own their own radios and tune in without family interference. A teenager could listen alone in her bedroom, or with her friends at the beach, to music that her parents might not enjoy or even condone.

Not many historians have looked at the connection between the development of rock 'n' roll and radio in the 1950s. Recording companies and radio stations, both struggling for a place in the entertainment industry after World War II, found that a relationship could be mutually beneficial. According to one estimate, record sales nearly tripled from 1954 to 1959. Record companies fueled this growth by providing radio stations with hit songs; the stations kept their operating costs low by restricting their programming staffs to the disc jockeys.

The reassignment of the FM spectrum in July 1962 by the FCC opened a new venue for experimentation, delighting a new generation of young listeners involved in alternative musics. After the war, the federal government had tried to promote a different set of radio frequencies in order to increase the number of radio stations available. Since most radios in the 1950s could not receive FM transmissions, many of the first FM stations were completely noncommercial, while commercial FM stations found sponsors difficult to attract or retain. As a result, FM radio developed a tradition of few interruptions and longer music sequences. Once again, the radio and recording industries found a synergy in the mid-1960s as rock performers began to focus on albums rather than singles. While AM radio became more rigid, the new FM stations had time for the music of the counterculture. Many middle-aged Americans today remember the days of "progressive" FM and "free-form" radio with the same fondness their parents reserve for 1930s programs.

Radio's move toward specialized formats was closely tied to a reemphasis within the advertising industry on market research. As the market for consumer goods grew after the war, advertisers worked to sell more services to manufacturers. Advertising professionals found demographic information particularly useful in explaining what advertising could do. Radio and then television became, in David Marc's memorable phrase, "demographic vistas."[11]

The 1970s and 1980s saw a proliferation of extremely specialized stations, many with automated play lists that assigned responsibility for what music went over the air to the station's marketing department. A recent essay on Top 40 radio called it "a fragment of the imagination" and listed twenty-four different station formats, including adult contemporary, album-oriented rock, beautiful music, big band, contemporary hit radio, country, easy-listening radio, gold, and music of your life.[12] The growing conservatism in radio music programming comes from advertising professionals' belief that most Americans prefer the music they already know. With the introduction of cable television stations (such as MTV) that broadcast video versions of top rock songs, much of the newest musical experimentation now reaches audiences on television before it is heard on radio. (College radio stations have remained the exception to this rule; noncommercial since the 1920s, they continue to promote new music and artists.)

The last twenty years have brought both a revival of noncommercial radio and a boom in so-called "talk" radio. The Corporation for Public Broadcasting, under the Public Broadcasting Act of 1967, funded National Public Radio (NPR) both as a production center for programming and as a network linking member stations. Controversial NPR membership requirements barred the small stations that had maintained the nonprofit radio option since 1920. Because most NPR stations are largely supported by listeners, their programming is aimed at those most likely to contribute; the stations therefore provide less diversity than the framers of the original legislation had hoped. On the other hand, talk radio, in several different formats, has grown wonderfully diverse. Call-in shows, with listeners offering opinions or experts giving answers to questions, take radio back to its community-based roots. Discussions of neighborhood issues fill many hours of local radio time, and the hosts of such programs often become influential political figures in their communities. National variations of such programs exist (Larry King interviews celebrities and invites audience questions; Rush Limbaugh ignites heated debate on conservative political issues; Bruce Williams dispenses business advice; and many doctors diagnose ailments from Alaska to Rhode Island), but the local programs sustain the bedrock audience for them.

In many ways the history of radio can be seen as a series of expansions and contractions. Technological developments (the audion, wired networks, the transistor), social and cultural changes (wars, migrations, and the increasing commercialization of everyday life), and innovative programming brought listeners new possibilities for entertainment and education. Yet as each possibility has appeared, various factors have worked to narrow it. Network radio brought the chance to hear national programs but turned listeners into passive rather than active participants. Commercialization promised to provide programming free to listeners but introduced rigid formats, bland content, and excessive advertising appeals. Various disenchanted listeners and critics protested throughout radio's evolution that commercialized broadcasting was blocking the development of more meaningful programming. Rock 'n' roll on 1950s radio allowed white teenagers to explore African American music and to participate in an emerging youth culture, but the industry's focus on demographics and the growth of formula Top 40 stations resulted in a homogenization that eliminated the diversity young listeners had sought. At the same time, as new possibilities brought conservative responses, other avenues sometimes appeared. When AM radio became predictable, FM became the home of musical experimentation; when individuals no longer used the radio to communicate, they traded that active participation for high-quality entertainment by famous vaudeville stars.

John Cheever was right that radio changed the Westcotts, but he portrayed them as helpless, resembling the accident victims they hear about on their new receiver. In reality, American listeners have frequently found ways of using the medium to further their own interests. The family in Woody Allen's film *Radio Days* is perhaps a better representation of radio audiences in the 1920s, 1930s, and 1940s: they integrate radio into their everyday lives, using it to reinforce and underline their activities. The narrator of the film shows how radio affected the shape and content of his memories, creating a warm picture of members of his extended family enjoying different radio programs and music. Broadcasting brought outside tragedies (a little girl dying from a fall down a well) into the home, but instead of inspiring fear (as in the Cheever story), such news served as a way to connect this family with people all over the country. Allen's narrator says, "Now it's all gone. Except for the memories." But Americans today continue to listen to and use radio in varied ways, to react against the commercialization of broadcasting, and to remember various earlier eras as radio's "golden age."

THE REST OF THE STORY IN TELEVISION

As World War I had both slowed radio development and allowed certain companies to better position themselves to profit from the new technology, World War II did the same for television. Developed before the war but first available for widespread use in the early 1950s, television enjoyed a much quicker acceptance than had almost any other consumer good. Advertisers and entertainers left radio in droves to sign up with the new medium on the block. Historian J. Fred MacDonald quotes *Variety's* description of this exodus as "the greatest exhibition of 'mass hysteria' in show biz annals." He goes on to report that in the last half of 1951, money spent on television advertising rose 195 percent, while radio advertising dropped 5 percent. The differences soon became even more striking.[13] Many radio stars and their shows moved to television, often performing the same scripts twice during the week, once for each medium. The structure and programming of television in the early 1950s remained what had been worked out for radio twenty years earlier.

Not until the late 1950s did broadcasting's commercial structure see any changes. Ostensibly in response to the quiz show scandals, the networks moved from having one sponsor for each program to selling time to many advertisers on any given program. The revelation that advertising agencies, as producers of quiz programs (as well as all other shows), had provided certain contestants with answers and coached them in order to make the shows more dramatic, gave the networks an excuse to assume control over programming. The networks and independent production companies now conceived, wrote, cast, and directed their programs, auctioning spot advertisements to the highest bidders. This change placated a public and an FCC shocked over the quiz show debacle, and enabled the networks to make greater profits by providing more individual units (each of which could be put out for bid) to sell.[14] The magazine approach (selling time on a single program to several sponsors)—first used in broadcasting to lure sponsors leery of advertising on the daytime radio programs aimed at women—now became a way to increase the price of broadcast time, as advertisers competed with each other in using television to promote their products.

Through the 1970s the television networks and their particular form of commercialized broadcasting remained phenomenally successful. Ninety-one percent of those watching prime-time television from 1978 through 1980 were viewing one of the three major networks, with 57 percent of all receivers in the United States tuned at least once during the day to one of the three.[15] Programmers claimed during the 1970s to be using a more segmented approach, appealing to the audiences advertisers most wanted to reach. But such audiences were not much different than those broadcasters had always sought: young, middle-class, and white. Television producers and advertising salespeople talked about programming differently, but not much had changed.[16]

Technology and economics brought the next set of changes to television. New ways of delivering the broadcast signal (cable, satellite) and new ways of using the television set (videocassettes, videodiscs, computers, video games) threatened the hold of the networks.[17] As Ken Auletta notes:

> In the war with the small but mobile armies of the new video democracy, the networks were being outflanked. In 1988 alone, the three networks' share of the prime-time audience would drop to 68 percent—compared to 92 percent in 1976; the number of channels available to the average home increased in a single year from twenty-two to twenty-eight, four times as many as were available in 1976; cable television entered 2.4 percent more homes, now reaching 51.1 percent of Americans, compared to just 15 percent in 1976.[18]

Such changes meant that the networks were losing some viewers and some profits. But whether the new technologies were contributing to democracy, or even making more genuine choices available, remained unclear in 1993. Using VCRs, audience members had more control over when they watched particular programs—but alternative programming was still often not available. Cable stations tended to schedule more of the same kind of programs—more sports, more news, more movies—rather than different forms of entertainment or education. And how were these new technologies, which were expensive and often featured commercials, contributing to "democracy"?

The television industry, now at a crossroads, might look to the history of radio for some ideas about how to respond to changing times. Radio is still with us today because of its postwar ability to search out new audiences and to remain flexible in its programming and economic structure.

Conclusion

THE END OF THE STORY

National radio service turned out rather differently than had been antici-
pated when broadcasting began in 1920. The large radio manufacturing
companies had believed national radio would rationalize broadcasting and
help increase profits, but they did not expect that broadcasting could directly make money. Intellectuals and futurists of the 1920s had seen broadcast radio as a means of improving morality and building a sense of nation-
hood. Amateur radio operators and the first broadcast listeners had looked
to national radio service as part of their hobby, an active rather than passive
enterprise. Many ordinary people had thought national radio would be a
way to maintain ethnic and regional loyalties.

Instead, the form national radio took in the United States proved to
be directly commercial, passive, and homogenized, promoting consumption as the way to happiness. The urge for national radio was an important
catalyst in generating early interest in American broadcasting, but once
most Americans agreed that national radio was a worthwhile goal other
factors shaped its eventual form and content. The choice of an expensive
wired network system to deliver national service brought broadcast advertising in its wake. Conventional wisdom soon claimed that advertising and
the network system went together like love and marriage. According to
this common belief, radio's search for financing inevitably led to advertising, and advertisers naturally insisted on large national audiences before
investing the amount of money needed to keep broadcasting afloat.

The link between advertising and the networks was not, however, pre-
ordained (like the link between love and marriage). The impulse toward
national radio had existed long before advertisers began clamoring for airtime; and when listeners and advertisers began demanding national radio,
options other than wired networks had existed to deliver the service. Yet
by the early 1930s, ten years after broadcast radio began, the question of
"who pays for radio?" had been answered. The commercialized radio network system had succeeded so well that earlier confusion surrounding the
shape, content, and financing of broadcasting was forgotten. Broadcasters
and many listeners regarded the "American system of broadcasting" not
only as a reflection of the American character, but as the only possible
form radio (and later television) could have taken in the United States.

The boosterism evident in the writing about broadcast advertising transformed all changes in radio programming and advertising into "progress."

Historians and listeners alike have often taken the view that advertising "saved" broadcasting from extinction. Yet the elaborate, calculated campaign to promote broadcast advertising, beginning in 1928, indicates that many within the radio and advertising industries believed that advertisers, advertising professionals, and consumers needed to be persuaded to accept it.[19] Many radio and business leaders thought in 1928 that another mode of financing would work better than advertising. Commercialized radio grew because of a systematic, sustained sales effort, not because advertisers flocked voluntarily to a new outlet.

Warren Susman's call for an "ecological" or interactive model in examining communications technologies, especially those that have presented themselves as "natural," can save communications historians from being blinded by such "progress talk." Susman believes that historians should focus on the interactions between media and culture. Ignoring the cultural contexts of communications technologies slights the stories of those who resist a new technology. In the case of radio, the story of those who resisted broadcast advertising—from the early stations funded in a variety of ways to those listeners, educators, broadcasters, and advertisers who imagined other systems or simply objected to broadcast advertising—shows that commercialized broadcasting was not a "characteristic cultural response" to a new technology.[20] While the promoters of broadcast advertising lived in a world that included stations funded in many ways, they constructed the network system as primary and pushed to involve advertising agencies in radio—actions that directly affected programming form and content.

Pre-network radio was not, of course, a golden age of listener-controlled local broadcasting, completely untainted by crude and manipulative advertising, nor did the commercialized network system suddenly spring into being within a vacuum. Early sponsored programs provided the models on which the networks later built commercialized programming. Sponsored shows were a minority among early radio programs, but the networks embraced them and applied their formats to all programming. Indirect advertising, anonymous performers, and regional sponsors could have continued to provide more diverse information and entertainment to American radio listeners, but broadcasting's increasingly national and commercial character determined the basis on which programming decisions were made. Programs and performers that had thrived in the 1920s were soon superseded.

The introduction of the networks also saw the disappearance of regional sponsors from the airwaves. Lacking an alternative way of reaching a smaller number of listeners, medium-sized companies such as the Happiness Candy Company and Clicquot Club Ginger Ale dropped out of radio sponsorship. Increasingly, the manufacturers who advertised on radio made "low-priced, packaged consumer goods"—products that people bought often. Today such companies continue to be among the heaviest advertisers.[21] Companies making consumer durables joined the packaged goods manufacturers on radio in the 1930s, but most radio advertising, like most advertising in general, remained for low-priced objects.

The increasingly commercialized airwaves sparked a new wave of protest in the early 1930s. The lack of public rallying behind this attempted reform movement left Congress without incentive to force change on an industry that, even in the midst of the Depression, was working smoothly. Yet the protesters raised important issues regarding radio's unrealized educational potential, the abuses of commercialism, the rights of alternative nonprofit stations, and the neglected needs of specialized audiences. Viewed as fanatics at best and crackpots at worst, these educators and reformers of the early 1930s perceived the problems inherent in a commercialized mass medium but failed to change the system. Some of their ideas were later adopted: in 1938 the FCC reserved certain FM frequencies for educational organizations; in 1952 certain television channels were also allocated for educational stations; and in 1962 Congress authorized funds "to assist [through matching grants] in the construction of educational television broadcasting facilities."[22] The relative lateness of these reforms ensured that nonprofit stations could not seriously challenge the already entrenched commercial stations, which held the best frequencies and were better financed. The commercialized national radio system thus withstood an attempted assault at a crucial time, the early 1930s, and emerged from the fight strengthened.

The passage of the 1934 Communications Act effectively brought protests against commercialized broadcasting to an end until after World War II. Various educators continued to lobby against the network system, but the reformers had lost their best chance to change the form and content of American radio. The 1934 Communications Act, by ignoring both advertising and the networks, gave government approval to the changes that had taken place in broadcasting. In only fourteen years radio had moved from amateur stations in garages airing phonograph records to elaborate studios with highly paid celebrity performers, and from a widespread rejection of commercialism to a system financed exclusively through direct advertising.

Who pays for radio? Who "bought" the broadcasting system that radio manufacturers were "selling"? All of us—radio listeners and television viewers, children, adults, PBS and Fox viewers, college radio station listeners and talk-show callers—continue to pay for the system used to finance American broadcasting. We should, occasionally, consider whether the cost is too high.

NOTES

INTRODUCTION

1. For one example of a discussion of earlier technologies, see Carolyn Marvin, *When Old Technologies Were New: Thinking about Electric Communication in the Late Nineteenth Century* (New York: Oxford University Press, 1988).

2. "Sponsoritis," *Radio Revue* 1 (March 1930): 16.

3. Carl Boggs, *The Two Revolutions: Gramsci and the Dilemmas of Western Marxism* (Boston: South End Press, 1984), 161.

4. Stuart Hall, "Notes on Deconstructing the Popular," in Raphael Samuel, ed., *People's History and Socialist Theory* (London: Routledge, 1981), 227–40. For additional insights, see George Lipsitz, "The Struggle for Hegemony," *Journal of American History* 75 (June 1988): 146–50.

5. Daniel Czitrom, *Media and the American Mind: From Morse to McLuhan* (Chapel Hill: University of North Carolina Press, 1982), 184.

6. For example, Alfred N. Goldsmith and Austin C. Lescarboura, *This Thing Called Broadcasting: A Simple Tale of an Idea, an Experiment, a Mighty Industry, a Daily Habit, and a Basic Influence in Our Modern Civilization* (New York: Henry Holt, 1930), 48; Paul Schubert, *The Electric Word: The Rise of Radio* (New York: Macmillan, 1928), 219. A critique of inevitability as presented in Erik Barnouw's

history of radio, particularly vol. 1, *A Tower in Babel: A History of Broadcasting in the United States to 1933* (New York: Oxford University Press, 1966), can be found in Philip T. Rosen, "The Marvel of Radio," *American Quarterly* 31 (Fall 1979): 572–81.

7. See J. Fred MacDonald, *Don't Touch That Dial: Radio Programming in American Life from 1920 to 1960* (Chicago: Nelson-Hall, 1979), 18–19, 38. MacDonald notes that "given the traditional distaste for governmental interference by free enterprise, given the inability of radio to finance itself with public donations, and given the necessity of finding sources of revenue to survive, the development of American radio as a commercialized medium was inevitable," concluding that "public approval of the entertainment more than offset public annoyance with . . . commercial messages" and that "in a single stroke network radio standardized, entertained, informed, and educated its mass audience." He might also have added that radio advertising now exploited, manipulated, and dictated programming to its audience.

8. Steven Lubar and Brooke Hindle, *Engines of Change* (Washington, D.C.: Smithsonian Institution Press, 1987), 7. See also Steven Lubar, "Culture and Technological Change in the 19th Century Pin Industry: John Howe and the Howe Manufacturing Company," *Technology and Culture* 28 (April 1987): 253–83.

9. Czitrom, *Media and the American Mind*; Susan Douglas, *Inventing American Broadcasting, 1899–1922* (Baltimore: Johns Hopkins University Press, 1987).

10. Roland Marchand, *Advertising the American Dream: Making Way for Modernity, 1920–1940* (Berkeley: University of California Press, 1985); Michael Schudson, *Advertising, the Uneasy Persuasion: Its Dubious Impact on American Society* (New York: Basic Books, 1984).

11. For a broad overview, see Jane P. Tompkins, ed., *Reader-Response Criticism: From Formalism to Post-Structuralism* (Baltimore: Johns Hopkins University Press, 1980). One early and important American study is Janice A. Radway, *Reading the Romance: Women, Patriarchy, and Popular Literature* (Chapel Hill: University of North Carolina Press, 1984). Radway combined the ethnographic techniques of British cultural studies with the psychoanalytic theories of Nancy Chodorow and close readings of romance novels to gain an understanding of how and why contemporary women read romances. While the book seems grounded in Radway's interviews with romance readers, the introduction to the latest edition (1991) explains that determining how readers use popular novels, or create meanings in conjunction with the text, remains difficult, despite the accessibility of the consumer population. Radway reminds us that simply searching out the audience response is not, by itself, enough.

12. Erik Barnouw, *The Sponsor: Notes on a Modern Potentate* (New York: Oxford University Press, 1978), 68–73, 114–15.

13. For a description of British cultural studies and an example of the Ameri-

can linkage between cultural studies and communications scholarship, see Andrea L. Press, *Women Watching Television: Gender, Class, and Generation in the American Television Experience* (Philadelphia: University of Pennsylvania Press, 1991). See also Daniel Czitrom, "Communication Studies as American Studies," *American Quarterly* 42 (December 1990): 678–83.

14. Raymond Williams, *Television: Technology and Cultural Form* (London: Fontana, 1974). See especially chapter 4, where Williams discusses his concept of "program flow."

CHAPTER 1. TOWARD NATIONAL RADIO

1. A. H. Folwell, "The Distance Fiend," *Radio Broadcast* 7 (May 1925): 35.

2. J. H. Morecroft, "The March of Radio: Preparing for Long Distance," *Radio Broadcast* 3 (September 1923): 361. See also "The Appetite for Distance," *Radio World* 9 (29 May 1926): 20.

3. Susan Douglas, *Inventing American Broadcasting, 1899–1922* (Baltimore: Johns Hopkins University Press, 1987), 195.

4. Susan Douglas, "Amateur Operators and American Broadcasting: Shaping the Future of Radio," in Joseph Corn, ed., *Imagining Tomorrow: History, Technology and the American Future* (Cambridge, Mass.: MIT Press, 1986), 53.

5. Douglas, *Inventing American Broadcasting*, 206, 295–97; Clinton DeSoto, *200 Meters and Down: The Story of Amateur Radio* (West Hartford, Conn.: American Radio Relay League, 1936), 38–43.

6. Douglas, *Inventing American Broadcasting*, 206.

7. "What Our Readers Write Us: Attention Announcers!" *Radio Broadcast* 4 (January 1924): 231–32. See also Pearcy W. Mack, "Men Are DX Hounds, Says Mack; Hear Call Letters, Not Programs," *Radio World* 7 (May 1925): 24; "A Lesson in Announcing by Mr. DX Listener," *Radio News* 7 (December 1925): 908–12.

8. "How Far Did You Hear Last Night?" *Radio Broadcast* 2 (January 1923): n.p.

9. "How Far Can I Hear with MR-6?" *Radio Broadcast* 2 (January 1923): n.p.

10. "Concerts from 14 Cities in One Evening," *Radio Broadcast* 2 (January 1923): n.p. See also "Daddy, Let's Get Los Angeles!" *Radio News* 6 (October 1924): 573.

11. "How Far Have You Heard?" *Radio Broadcast* 2 (November 1922): 61.

12. "How Far Have You Heard?" *Radio Broadcast* 2 (January 1923): 228; "How Far Have You Heard on One Tube?" *Radio Broadcast* 2 (February 1923): 336.

13. "How Far Have You Heard?" *Radio Broadcast* 2 (December 1922): 115.

14. "How Far Have You Heard on One Tube?" *Radio Broadcast* 2 (April 1923): 504–14.

15. "Porto Rico Fan Wins 'How Far?' Contest," *Radio Broadcast* 3 (August 1923): 304; Richard Bartholomew, "A Neighbor at Three Thousand Miles," *Radio Broadcast* 3 (August 1923): 305–11.

16. Abbye M. White, "Hearing North America," *Radio Broadcast* 3 (September 1923): 421–25.

17. "Comments on the Contest," *Radio Broadcast* 3 (October 1923): 492.

18. "Results of the 'How Far' Contest," *Radio Broadcast* 5 (July 1924): 266.

19. Credo Fitch Harris, *Microphone Memoirs of the Horse and Buggy Days of Radio* (New York: Bobbs-Merrill, 1937), 252–53.

20. "The Month in Radio," *Radio Broadcast* 7 (September 1925): 601.

21. Kingsley Welles, "The Listeners' Point of View: Do We Need Silent Nights for Radio Stations?" *Radio Broadcast* 7 (October 1925): 751–54.

22. John Wallace, "The Listeners' Point of View: In Defense of the DX Fishers," *Radio Broadcast* 8 (February 1926): 447–48. See also "Radio Editorials," *Radio Age* 4 (November 1925): 4.

23. Erik Barnouw, *A Tower in Babel: A History of Broadcasting in the United States to 1933* (New York: Oxford University Press, 1966), 93, 167.

24. J. H. Morecroft, "The March of Radio: What Is the Range of a Broadcasting Station?" *Radio Broadcast* 3 (May 1923): 12.

25. Robert Marriott, "United States Broadcasting Development," *Proceedings of the Institute of Radio Engineers* 17 (August 1929): 1409.

26. A. J. Haynes, "The Factor That Limits Long-Distance Reception: Why the Most Sensitive and Selective Set Possible Cannot Hear Any Station Anywhere," *Radio Broadcast* 4 (February 1924): 283–84. See also Felix Anderson, "Tuning Out Interference," *Radio Age* 3 (January 1924): 5.

27. Ralph Brown and G. D. Gillett, "Distribution of Radio Waves from Broadcasting Stations over City Districts," *Proceedings of the Institute of Radio Engineers* 12 (August 1924): 395. See also Edwin Armstrong, "The Super-Heterodyne," *Proceedings of the Institute of Radio Engineers* (October 1924): 539–52; C. M. Jansky, "Some Studies of Radio Broadcast Coverage in the Middle West," *Proceedings of the Institute of Radio Engineers* 16 (October 1928): 1356–67; Eugene Van Cleef, "Do Weather Conditions Influence Radio?" *Radio Broadcast* 7 (May 1925): 90–94; Carl Dreher, "As the Broadcaster Sees It: Computing How Far a Radio Station Can Be Heard," *Radio Broadcast* 7 (June 1925): 229–30; Carl Dreher, "As the Broadcaster Sees It: High Power and the Elimination of Static," *Radio Broadcast* 7 (July 1925): 350–52.

28. Leslie Page, "The Nature of the Broadcast Receiver and Its Market in the United States from 1922 to 1927," *Journal of Broadcasting* 14 (Spring 1960): 178.

29. "Atwater Kent Radio," *Radio Broadcast* 7 (July 1925): 421; "Music Master Reproducer," *Radio Broadcast* 7 (July 1925): 413; and "The Finer Side of Radio,"

Radio Broadcast 7 (May 1925): 121. See also "Mr. Everyman Says," *Radio News* 7 (April 1926): 1393.

30. O. E. Roberts, Jr., "Correspondence from Readers: The Itch for Distance," *Radio News* 5 (August 1923): 161. This was written in response to Armstrong Perry, "The Itch for Distance," *Radio News* 4 (April 1923): 1777.

31. Harry A. Mount, "Radio—The New Farm Hand" *Popular Radio* 4 (August 1923): 152.

32. General James G. Harbord, "Big Things Are Coming for Radio on the Farm," *Radio Age* 3 (August 1924): 35.

33. W. A. Wheeler, "Down on the Farm in 1923," *Radio Broadcast* 2 (January 1923): 212. See also "The Radio Market News Service," *Radio News* 4 (June 1922): 54, 108.

34. S. R. Winters, "What Does He Hear?" *Wireless Age* 10 (February 1923): 35.

35. Reynold M. Wik, "The Radio in Rural America During the 1920s," *Agricultural History* 55 (October 1981): 341.

36. "Radio on the Farm?—Let These Farmers Tell You," *Radio Age* 5 (June 1923): 16.

37. John C. Baker, *Farm Broadcasting: The First Sixty Years* (Ames: University of Iowa Press, 1981), 11. Slightly different figures can be found in Wik, "The Radio in Rural America," 342.

38. "Farmers Find Radio Can Save Them Much Money," *Radio World* 9 (17 April 1926): 24. See also "The Benefits of the Radio Telephone in Rural Communities," *Radio News* 4 (June 1922): 55, 120; J. Farrell, "Radio Proves a Boon to Farmers," *Radio News* 4 (May 1923): 193; and H. R. Kibler, "Sets That Earn Incomes," *Popular Radio* 10 (October 1926): 525–27.

39. M. S. Eisenhower, "U.S. Will Broadcast Often to Million Farm Audience," *Radio World* 9 (19 June 1926): 29; Sam Pickard, "National Radio Farm School," *Radio Age* 5 (August 1926): 19–21; M. S. Eisenhower, "Papa Bedbug Takes to Radio: Vital Information Given to Farmers by New Means," *Radio Age* 5 (September 1926): 3–6; Thomas Stevenson, "Radio Farm School Has 250,00 on Roll," *Radio World* 10 (25 September 1926): 19; M. S. Eisenhower, "Uncle Sam Chats with His Dairymen: Radio Is a Potential Force in Farm Education," *Radio Age* 5 (October 1926): 37–40; J. Farrell, "Farm Radio Making Rapid Progress," *Radio News* 6 (January 1925): 1143.

40. Baker, *Farm Broadcasting*, 16.

41. Many of the USDA lessons involved the proper role of women as consumers in the home rather than as farm workers. See Sarah Elbert, "Women and Farming: Changing Structures, Changing Roles," in Wava G. Haney and Jane B. Knowles, eds., *Women and Farming: Changing Roles, Changing Structures* (Boulder,

Colo.: Westview Press, 1988), 245–65; Mary Neth, "Preserving the Family Farm: Farm Families and Communities in the Midwest, 1900–1940" (Ph.D. diss., University of Wisconsin, 1987), 413–25.

42. James F. Evans, *Prairie Farmer and WLS: The Burridge D. Butler Years* (Chicago: University of Illinois Press, 1969), 162–63.

43. Charles Wolfe, "The Triumph of the Hills: Country Radio, 1920–50," in Paul Kingsbury and Alan Axelrod, eds., *Country: The Music and Musicians* (New York: Abbeville Press, 1988), 59.

44. Wolfe, "The Triumph of the Hills," 57. See also Charles Wolfe, "Nashville and Country Music, 1926–1930: Notes on Early Nashville Media and Its Response to Old-Time Music," *Journal of Country Music* 4 (Spring 1973): 8, 14; Charles Wolfe, *The Grand Ole Opry: The Early Years, 1925–35* (Old Woking, Surrey, England: Old Time Music, 1975), 15–16; George C. Biggar, "The WLS National Barn Dance Story: The Early Years," *John Edwards Memorial Foundation Quarterly* 7 (August 1971): 106; and Richard Stockdell, "The Evolution of the Country Radio Format," *Journal of Popular Culture* 16 (Spring 1983): 144–47.

45. Bill Malone, *Country Music, USA* (Austin: University of Texas Press, 1985), 1–31; Jack Temple Kirby, *Rural Worlds Lost: The American South, 1920–1960* (Baton Rouge: Louisiana State University Press, 1988), 229–30; Pete Daniel, *Standing at the Crossroads: Southern Life in the Twentieth Century* (New York: Hill and Wang, 1986), 99–103; George Lipsitz, *Class and Culture in Cold War America: "A Rainbow at Midnight"* (New York: Praeger, 1981), 195–204.

46. For the difficulty in describing audiences, see Malone, *Country Music, USA*, 42. On the conflicting strains in country music, see Malone, 33; see also George O. Carney, "Country Music and the Radio," *Rocky Mountain Social Science Journal* 19 (April 1974): 19–32.

47. Lipsitz, *Class and Culture in Cold War America*, 195–225.

48. F. C. Gilbert, "Rural Life Modernized," *Wireless Age* 12 (March 1925): 24–27, 69–71; William Hurd, "Harvest Time on the Air," *Wireless Age* 12 (November 1924): 19.

49. Kirby, *Rural Worlds Lost*, 309–10.

50. Biggar, "The WLS National Barn Dance Story," 105.

51. Loyal Jones, *Radio's Kentucky Mountain Boy: Bradley Kincaid* (Berea College, Kentucky: Appalachian Center, 1980); Biggar, "The WLS Barn Dance Story," 107; Malone, *Country Music, USA*, 55; Archie Green, "Bradley Kincaid's Folios," *John Edwards Memorial Foundation Quarterly* 13 (Summer 1977): 21–28.

52. Daniel, *Standing at the Crossroads*, 102. See also Archie Green, "Hillbilly Music: Source and Symbol," *Journal of American Folklore* 78 (July-September 1965): 204–28.

53. On black ownership of radios, see J. Fred MacDonald, *Don't Touch That Dial: Radio Programming in American Life from 1920 to 1960* (Chicago: Nelson-

Hall, 1979), 333. On race records and radio, see Barnouw, *A Tower in Babel*, 128–31, and Norman Spalding, "History of Black Oriented Radio in Chicago, 1929–1963" (Ph.D. diss., University of Illinois at Urbana-Champaign, 1981), 20. Paul Oliver quotes a study from the early 1930s of 612 African American families living in rural Alabama: "There are no radios, but 76 families had victrolas, bought on the installment plan from agents in the community." Paul Oliver, *Screening the Blues: Aspects of the Blues Tradition* (New York: Da Capo Press, 1968), 5.

54. Timothy Patterson, "Hillbilly Music among the Flatlanders: Early Midwestern Radio Barn Dances," *Journal of Country Music* 6 (Spring 1975): 12–18.

55. Wolfe, "The Triumph of the Hills," 72; Wolfe, "Nashville and Country Music," 5; Biggar, "The WLS Barn Dance," 106.

56. George B. Chadwick, "Football by Radio," *Popular Radio* 3 (January 1923): 53.

57. Elliot Gorn, "The Manassa Mauler and the Fighting Marine," *Journal of American Studies* 19 (April 1985): 31.

58. John F. Rooney, *A Geography of American Sport: From Cabin Creek to Anaheim* (Reading, Mass.: Addison-Wesley, 1974), 23; John F. Rooney, "Up from the Mines and Out from the Prairies: Some Geographic Implications of Football in the United States," *Geographical Review* 59 (October 1969): 472–91; Steven A. Reiss, *Touching Base: Professional Baseball and American Culture in the Progressive Era* (Westport, Conn.: Greenwood Press, 1980), 19.

59. Reiss, *Touching Base*, 5, 15, 30–31.

60. Elliot Gorn, *The Manly Art: Bare Knuckle Prize Fighting in America* (Ithaca, N.Y.: Cornell University Press, 1986), 179, 248; Gorn, "The Manassa Mauler and the Fighting Marine," 29–31.

61. Reiss, *Touching Base*, 35.

62. John Wallace, "The Listener's Point of View: The Requirements of a Football Announcer," *Radio Broadcast* 10 (December 1926): 160.

63. "They All Tried It," *Radio Broadcast* 8 (January 1926): 411.

64. Curt Smith, *Voices of the Game: The First Full-Scale Overview of Baseball Broadcasting, 1921 to the Present* (South Bend, Ind.: Diamond Communications, 1987), 10.

65. Myra May, "Meet J. Andrew White, the Most Famous Announcer in Radio," *Radio Broadcast* 5 (October 1924): 447.

66. Gleason Archer, *History of Radio to 1926* (New York: American Historical Society, 1938), 213–25; May, "Meet J. Andrew White," 448. For an early recreation of a baseball game, see Smith, *Voices of the Game*, 8–9.

67. Archer, *History of Radio to 1926*, 319; J. H. Morecroft, "The March of Radio: The Dempsey-Tunney Fight—A Dangerous Precedent," *Radio Broadcast* 10 (December 1926): 149.

68. John Wallace, "The Listener's Point of View: The Dempsey-Tunney

Fight," *Radio Broadcast* 10 (December 1926): 161; Alfred N. Goldsmith and Austin C. Lescarboura, *This Thing Called Broadcasting* (New York: Henry Holt, 1930), 213–37.

69. May, "Meet J. Andrew White," 449; Wallace, "Requirements of a Football Announcer," 160. See also Wayne Towers, "World Series Coverage in New York City in the 1920s," *Journalism Monographs* 73 (August 1981): 15–16.

70. Towers, "World Series Coverage in New York City in the 1920s," 8. For a general description of early World Series coverage, see Smith, *Voices of the Game*, 9–14.

71. C. W. Horn, "Broadcasting the World Series Baseball Games," *Radio Age* 1 (December 1922): 32.

72. MacDonald, *Don't Touch That Dial*, 24; Archer, *History of Radio to 1926*, 279.

73. Robert C. Toll, *The Entertainment Machine: American Show Business in the Twentieth Century* (New York: Oxford University Press, 1982), 9. For the influence of the railroad on the location of baseball teams, see Ronald Abler, John S. Adams, and Peter Gould, *Spatial Organization: The Geographer's View of the World* (Englewood Cliffs, N.J.: Prentice-Hall, 1971), 377–79.

74. For the story of one attempt to use the radio to maintain ethnic and class ties even after the triumph of the networks, see Mary Cygan, "A 'New Art' for Polonia: Polish American Radio Comedy During the 1930s," *Polish American Studies* 45 (Autumn 1988): 5–21.

75. Daniel J. Czitrom, *Media and the American Mind: From Morse to McLuhan* (Chapel Hill: University of North Carolina Press, 1982), 91.

76. Stephen Kern, *The Culture of Time and Space, 1880–1918*, (Cambridge, Mass.: Harvard University Press, 1983), 314.

77. Susan Douglas, "Amateur Operators and American Broadcasting: Shaping the Future of Radio," in Joseph Corn, ed., *Imagining Tomorrow: History, Technology and the American Future* (Cambridge, Mass.: MIT Press, 1986), 35–55; Clayton R. Koppes, "The Social Destiny of Radio: Hope and Disillusionment in the 1920s," *South Atlantic Quarterly* 68 (Summer 1969): 363–76; Mary Mander, "The Public Debate about Broadcasting in the 1920s," *Journal of Broadcasting* 28 (Spring 1984): 167–85; and Joseph Corn, "Epilogue" in Joseph Corn, ed., *Imagining Tomorrow*, 228. For a slightly contrary view, see Catherine L. Covert, "We May Hear Too Much: American Sensibility and the Response to Radio, 1919–1924," in Catherine L. Covert and John D. Stevens, eds., *Mass Media between the Wars: Perceptions of Cultural Tension, 1919–1941* (Syracuse, N.Y.: Syracuse University Press, 1984), 199–220.

78. Quoted in Douglas, "Amateur Operators and American Broadcasting," 54.

79. Alfred D. Chandler, Jr., *The Visible Hand: The Managerial Revolution in American Business* (Cambridge, Mass.: Harvard University Press, 1977), 200–207.

80. Mander, "The Public Debate about Broadcasting in the 1920s," 171. On transportation metaphors, see also William Boddy, "The Rhetoric and Economic Roots of the American Broadcasting Industry," *Cine-Tracts* 2 (Spring 1979): 38–40.

81. Robert Luther Thompson, *Wiring a Continent: The History of the Telegraph Industry in the United States, 1832–1866* (New York: Arno Press, 1972), 253.

82. Chandler, *The Visible Hand*, 200.

83. Czitrom, *Media and the American Mind*, 31, 59.

84. John Brooks, *Telephone: The First Hundred Years* (New York: Harper and Row, 1976), 137.

85. Brooks, *Telephone*, 136.

86. Carolyn Marvin, *When Old Technologies Were New: Thinking about Communications in the Late Nineteenth Century* (New York: Oxford University Press, 1988), 63–108.

87. Philip Rosen, *The Modern Stentors: Radio Broadcasters and the Federal Government, 1920–1934* (Westport, Conn.: Greenwood Press, 1980), 3–76.

88. Douglas, *Inventing American Broadcasting*, 290.

89. Thomas P. Hughes, "The Electrification of America: The System Builders," *Technology and Culture* 20 (January 1979): 124–61; "The Order of the Technological World," in A. Rupert Hall and Norman Smith, eds., *History of Technology*, vol. 5 (London: Mansell Publishing, 1980), 1–16.

CHAPTER 2. THE RISE OF THE NETWORK SYSTEM

1. David Sarnoff, "Why Super-Broadcasting Means Better Service: Broadcast Address over Station KGO, Oakland, California," 26 October 1924, Addresses, Press Releases, and Articles by David Sarnoff, vol. 3, David Sarnoff Library (hereafter cited as DSL), Princeton, N.J.

2. George P. Stone, "Radio Has Gripped Chicago," *Radio Broadcast* 1 (October 1922): 507.

3. David Sarnoff, "Address before the Chicago Association of Commerce," 23 April 1924, Addresses, Press Releases, and Articles by David Sarnoff, vol. 3, DSL.

4. "Delegates Oppose High Power Radio," *New York Times*, 8 October 1924. See also S. R. Winters, "Huge Stations Still a Dream," *Radio Age* 3 (December 1924): 7–9.

5. Edward F. Sarno, Jr., "The National Radio Conferences," *Journal of Broadcasting* 12 (Spring 1969): 189–98. See also Philip Rosen, *The Modern Stentors: Radio Broadcasters and the Federal Government, 1920–1934* (Westport, Conn.: Greenwood Press, 1980), 39–41, 55–59, 74–76.

6. Third National Radio Conference, *Recommendations for the Regulation of Radio* (Washington, D.C.: Government Printing Office, 1924), 32.

7. See, for example, Alfred N. Goldsmith and Austin C. Lescarboura, *This Thing Called Broadcasting* (New York: Henry Holt, 1930), 144–45.

8. Allan Harding, "What Radio Has Done and What It Will Do Next," *American Magazine* 101 (March 1926): 170.

9. Winfield Barton, "What Broadcasting Does For a Newspaper," *Radio Broadcast* 4 (February 1924): 344. See also R. J. McLauchlin, "What the Detroit 'News' Has Done in Broadcasting," *Radio Broadcasting* 1 (June 1922): 136–41; C. Joseph Pusateri, *Enterprise in Radio: WWL and the Business of Broadcasting in America* (Washington: University Press of America, 1980), 15–16.

10. Hiram Jome, *The Economics of the Radio Industry* (New York: A. W. Shaw Company, 1929), 174.

11. Ibid., 178.

12. Erik Barnouw, *A Tower in Babel: A History of Broadcasting in the United States to 1933* (New York: Oxford University Press, 1966), 119–20.

13. Gleason Archer, *Big Business and Radio* (New York: American Historical Company, 1939), 51–52.

14. Ibid., 4.

15. David Sarnoff, "General Statement at the Third National Radio Conference in Washington, D.C.," 6 November 1924, Addresses, Press Releases, and Articles by David Sarnoff, vol. 3, DSL.

16. Powel Crosley, "Should There Be a Monopoly of Broadcasting?" *Popular Radio* 5 (June 1924): 599. See also "Thought Waves from the Editorial Tower," *Radio Age* 2 (January-February 1923): 17; "Delegates Oppose High Power Radio," *New York Times*, 8 October 1924.

17. Herbert Hoover, "Opening Address," Third National Radio Conference, *Recommendations for the Regulation of Radio* (Washington, D.C.: Government Printing Office, 1924), 3–6.

18. Ibid., 1.

19. David Sarnoff, "Statement on General Problems of Radio Broadcasting at Meeting of Sub-Committee Number 3, Third Annual Radio Conference, Washington, D.C.," 8 October 1924, Addresses, Press Releases, and Articles by David Sarnoff, vol. 3, DSL.

20. Barnouw, *A Tower in Babel*, 57–61, 72–82; Gleason Archer, *History of Radio to 1926* (New York: American Historical Society, 1938), 156–89; Susan Douglas, *Inventing American Broadcasting* (Baltimore: Johns Hopkins University Press, 1987), 240–91.

21. Carl Dreher, *Sarnoff: An American Success* (New York: Quadrangle, 1977), 2–84; Eugene Lyons, *Sarnoff: A Biography* (New York: Harper and Row, 1966), 1–89; David Sarnoff, as told to Mary Margaret McBride, "Radio," *Saturday Evening Post*, 7 August 1926, 8–9, 141–49.

22. David Sarnoff, *Looking Ahead* (New York: McGraw-Hill, 1968), 31.

23. David Sarnoff, "The Message of Radio: Address to the Engineering Society, Buffalo, New York," 9 January 1923; David Sarnoff, "The Message of Radio: Address to the Chamber of Commerce, Atlantic City, New Jersey," 26 January 1923. Both contained in Addresses, Press Releases, and Articles by David Sarnoff, vol. 2, DSL.

24. Elmer Bucher, "Radio and David Sarnoff," 1943, unpublished manuscript, p. 358, DSL.

25. David Sarnoff, "When Radio Reaches Half a Billion," 15 November 1923, Addresses, Press Releases, and Articles by David Sarnoff, vol. 2, DSL.

26. David Sarnoff, "Voice of the Sea: Address before the Boston City Club, Boston, Massachusetts," 13 December 1923, vol. 2; "Address before the Municipal Club of Brooklyn, Princeton Club, New York, New York," 27 February 1924, vol. 3; "Address before the Association of Commerce, Chicago, Illinois," 23 April 1924, vol. 3; "Radio and Its Relation to the Central Station Industry: Address before the National Electric Light Association Convention, Atlantic City, New Jersey," 21 May 1924, vol. 3; "An Open Road in Radio: Address Before the Electrical Jobbers Association, Hot Springs, Virginia," 4 June 1924, vol. 3; all in Addresses, Press Releases, and Articles by David Sarnoff, DSL. David Sarnoff, *Statement of Mr. David Sarnoff before the Committee on Merchant Marine and Fisheries on HR 7357*, 13 March 1924 (Washington, D.C.: Government Printing Office, 1924). Just days after the Third National Radio Conference, Sarnoff spoke of super-power for the final time; see David Sarnoff, "Why Super-Broadcasting Means Better Service: Broadcast Address Over KGO, Oakland, California," 26 October 1924, Addresses, Press Releases, and Articles by David Sarnoff, vol. 3, DSL.

27. David Sarnoff, "Address before the Municipal Club of Brooklyn," 27 February 1924, Addresses, Press Releases, and Articles by David Sarnoff, vol. 3, DSL. In April 1924, before the Chicago Association of Commerce, Sarnoff made his strongest case for super-power. Believing that the presentation of the presidential campaign on radio would show the American people national radio's power and importance, he explained that "in seeking for an economic solution of the broadcasting problem, broadcasting on a national scale is found to be a very convincing answer." David Sarnoff, "Address before the Chicago Association of Commerce," 23 April 1924, Addresses, Press Releases, and Articles by David Sarnoff, vol. 3, DSL.

28. J. H. Morecroft, "The March of Radio: The Radio Corporation View," *Radio Broadcast* 5 (July 1924): 220–21. See also a reprinting of Sarnoff's testimony before the House Committee on Merchant Marine and Fisheries, in David Sarnoff, "Broadcasting by Super-Power Stations," *Radio World* 5 (5 April 1924): 32.

29. Sarnoff, "General Statement at Third Annual Radio Conference," 6 November 1924, DSL.

30. Ibid.

31. "Delegates Oppose High Power Radio," *New York Times;* "Radiotorials," *Radio Age* 3 (December 1924): 5.

32. David Sarnoff, "Statement at Meeting of Sub-Committee #3, Third Annual Radio Conference," 9 October 1925, Addresses, Press Releases, and Articles by David Sarnoff, vol. 3, DSL.

33. Archer, *Big Business and Radio*, 57, 84–85.

34. Ibid., 169–72, 267–72.

35. On the patent renegotiation, see Archer, *Big Business and Radio*, 36–191; Barnouw, *A Tower in Babel*, 181–86.

36. Alfred N. Goldsmith, "Reduction of Interference in Broadcast Reception," *Proceedings of the Institute of Radio Engineers* 14 (October 1926): 598.

37. Ibid., 581. See also Alfred N. Goldsmith, "And Now Engineers Are Predicting 1,000,000-Watt Broadcasting," *Popular Radio* 12 (December 1927): 411.

38. Herbert Hoover, "Opening Address," Fourth National Radio Conference, *Proceedings of the Fourth National Radio Conference and Recommendations for Regulation of Radio* (Washington, D.C.: Government Printing Office, 1925), 3.

39. Robert Marriott, "United States Broadcasting Development," *Proceedings of the Institute of Radio Engineers* 17 (August 1929): 1407. See also L. J. Lesh, "The Super-Radio Survey," *Radio Age* 2 (April 1923): 11–13, 30; Thomas Stevenson, "Super-Power Blanketing of Small Stations Only a Myth, Experts Find," *Radio World* 8 (26 September 1925): 20; Carl Dreher, "As the Broadcaster Sees It: How Much Power Is Super-Power?" *Radio Broadcast* 7 (May 1925): 74–76; Carl Dreher, "As the Broadcaster Sees It: Computing How Far a Radio Station Can Be Heard," *Radio Broadcast* 7 (June 1925): 229–30; Carl Dreher, "As the Broadcaster Sees It: Radio Power and Noise Level," *Radio Broadcast* 7 (September 1925): 615–17; S. R. Winters, "The Service Area of a Broadcast Station" *Radio News* 9 (July 1927): 12–13.

40. On international shortwave experiments, see H. E. Hallborg, L. A. Briggs, and C. W. Hansell, "Short Wave Commercial Long-Distance Communication," *Proceedings of the Institute of Radio Engineers* 15 (July 1927): 467–99; Holly Cowan Shulman, "The Voice of Victory: The Development of American Propaganda and the Voice of America, 1920–1942" (Ph.D. diss., University of Maryland, 1984), 63–109; "Broadcasting by Repeating Will Enable Radio To Encircle Globe," *Radio Age* 3 (August 1924): 13–14.

41. W. W. Rodgers, "Is Short-Wave Relaying a Step toward National Broadcasting Stations?" *Radio Broadcast* 3 (June 1923): 119. See also D. G. Little and E. Falknor, "KFKX, The Repeating Broadcasting Station," *Radio Age* 3 (March 1924): 37; "Re-broadcasting: A New Era in Radio," *Radio News* 5 (March 1924): 1242, 1322, 1324; "Judge S. B. Davis," *Radio Broadcast* 6 (March 1925): 899.

42. "WGY on Wheels," *Radio Broadcast* 6 (December 1924): 258.

43. W. J. Purcell, "The Rebroadcasting Set at WGY," *Radio Broadcast* 5 (September 1924): 389–90.

44. Ibid., 389.

45. "Proposed Plan for the Phantom Dinner," 19 January 1926, Box 97, Folder 4, National Broadcasting Company Papers (hereafter cited as NBC Papers), Mass Communications History Center, Wisconsin State Historical Society, Madison. See also "How Radio Relay Linked Six Stations," *Radio World* 5 (29 March 1924): 11.

46. David Sarnoff, "Broadcast Address at the MIT Phantom Dinner," 19 January 1926, Addresses, Press Releases, and Articles by David Sarnoff, vol. 4, DSL.

47. Charles Popenoe to H. P. Davis, 27 November 1925, Box 97, Folder 1, NBC Papers.

48. Charles Popenoe to M. P. Rice, 28 November 1925, Box 97, Folder 1, NBC Papers.

49. For example, H. P. Davis to Charles Popenoe, 3 March 1925; Telegram, Charles Popenoe to H. P. Davis, 16 January 1926, Box 97, Folder 1, NBC Papers.

50. Rodgers, "Is Short-Wave Relaying a Step toward National Broadcasting?" 119; Joe Beaudino, "The History of Short Wave Broadcasting," unpublished manuscript, Division of Electricity, National Museum of American History (hereafter cited as NMAH), Smithsonian Institution, Washington, D.C.

51. "Short Waves Should Be Conserved," *Radio Broadcast* 6 (December 1924): 253–54; "Receiving Short Broadcast Waves," *Radio Broadcast* 6 (April 1925): 1067–68; Frank D. Pearne, "Short Wave Transmission and Reception," *Radio Age* 3 (July 1924): 10–11. For other early experiments in shortwave rebroadcasting, see Beaudino, "History of Short Wave Broadcasting," 4–5; W. J. Purcell, "The Rebroadcasting Set at WGY," 389; Donald G. Little, "The Reminiscences of Donald G. Little," Oral History Research Office, Columbia University, New York, 36; "KDKA's Powerful Short Wave Station," and "The Sensitive Short Wave Receiving Apparatus at WBZ," *Radio News* 6 (September 1924): 292–93, 422–33; Walter C. Evans, "Now You'll Know How Rebroadcasting Is Handled," *Radio Age* (January 1926): 17.

52. Beaudino, "History of Short Wave Broadcasting," 5–6.

53. William E. Barrett, "Hastings Is Now Radio Center of United States," *Hastings Chamber of Commerce Journal* 1 (December 1923).

54. "Westinghouse Repeating Station KFKX," H. D. Roess Collection, Division of Electricity, NMAH; Beaudino, "History of Short Wave Broadcasting," 7. See also Little, "Reminiscences," 36–37.

55. William Peck Banning, *Commercial Broadcasting Pioneer: The WEAF Experiment 1922–1926* (Cambridge, Mass.: Harvard University Press, 1946), 59.

56. Elam Miller to W. E. Harkness, 17 July 1924, Box 1, Folder 4, E. P. H.

James Papers (hereafter cited as James Papers), Mass Communications History Center, Wisconsin State Historical Society, Madison.

57. Leonard S. Reich, "Research, Patents, and the Struggle To Control Radio: A Study of Big Business and the Uses of Industrial Research," *Business History Review* 51 (Summer 1977): 234.

58. N. R. Danielian, *AT&T: The Story of Industrial Conquest* (New York: Vanguard Press, 1939), 104–5.

59. M. D. Fagen, ed., *A History of Engineering and Science in the Bell System* (New York: Bell Telephone Laboratories, 1975), 426–28.

60. Banning, *Commercial Broadcasting Pioneer*, 111–12.

61. Ibid., 112–13. This *Aida* broadcast, while it may well have involved Metropolitan Opera artists, does not seem to have been held under the official auspices of the company, since it is not included in the *Annals of the Metropolitan Opera*, which show that the 1922–23 season opened two days later, on November 13, with Puccini's *Tosca*. See Gerald Fitzgerald, ed., *Annals of the Metropolitan Opera: The Complete Chronicle of Performances and Artists* (Boston: G. K. Hall, 1989), 320. Apart from early experiments by Lee De Forest, the first broadcast from the stage of the Metropolitan did not occur until December 25, 1931, with *Hänsel und Gretel*. See Peter Allen, "Broadcasting," in David Hamilton, ed., *The Metropolitan Opera Encyclopedia* (New York: Simon and Schuster, 1987), 56–57.

62. William H. Easton, "Out of Studio Broadcasting," *Radio Broadcast* 2 (March 1923): 364–68.

63. Banning, *Commercial Broadcasting Pioneer*, 65.

64. Ibid., 72.

65. Banning, *Commercial Broadcasting Pioneer*, 165–69.

66. Barnouw, *A Tower in Babel*, 144–45.

67. Archer, *History of Radio*, 324.

68. Ibid., 113–14.

69. James C. Young, "Broadcasting Personality," *Radio Broadcast* 5 (July 1924): 249. On the Rothafel visit to Washington, see also Bruce Bliven, "How Radio Is Remaking Our World," *Century* 108 (July 1924): 147.

70. Banning, *Commercial Broadcasting Pioneer*, 228.

71. Ibid., 232.

72. AT&T sought stations "equipped or licensed by AT&T," which excluded those owned by other patent pool members. Barnouw, *A Tower in Babel*, 145, 148, 150–51.

73. George E. Chadwick, "Symphonies by Telegraph," *Popular Radio* 3 (February 1923): 120–23. Chadwick explained that Western Union used a "special kind of circuit" to successfully pick up the City Symphony of New York.

74. "Expensive Service," *Radio Broadcast* 5 (May 1924): 23.

75. Danielian, *AT&T*, 123; Reich, "Research, Patents, and the Struggle To Control Radio," 222.

76. Banning, *Commercial Broadcasting Pioneer*, 209.

77. "Outlaw Station To Be Closed," *Radio Broadcast* 5 (July 1924): 130–32.

78. Reich, "Research, Patents, and the Struggle To Control Radio," 224.

79. Barnouw, *A Tower in Babel*, 184–86; Reich, "Research, Patents, and the Struggle To Control Radio," 229–30; Archer, *Big Business and Radio*, 250–76.

80. "The Radio Act of 1927," in Frank J. Kahn, ed., *Documents of American Broadcasting* (Englewood Cliffs, N.J.: Prentice-Hall, 1973), 36–51.

81. *Congressional Record*, 70th Cong., 1st sess., 6 February 1928, 2545.

82. Ibid., 4474.

83. Ibid., 4569.

84. Ibid., 4574.

85. Ibid., 5117–18.

86. On the reactions to and results of the Davis amendment, see "To Break the East's Radio Monopoly," *Literary Digest* (7 April 1928): 13; Louis G. Caldwell, "Problems Raised by the Davis Amendment," *Congressional Digest* 7 (October 1928): 262–63, 286; E. L. Davis and Emanuel Celler, "Will the Davis Amendment Bring Better Radio?" *Congressional Digest* 7 (October 1928): 268–69; "Davis Amendment Criticized," *Air Law Review* 1 (January 1930): 117–20; "The Davis Amendment Again," *Air Law Review* 1 (July 1930): 402; J. M. Herring, "Equalization of Broadcasting Facilities within the United States," *Harvard Business Review* 9 (July 1931): 417–29.

87. F. J. Brown, "The Story of Broadcasting in England," *Radio Broadcast* 7 (June 1925): 175–82; John Wallace, "The Listener's Point of View: Germany and America Compared," *Radio Broadcast* 9 (October 1926): 492; Kurt Bronisch, "Broadcast Advertising in Germany," *Broadcast Advertising* 5 (June 1932): 22.

88. David Worrall, "Radio Conditions in Australia Are Rapidly Improving," *Broadcast Advertising* 3 (July 1930): 11.

89. Rose Ziglin, "Radio Broadcasting in the Soviet Union," *Annals of the American Academy of Political and Social Science* 177 (January 1935): 66–72.

90. J. H. Morecroft, "The March of Radio: How They Run Radio in Canada," *Radio Broadcast* 8 (April 1926): 655.

91. Bill McNeill and Morris Wolfe, *Signing On: The Birth of Radio in Canada* (Garden City, N.Y.: Doubleday, 1982), 177–227.

92. "National Broadcasting Company Inc.," *Fortune* 2 (December 1930): 116.

93. Barnouw, *A Tower in Babel*, 250. See also "An Appraisal of Radio Advertising Today," *Fortune* 6 (September 1932): 37–44, 91–93.

94. Barnouw, *A Tower in Babel*, 220–23, 250; Lawrence Bergreen, *Look Now, Pay Later: The Rise of Network Broadcasting* (New York: New American Library, 1980), 1–9; David Halberstam, *The Powers That Be* (New York: Alfred Knopf,

1979), 21–33; Robert Metz, *CBS: Reflections in a Bloodshot Eye* (New York: New American Library, 1975), 1–25.

95. Morris L. Ernst, "Who Shall Control the Air?" *The Nation* (21 April 1926): 443–44.

CHAPTER 3. ARGUMENTS OVER BROADCAST ADVERTISING

1. Zeh Bouck, "Can We Solve the Broadcasting Riddle?" *Radio Broadcast* 6 (April 1925): 1040–43; "The Decision in the 'Who Is To Pay for Broadcasting?' Contest," *Radio Broadcast* 6 (February 1925): 736. See also Halsey D. Kellog, Jr., "Who Is To Pay for Broadcasting—And How: The Plan Which Won *Radio Broadcast*'s Prize of $500," *Radio Broadcast* 6 (March 1925): 864. For another contest, see "Prize Offered for Best Solution of Broadcasting Problem," *Radio World* 5 (29 March 1924): 29. For other contemporary discussions of the issue, see "Thought Waves from the Editorial Tower," *Radio Age* 1 (October 1922): 17; Waldemar Kaempffert, "Who Will Pay for Broadcasting? A Frank and Searching Outline of Radio's Most Pressing Problem and the Possible Ways of Solving It," *Popular Radio* 2 (December 1922): 236–46.

2. "Experts Foresee End of Present Easy Broadcasting Arrangements," *New York Times*, 18 May 1924, Section 8, 3.

3. Erik Barnouw, *A Tower in Babel: A History of Broadcasting in the United States to 1933* (New York: Oxford University Press, 1966), 99.

4. J. H. Morecroft, "Radio Currents: An Editorial Interpretation," *Radio Broadcast* 1 (May 1922): 3. See also J. H. Morecroft, "The March of Radio: Who Will Endow Broadcasting?" *Radio Broadcast* 10 (January 1927): 257–58. Robert J. Landry, *This Fascinating Radio Business* (New York: Bobbs-Merrill Company, 1946), 44–45; Philip Rosen, *The Modern Stentors: Radio Broadcasters and the Federal Government, 1920–1934* (Westport, Conn.: Greenwood Press, 1980), 68; J. H. Morecroft, "The March of Radio: Great Minds Still Disagree on Broadcasting Payment," *Radio Broadcast* 5 (August 1924): 304. For another editorial call for stations supported by philanthropy, see "Broadcasting from the Editor's Chair," *Radio Digest* 26 (January 1921): 61.

5. "Experts Foresee End," *New York Times*; S. E. Frost, Jr., *Education's Own Stations* (Chicago: University of Chicago Press, 1937), 4.

6. James C. Young, "Radio—The Voice of the City," *Radio Broadcast* 6 (January 1925): 448.

7. Saul N. Scher, "An Old City Hall Tradition: New York's Mayors and WNYC," *Journal of Broadcasting* 10 (Spring 1966): 138; Logbook 1 of Radio-phone WNYC: Municipal Station City of New York, 5 July 1924–10 December

1924, Museum of the City of New York. See also Grover Whalen, "Radio Control," *The Nation* 119 (23 July 1924): 90; "CONY Sought as Letters of City's Station," *Radio World* 5 (19 April 1924): 35; Irving Foulds Luscombe, "WNYC: 1922–1940—The Early History of a Twentieth-Century Urban Service" (Ph.D. diss., New York University, 1968); Milton Nobel, "The Municipal Broadcasting System: Its History, Organization and Activities" (MPA thesis, City College of New York, 1953); "History of WNYC," unpublished publicity pamphlet, WNYC, New York. For a description of municipal broadcasting in Chicago, see "The City of Chicago in Radio," *Radio Age* 1 (July-August 1922), 7. I want to thank Betsy Smulyan for her help in researching the WNYC logbook.

8. For "not the most attractive," see newspaper clipping, 26 June 1926, WNYC scrapbook, WNYC, New York. For "resent lavish expenditure," see Dudley Siddall, "Who Owns Our Broadcasting Stations?" *Radio Broadcast* 6 (February 1925): 707–8. For "group picture," see Edgar H. Felix, *Using Radio in Sales Promotion* (New York: McGraw-Hill, 1927), 44.

9. For an example of network propaganda against federal support of broadcasting, see M. H. Aylesworth, "Radio's Accomplishment," *Century* (June 1929): 216, and Zeh Bouck, "Can We Solve the Broadcasting Riddle?" For an example of the listener's point of view (albeit heavily influenced by the radio industry), see J. H. Morecroft, "The March of Radio," *Radio Broadcast* 7 (May 1925): 39.

10. Rothafel and Yates, *Broadcasting: Its New Day*, 149; "Success Promised," *Radio World* 5 (19 April 1924): 26. For a similar plan, see "A Scheme for Paying Artists for Broadcasting," *Popular Radio* 2 (September 1922): 71–72.

11. "Broadcaster Asks Listeners To Pay," *New York Times*, 26 March 1924, 22; J. H. Morecroft, "The March of Radio: Voluntary Contributions for Radio Programs," *Radio Broadcast* 5 (July 1924): 220; Rothafel and Yates, *Broadcasting: Its New Day*, 150–53.

12. "Radio—The New Social Force," *Outlook* 136 (19 March 1924): 456–57.

13. Jennie Irene Mix, "The Listeners' Point of View: Who Will Pay for Broadcasting?" *Radio Broadcast* 4 (April 1924): 479; Rothafel and Yates, *Broadcasting: Its New Day*, 150.

14. "Radio Editorials," *Radio Age* 4 (May 1925): 4.

15. Joseph H. Jackson, "Should Radio Be Used for Advertising?" *Radio Broadcast* 2 (November 1922): 76.

16. Rothafel and Yates, *Broadcasting: Its New Day*, 156. See also "Advertising Takes Its Place in Radio Programs," *Radio Age* 5 (July 1925): 67; J. C. McQuiston, "Advertising by Radio: Can It and Should It Be Done?" *Radio News* 4 (August 1922): 232.

17. E. J. Van Brook, "How Bombastic Advertising Can Be Suppressed," *Broadcast Advertising* 1 (July 1929): 18. See also H. Gernsback, "Future Developments of Radio," *Radio News* 5 (March 1924): 1221.

18. "Radio, An Objectionable Advertising Medium," *Printer's Ink* 8 (February 1923): 175–76.

19. Bruce Bliven, "How Radio Is Remaking our World," *Century* 108 (July 1924): 149.

20. "Radio Men Oppose 'Ad' in Programs," *New York Times*, 2 April 1924, 8.

21. Fourth National Radio Conference, *Proceedings of the Fourth National Radio Conference and Recommendations for Regulation of Radio* (Washington, D.C.: Government Printing Office, 1925), 18.

22. J. H. Morecroft, "Radio Currents: An Editorial Interpretation," *Radio Broadcast* 1 (May 1922): 1.

23. Stuart Chase, "An Inquiry into Radio," *Outlook* 148 (18 April 1928): 617.

24. Jackson, "Should Radio Be Used for Advertising?" 75.

25. "Celler Would Curb Radio Advertising," *New York Times*, 24 March 1924, 24.

26. Marvin Robert Bensman, "The Regulation of Radio Broadcasting by the Department of Commerce" (Ph.D. diss., University of Wisconsin, 1969), 113.

27. Ibid., 233–34.

28. R. D. Heinl, "Problems the Conference Must Face," *New York Times*, 13 September 1925, Section 11, 2.

29. Third National Radio Conference, *Recommendations*, 4.

30. Fourth National Radio Conference, *Proceedings*, 5.

31. Glenn Johnson, "Secretary of Commerce Herbert Hoover: The First Regulator of Broadcasting" (Ph.D. diss., University of Iowa, 1970), 152, 277. For Hoover's flip-flop on government support, see Samuel L. Rothafel and Raymond F. Yates, *Broadcasting: Its New Day* (New York: Century, 1925), 159; "Topics of the Times: He Feels a Need for Action," *New York Times*, 23 November 1924, Section 18, 5; "Hoover Advocates Tax on Radio Sales," *New York Times*, 22 December 1924, Section 20, 1; "Topics of the Times: He Did Not Propose a Radio Tax," *New York Times*, 25 December 1924, Section 16, 15; J. H. Morecroft, "The March of Radio: Hoover Not for a Radio Sales Tax," *Radio Broadcast* 6 (March 1925): 898. For a pro-tax position, see Raymond Francis Yates, "Shall We Have a Federal Radio Tax?" *Radio News* 5 (January 1924): 867, 976–77.

32. David Burner, *Herbert Hoover: A Public Life* (New York: Alfred A. Knopf, 1979), 163; Ellis Hawley, "Herbert Hoover and Economic Stabilization, 1921–22," in Ellis Hawley, ed., *Herbert Hoover as Secretary of Commerce: Studies in New Era Thought and Practice* (Iowa City: University of Iowa Press, 1981), 60; Joan Hoff Wilson, *Herbert Hoover: Forgotten Progressive* (Boston: Little, Brown & Company, 1975), 112; C. M. Jansky, "The Contribution of Herbert Hoover to Broadcasting," *Journal of Broadcasting* 1 (Summer 1957): 241–49; Herbert Hoover, *The Memoirs of Herbert Hoover: The Cabinet and the Presidency* (New York: Macmillan Company, 1952), 139–48; Edward F. Sarno, Jr., "The National Radio Conferences," *Journal of Broadcasting* 13 (Spring 1969): 189–202.

33. For contemporary writing that presents radio as essentially commercial, see John Wallace, "The Listeners' Point of View: Communication," *Radio Broadcast* 9 (May 1926): 38–39; Austin C. Lescarboura, "How Much It Costs To Broadcast," *Radio Broadcast* 9 (September 1926): 367–71; "Is All Broadcasting Advertising?" *Radio Broadcast* 8 (January 1926): 398; James C. Young, "How Will You Have Your Advertising?" *Radio Broadcast* 6 (December 1924): 245–46; Hugo Gernsback, "Who Pays for Radio Broadcasting?" *Radio News* 7 (November 1925): 585; Raymond Francis Yates, "The Broadcast Listener: The Broadcasting of Advertising," *Popular Radio* 8 (July 1925): 90. For examples of historians adopting this view, see Alfred N. Goldsmith and Austin C. Lescarboura, *This Thing Called Broadcasting* (New York: Henry Holt, 1930), 48; Paul Schubert, *The Electric Word: The Rise of Radio* (New York: Macmillan, 1928), 219.

34. Susan Strasser, *Satisfaction Guaranteed: The Making of the American Mass Market* (New York: Pantheon, 1989), 93–95.

35. In discussing the campaign I've concentrated on the following books: Frank A. Arnold, *Broadcast Advertising: The Fourth Dimension* (New York: J. Wiley and Sons, 1931); Orrin Elmer Dunlap, *Radio in Advertising* (New York: Harper and Brothers, 1931); Edgar Felix, *Using Radio in Sales Promotion* (New York: McGraw-Hill, 1927); Herman S. Hettinger, *A Decade of Radio Advertising* (Chicago: University of Chicago Press, 1933); Neville O'Neill, ed., *The Advertising Agency Looks at Radio* (New York: D. Appleton and Company, 1932); and one magazine, *Broadcast Advertising*, published in Chicago between April 1929 and December 1932.

36. Frank Arnold, "The Reminiscences of Frank Arnold," Oral History Research Office, Columbia University, New York, 15.

37. Barnouw, *A Tower in Babel*, 192; Arnold, "Reminiscences," 20, 50, 65.

38. Arnold, *Broadcast Advertising*, 40, 54–55.

39. Edgar Felix, "The Reminiscences of Edgar Felix," Oral History Research Office, Columbia University, New York, 6.

40. "Our Respects To: Major Edgar Herbert Felix," *Broadcasting* 27 (30 October 1944): 38–40; Barnouw, *A Tower in Babel*, 28–29; "We Pay Our Respects To: Orrin Elmer Dunlap, Jr.," *Broadcasting* 23 (5 October 1942): 37.

41. Dunlap, *Radio in Advertising*, 104; Felix, *Using Radio in Sales Promotion*, 9.

42. *National Cyclopedia of American Biography*, 1977, s.v. "Hettinger, Herman Strecker." See also "We Pay Our Respects To: Herman Strecker Hettinger, Ph.D.," *Broadcasting* 11 (15 December 1936): 49.

43. O'Neill, *The Advertising Agency Looks at Radio*, v.

44. Frank A. Arnold, "High Spots in Broadcast Techniques: Procedures in Broadcast Advertising That Are Foreign to the Uninitiated," *Broadcast Advertising* 1 (May 1929): 6–7, 31; Orrin E. Dunlap, "Gauging Listener Interest in Radio Broadcasts: Methods Used by Advertisers to Determine Public's Opinion," *Broadcast Advertising* 1 (August 1929): 17–22; Howard Angus, "Preparation of Commer-

cial Copy Is Hardest Task of Radio Advertiser," *Broadcast Advertising* 4 (December 1931): 7–8; Angus, "The Importance of Stars in Your Radio Program," *Broadcast Advertising* 4 (February 1932): 12, 26–27; Angus, "Intelligent Broadcast Merchandising," *Broadcast Advertising* 5 (August 1932): 8, 20–22; L. Ames Brown, "Broadcast Advertising—Its Possibilities and Limitations: Mass Psychology Plays Important Part in Radio Advertising," *Broadcast Advertising* 1 (April 1929): 22–29; Brown, "Broadcasting Is Vigorous, Effective, Successful," *Broadcast Advertising* 3 (June 1930): 3–4, 18, 20; Brown, "The Development of Radio as an Advertising Medium: A Report of Changing Concepts," *Broadcast Advertising* 4 (June 1931): 5–6, 26–30; Charles F. Gannon, "The Agency's Place in American Broadcasting," *Broadcast Advertising* 4 (August 1931): 15, 28; M. A. Hollinshead, "Recordings: Their Place in Broadcasting," *Broadcast Advertising* 4 (July 1931): 5–7, 22–26; H. H. Kynett, "The Agency's Needs in Broadcasting," *Broadcast Advertising* 3 (July 1930): 8–9, 32; Kynett, "Spot Broadcasting as Viewed by the Advertising Agency," *Broadcast Advertising* 3 (December 1930): 14–18, 40–42; Hubbell Robinson, "How True Detective Mysteries, Broadcasting Dramatized Sample Stories, Won Half a Million New Readers in Less Than a Year," *Broadcast Advertising* 2 (March 1930): 10–12.

45. "NAB Committees Make Constructive Reports: Embrace Legislation, Ethics, Commercial Broadcasting," *Broadcast Advertising* 2 (November 1929): 23, 26–27; "Broadcasters Talk about Rates and Representatives at San Francisco Meeting," *Broadcast Advertising* 4 (October 1931): 20–21, 54–60; L. Ames Brown, "Broadcasting Is Vigorous, Effective, Successful: An Address Delivered before the Annual Convention of the AAAA," 3–4, 18–20.

46. "The 'Invisible Guest,'" *Popular Radio* 8 (September 1925): 273.

47. On the beliefs of those who worked in the industry about how advertising worked in the 1920s, see Roland Marchand, *Advertising the American Dream: Making Way for Modernity, 1920–1940* (Berkeley: University of California Press, 1985).

48. Felix, *Using Radio in Sales Promotion*, 216.

49. Arnold, *Broadcast Advertising*, 85.

50. Henry Adams Bellows, "A Defense of the American System of Broadcasting," *Broadcast Advertising* 4 (July 1931): 16–17, 44; Arnold, *Broadcast Advertising*, 85; Hettinger, *Decade of Radio Advertising*, viii.

51. Arnold, *Broadcast Advertising*, xviii, 38–44.

52. William Boddy, "The Rhetoric and Economic Roots of the American Broadcasting Industry," *Cine-Tracts* 2 (Spring 1979): 38–40. I am grateful to Sally Stein for calling Boddy's work to my attention.

53. For example, AT&T had claimed that the telephone provided a "Sixth Sense—The Power of Personal Projection," and advertisements for radio receiving sets stressed their "magical" capabilities. See T. Jackson Lears, "Some Ver-

sions of Fantasy: Toward a Cultural History of American Advertising, 1880–1920," *Prospects: The Annual of American Cultural Studies* 9 (1984): 349–406.

54. "Radio's Magic Carpet: Extensive Printed Advertising Re-enforces Broadcast Campaign," *Broadcast Advertising* 1 (July 1929): 5–10, 23–26; E. A. Fellers, "Broadcasting Barn Dances Sells Kerosene Lamps: Putting Aladdin Lamps on the Air Puts Them into Farmers' Homes," *Broadcast Advertising* 2 (December 1929): 18–20, 34; Showalter Lynch, "The Cinderella of Broadcasting, Continuity, Is Paging the Fairy Prince," *Broadcast Advertising* 3 (January 1931): 11, 30–31.

55. Arnold, *Broadcast Advertising*, 21, 44; Dunlap, *Radio in Advertising*, 7; Harrison J. Cowan, "Broadcasting a Perfume: Methods Pursued in Bourjois' 'Evening in Paris' Campaign," *Broadcast Advertising* 2 (October 1929): 1–5, 30–32; Harry C. Butcher, "The Sponsor's Place in Broadcasting," *Broadcast Advertising* 3 (November 1930): 10–11, 22, 24.

56. The most organized attempt to present advertising as sincere and trustworthy was the Truth in Advertising movement of the Progressive era. See Daniel Pope, *The Making of Modern Advertising* (New York: Basic Books, 1983), 202–26.

57. T. J. Jackson Lears, "The Rise of American Advertising," *Wilson Quarterly* 7 (Winter 1983): 157. See also T. J. Jackson Lears, "From Salvation to Self-Realization: Advertising and the Therapeutic Roots of the Consumer Culture, 1880–1930," in *The Culture of Consumption*, eds. T. J. Jackson Lears and Richard Fox (New York: Pantheon, 1983), 20; and T. J. Jackson Lears, "Some Versions of Fantasy: Toward a Cultural History of American Advertising, 1800–1920," *Prospects: The Annual of American Cultural Studies* 9 (1984): 368.

58. Dunlap, *Radio in Advertising*, 139.

59. Alan Trachtenberg, with Amy Weinstein Meyers, *Classic Essays on Photography* (New Haven, Conn.: Leete's Island Books, 1980), 1–108; Marchand, *Advertising the American Dream*, 149–53; Judy Babbitts, "'To See Is To Know': Stereographs Educate Americans about East Asia, 1890–1930" (Ph.D. diss., Yale University, 1987). I want to thank Judy Babbitts for this insight.

60. O'Neill, *The Advertising Agency Looks at Radio*, 3.

61. Marchand, *Advertising the American Dream*, 13–24.

62. Stephen Fox's tracing of the cycles of advertising practice from hard sell to soft sell and back again, demonstrates that different approaches never vanish, just go in or out of favor. See Stephen Fox, *The Mirrormakers* (New York: Vintage Books, 1984).

63. A. Michael McMahon, "An American Courtship: Psychologists and Advertising Theory in the Progressive Era," *American Studies* 3 (Fall 1972): 9. See also Otis Pease, *The Responsibilities of American Advertising: Private Control and Public Influence, 1920–1940* (New Haven, Conn.: Yale University Press, 1958), 20–26; Stephen Richard Shapiro, "The Big Sell—Attitudes of Advertising Writers about

Their Craft in the 1920's and 1930's" (Ph.D. diss., University of Wisconsin, 1969), 43, 53, 227.

64. Merle Curti, "The Changing Concept of 'Human Nature' in the Literature of American Advertising," *Business History Review* 41 (Winter 1967): 347.

65. Hal Johnson, "We Made the Program Fit the Product," *Broadcast Advertising* 2 (March 1930): 6–8; "Reproduce Product's Tempo in Program, Says Woolley," *Broadcast Advertising* 4 (May 1931): 26, 28; Robert T. Colwell, "The Program as Advertisement," in O'Neill, *The Advertising Agency Looks at Radio*, 22–41.

66. Hettinger, *Decade of Radio Advertising*, 23.

67. Ibid., 14.

68. Ibid., 3–40.

69. Dunlap, *Radio in Advertising*, 110–11.

70. Arnold, *Broadcast Advertising*, 112.

71. On the history of branding, see Strasser, *Satisfaction Guaranteed*, 29–57 and passim. On convenience goods, see Pope, *Making of Modern Advertising*, 46–48; Michael Schudson, *Advertising, the Uneasy Persuasion: Its Dubious Impact on American Society* (New York: Basic Books, 1984), 97–98.

72. Pope, *Making of Modern Advertising*, 92–96; Strasser, *Satisfaction Guaranteed*, 21–23, 57–88.

73. Arnold, *Broadcast Advertising*, 97.

74. National Broadcasting Company, *Making Pep and Sparkle Typify a Ginger Ale*, 18. See also National Broadcasting Company, *Selling Goods, Selling Service, Selling the Consciousness of a Great Ideal: The Broadcast Advertising of Cities Service Company*, 1928, p. 11, Box 3, Folder 6, E. P. H. James Papers (hereafter cited as James Papers), Mass Communications History Center, Wisconsin State Historical Society, Madison.

75. Pope, *Making of Modern Advertising*, 94.

76. National Broadcasting Company, *Improving the Smiles of a Nation! Advertising Has Worked for the Makers of Ipana Tooth Paste*, 1928, Broadcast Pioneers Library, Washington, D.C., 5.

77. Ibid., 15.

78. Hettinger, *Decade of Radio Advertising*, 162. On agency reaction, see M. O. Hastings, "You're Not Quite Ready for That As Yet!" *Broadcast Advertising* 1 (April 1929): 10; "Should Stations Pay Commission on Talent? Broadcasters and Advertising Agencies Express Varying Views," *Broadcast Advertising* 3 (September 1930): 6–7, 22; Ralph Hower, *The History of an Advertising Agency: N. W. Ayer & Son at Work, 1869–1949* (Cambridge, Mass.: N. W. Ayer & Son, 1949), 168.

79. Gordon Best, "Radio Has Brought a New Responsibility to Advertising Agencies," *Broadcast Advertising* 5 (July 1932): 6. See also Roy S. Durstine, "Function of the Agency in Broadcast Advertising," *Broadcast Advertising* 1 (June 1929): 29.

80. O'Neill, *The Advertising Agency Looks at Radio*, v.

81. Ray R. Morgan and H. K. Carpenter, "West Coast Advertising Man's Complaint 'Let's Get Down to Business' Is Answered by Eastern Station Manager 'All Right—Let's,'" *Broadcast Advertising* 3 (August 1930): 6–8, 22, 26; "Should Stations Pay Commission on Talent?" *Broadcast Advertising* 3 (September 1930): 6–7, 22; "A Station-Agency Symposium: What the Station Wants from the Agency" and "How Can We Improve Radio? What the Agency Wants from the Station," *Broadcast Advertising* 5 (April 1932): 4–5, 24–27. See also John Benson, "The Advertising Agency and Broadcasting," *Broadcast Advertising* 3 (January 1931): 4; John Benson, "Radio's Advertising Problems May Be Solved Jointly by Broadcasters and Agencies," *Broadcast Advertising* 4 (January 1932): 5, 42–46.

82. Mark Woods, "The Reminiscences of Mark Woods," Oral History Research Office, Columbia University, New York, 21, 29.

83. "Should Stations Pay Commission on Talent?" 6.

84. Morgan and Carpenter, "West Coast Advertising Man's Complaint," 6–8, 22, 26; William S. Hedges, "Agencies and Broadcasters Should Cooperate," *Broadcast Advertising* 3 (July 1930): 5–6, 28, 30; "Should Stations Pay Commission on Talent?" 6–7, 22. See also A. A. Cormier, "What the Radio Station Wants from the Agency," *Broadcast Advertising* 3 (December 1930): 19–20; "A Station-Agency Symposium: What the Station Wants from the Agency," *Broadcast Advertising* 5 (April 1932): 4.

85. Barnouw, *A Tower in Babel*, 239. See also J. Fred McDonald, *Don't Touch That Dial: Radio Programming in American Life, 1920 to 1960* (Chicago: Nelson-Hall, 1979), 31–33.

86. "Merchandising a Radio Campaign,: How Carson Pirie Scott and Company Sold Their Dealers on the Bobolink Broadcasts," *Broadcast Advertising* 3 (October 1930): 6.

87. For "don't confuse," see Russell Bryon Williams, "In Radio, It Pays To Advertise," *Broadcast Advertising* 5 (June 1932): 23. For "within the advertiser's own organization," see Harry Shinnick and Irwin Borders, "Merchandising in Its Relation to Radio," in O'Neill, *The Advertising Agency Looks at Radio*, 153.

88. Shinnick and Borders, "Merchandising in Its Relation to Radio," 155–70; Bernard Grimes, "How Radio Programs Are Merchandised," *Printer's Ink* 155 (25 June 1931): 53–56; "Merchandising the Radio Program," *Printer's Ink* 156 (23 July 1931): 118; "Chain Advertisers To Use Listener Magazines," *Broadcast Advertising* 5 (June 1932): 26; Dunlap, *Radio in Advertising*, 189–212; Hettinger, *Decade of Radio Advertising*, 276–88.

89. "How Quaker Products Company 'Sells' Radio to Salesmen," *Broadcast Advertising* 1 (July 1929): 14. See also E. P. H. James, "Why Dealer Cooperation Is Important," *Broadcasting* 3 (January 1933): 11.

90. For "leads the horse to water," see Dunlap, *Radio in Advertising*, 189. On

program quality, see Howard Angus, "Intelligent Broadcast Merchandising Means Building a Good Program and Exploiting It in Every Way Possible," *Broadcast Advertising* 5 (August 1932): 8.

91. "Here's an Explanation of Chains' Financial Arrangements with Affiliated Stations," *Broadcast Advertising* 5 (October 1932): 13.

92. Arnold, *Broadcast Advertising*, "Appendix G: General Rate Card of National Broadcasting Co., Inc., as of July 19, 1931," 232–36; Arnold, *Broadcast Advertising*, "Appendix J: General Rate Card of Columbia Broadcasting System, Inc., as of June 1, 1931," 249–53; Dunlap, *Radio in Advertising*, "Appendix A: National Broadcasting Company, Inc., Rate Card, May 1, 1931," 302–9; Dunlap, *Radio in Advertising*, "Appendix B: Columbia Broadcasting System, Rate Card No. 10," 310–18.

93. Ted Hill, "Let's Standardize Our Rate Cards," *Broadcast Advertising* 4 (September 1931): 18–19, 26.

94. "Broadcasters Strengthen Ranks To Resist Outside Domination," *Broadcast Advertising* 15 (December 1932): 12–13.

95. Goldsmith and Lescarboura, *This Thing Called Broadcasting*, 98.

96. Jessica Dragonette, *Faith Is a Song: The Odyssey of an American Artist* (New York: David McKay Company, 1951), 104.

97. Pope, *The Making of Modern Advertising*, 168, 139–43.

98. Arnold, *Broadcast Advertising*, xv.

99. Ray A. Sweet, "Daylight Broadcasting," *Radio News* 5 (June 1924): 1727–1821.

100. On the first wave of boy enthusiasts, who by the 1920s were teaching their sons about radio, see Susan Douglas, *Inventing American Broadcasting* (Baltimore: Johns Hopkins University Press, 1987), 187–215.

101. Crystal D. Tector, "Radio and the Woman" *Radio World* 1 (20 May 1922): 20. See also subsequent issues, (3 June 1922): 14; (17 June 1922): 15; (15 July 1922): 15; (29 July 1922): 15; (5 August 1922): 15; and (12 August 1922): 15. "At Wellesley College," *Radio Broadcast* 7 (July 1925): 336. For other examples, see "The Autobiography of a Girl Amateur: Being a True Account of the Trials and Tribulations of a Lady Member of the Honorable Body of 'Hams,'" *Radio Amateur News* 1 (March 1920): 490; Marianne C. Brown, "One of the Gang," *Radio News* 3 (September 1920): 148; Abbye M. White, "Hearing North America," *Radio Broadcast* 3 (September 1923): 421; S. R. Winters, "A Lady (Radio) Bug," *Radio News* 4 (July 1922): 52; Alfred M. Caddell, "A Woman Who Makes Receiving Sets," *Radio Broadcast* 4 (November 1923): 29.

102. Otis Pease, *The Responsibilities of American Advertising* (New Haven: Yale University Press, 1958), 34; Lears, "From Salvation to Self-Realization," 23. See also Dolores Hayden, *The Grand Domestic Revolution: A History of Feminist Designs for American Homes, Neighborhoods, and Cities* (Cambridge, Mass.: MIT Press,

1981), 283–86; Stuart Ewen, *Captains of Consciousness: Advertising and the Social Roots of the Consumer Culture* (New York: McGraw-Hill, 1976), 113–24.

103. Arnold, *Broadcast Advertising*, 42.

104. Marchand, *Advertising the American Dream*, 66.

105. Claudine MacDonald to John Royal, 15 January 1932, Box 15, Folder 25, NBC Papers (hereafter cited as NBC Papers), Mass Communications History Center, Wisconsin Historical Society, Madison.

106. Mary Loomis Cook, "Programs for Women," in O'Neill, *The Advertising Agency Looks at Radio*, 132.

107. Nena Wilson Badenoch, "Meet Our Radio Mother," *Radio Age* 4 (February 1925): 33; "WJZ: Facts for Feminine Fans," *WJZ Program Guide*, 18 December 1926, Box 1, Folder 7, James Papers.

108. William D. Jenkins, "Housewifery and Motherhood: The Question of Role Change in the Progressive Era," in Mary Kelley, ed., *Woman's Being, Woman's Place: Female Identity and Vocation in American History* (Boston: G. K. Hall, 1983), 142–53. See also Susan Strasser, *Never Done: A History of American Housework* (New York: Pantheon, 1982), 202–23; Laura Shapiro, *Perfection Salad: Women and Cooking at the Turn of the Century* (New York: Farrar, Straus, and Giroux, 1986); Emma Seifert Weigley, "It Might Have Been Euthenics: The Lake Placid Conferences and the Home Economics Movement," *American Quarterly* 26 (March 1974): 79–96.

109. Jean Gordon and Jan McArthur, "Interior Decorating Advice as Popular Culture: Women's Views Concerning Wall and Window Treatments, 1870–1920," *Journal of American Culture* 9 (Fall 1986): 15–16; Warren Susman, *Culture as History: The Transformation of American Society in the Twentieth Century* (New York: Pantheon, 1984), 201. Roland Marchand writes that "the inadequacy ascribed to women was only one salient example of the wider public incompetence that advertisers assumed, and sought to reinforce, by their constant celebration of experts." See Marchand, *Advertising the American Way*, 350–51.

110. Marjorie Presnell, "Women Strong for Home Hints," *Radio Digest* 24 (February 1930): 51.

111. Martin Grief, "Introduction," in Ruth Van Deman and Fanny Walker Yeatman, *Aunt Sammy's Radio Recipes* (New York: Universe Books, 1975), n.p.

112. Ibid. The U.S. Department of Agriculture still has in print a selection of "Aunt Sammy's Radio Recipes" as Home and Garden Bulletin No. 215, available from the U.S. Government Printing Office, Stock Number 001-000-03523.

113. On the USDA's efforts to teach farm families to consume, see Mary Neth, "Preserving the Family Farm: Farm Families and Communities in the Midwest, 1900–1940" (Ph.D. diss., University of Wisconsin, 1987), particularly chapter 8.

114. James Gray, *Business without Boundary: The Story of General Mills* (Minneap-

olis: University of Minnesota Press, 1954) 177–78. See also "National Exchange of Radio Recipes," *Radio Age* 4 (December 1925): 29; "Thousands of Cooking Students Are Graduated in Our Homes," *Radio World* 8 (23 January 1926): 31; Pauline Chestnut, "Recipes via Radio," *Radio Digest* 26 (January 1926): 80.

115. Florence Roberts, "Radio Reminiscences," *Radio Digest* 26 (April 1931): 53.

116. "New Women's Hour on CBS," *Radio Revue* 1 (30 January 1930): 47; Eve M. Conradt-Eberlin, "Real Homemaking in the Studio," *Radio Digest* 25 (June 1930): 78.

117. See "The Woman's Magazine of the Air" 2 (15 August 1930); 3 (1 September 1930); 4 (15 September 1930); 5 (1 October 1930); and 6 (15 October 1930) in Box 5, Folder 79, James Papers. For another example of a magazine program, see the "Women's Radio Revue" as described in internal NBC memos, such as J. V. McConnell to D. C. Williams, 13 August 1931 and 2 December 1931, and Christine MacDonald to John Royal, 15 January 1932, with listener comments, Box 15, Folder 25, NBC Papers; National Broadcasting Company, "The Woman's Radio Revue: Let Us Join the Ladies: They Buy about 85% of Everything That Goes into the Home," 15 April 1931, Box 2, Folder 8, James Papers.

118. Hettinger, *Decade of Radio Advertising*, 201.

119. Niles Trammel to John Royal, 23 August 1933, Box 90, Folder 9, NBC Papers.

120. Pamphlets in Box 4, Folder 1, James Papers. See also Halsey D. Kellog and Abner G. Walters, "How To Reach Housewives Most Effectively," *Broadcasting* (15 April 1932): 7, 31.

121. Marleen Getz Rouse, "Daytime Radio Programming for the Homemaker, 1926–1956," *Journal of Popular Culture* 12 (Fall 1979): 317. See also "Exploiting Women's Interest in People To Create an Interest in Products: Sponsors of Morning Broadcasts Find Success with 'Human Interest' Skits," *Broadcast Advertising* 5 (July 1923): 200.

122. Robert C. Allen, *Speaking of Soap Operas* (Chapel Hill: University of North Carolina Press, 1985), 96–121.

123. MacDonald, *Don't Touch That Dial*, 233.

124. Marchand, *Advertising the American Dream*, 66–69.

CHAPTER 4. TWISTING THE DIALS: CHANGES IN RADIO PROGRAMMING

1. Raymond Francis Yates, "The Broadcast Listener: Some Pretty Bad Stations," *Popular Radio* 8 (November 1925): 474. On amateur performers, see James H. Collins, "How To Get on a Radio Program," *Popular Radio* 7 (February 1925):

109–17. For variety of programs on any given evening, see newspaper schedules such as *Boston Evening American*, 7 October 1926, and others in series 134, George H. Clark Radioana Collection (hereafter cited as Clark Collection, NMAH), Archives Center, National Museum of American History, Smithsonian Institution, Washington, D.C.

2. George P. Stone, "Radio Has Gripped Chicago," *Radio Broadcast* 1 (October 1922): 503–6.

3. Michael Biel, "The Making and Use of Recordings in Broadcasting before 1935" (Ph.D. diss., Northwestern University, 1977), 228–33; Philip Rosen, *The Modern Stentors: Radio Broadcasters and the Federal Government, 1920–1934* (Westport, Conn.: Greenwood Press, 1980), 38; "A Brief Historical Note on the Mechanical Reproduction Announcement Requirement," *Journal of Broadcasting* 4 (Spring 1960): 119–22. I would like to thank Sam Brylawski of the Library of Congress for calling my attention to Biel's work.

4. "Do You Want Better Broadcasting?" *Popular Radio* 3 (June 1923): 6–8.

5. Credo Fitch Harris, *Microphone Memoirs of the Horse and Buggy Days of Radio* (New York: Bobbs-Merrill, 1937), 43–44.

6. H. M. Taylor, "Random Observations on Running a Broadcasting Station," *Radio Broadcast* 1 (July 1922): 224–26; John Wallace, "The Listeners' Point of View: A Genuinely New Type of Radio Program," *Radio Broadcast* 9 (July 1926): 236–37; Armstrong Perry, "Broadcasters, Broadcatchers and Broadcashers," *Radio News* 6 (July 1924): 16–17, 127–29. Several archives contain boxes of letters from listeners. For the first solicited mail, called QSL cards, from the early part of the century, see H. D. Roess Collection, Division of Electricity, and the Clark Collection, Archives Center, both at the National Museum of American History, Smithsonian Institution, Washington D.C. A sampling of listener letters to a variety of stations in 1925 and 1926 can be found in Box 1, Folder 7, E. P. H. James Papers (hereafter cited as James Papers), Mass Communications History Center, Wisconsin State Historical Society, Madison. Thanks to Elliot Sivowitch, Division of Electricity, National Museum of American History, Smithsonian Institution, for information on the QSL cards.

7. Kingsley Welles, "Meet Mr. Average Radio Enthusiast," *Radio Broadcast* 9 (October 1926): 531–32. For another early survey, see John Wallace, "The Listeners' Point of View: What the Farmer Listens To," *Radio Broadcast* 9 (August 1926): 316.

8. John Wallace, "The Listeners' Point of View: The Listeners Speak for Themselves," *Radio Broadcast* 8 (April 1926): 669–71. See also Maxwell Alper, "Jazz Defeat Is Complete: Better Music Demanded," *Radio World* 11 (16 April 1927): 17.

9. "Broadcast Program Analysis," *Radio Age* 13 (January 1924): 30–31.

10. J. H. Morecroft, "The March of Radio: The Day of Good Music," *Radio Broadcast* 7 (May 1925): 42–43; "The Ever Present Jazz vs. 'Classical Music' Con-

troversy," *Radio Broadcast* 9 (July 1926): 240; Raymond Francis Yates, "The Broad-cast Listener: The Waning 'Art of Jazz,'" *Popular Radio* 8 (July 1925): 88.

11. "Tell Us What You Like in Radio Programs," *Radio Broadcast* 10 (February 1927): 376; John Wallace, "The Listeners' Point of View: Answers the Question-naire Brought Forth," *Radio Broadcast* 10 (March 1927): 475–76; John Wallace, "The Listeners' Point of View: What Many Listeners Think about Broadcast-ing," *Radio Broadcast* 10 (April 1927): 566–69; "What the Listener Likes and How He Likes It," *Radio Broadcast* 11 (May 1927): 32. Another survey of radio listen-ers, conducted in October and November 1927, reported that "programs of na-tional advertisers which were of high quality and had been carried over a long period of time had a large following among listeners." J. H. Palmer, "Study of the Use of Radio as an Advertising Medium," *Journal of Business* 1 (October 1928): 495–96.

12. James C. Young, "New Fashions in Radio Programs: How the Present Trend of Radio Advertising Is Improving the Quality of Broadcast Programs," *Radio Broadcast* 7 (May 1925): 83.

13. Raymond Francis Yates, "Broadcast Listener: What Competitive Programs Are Doing to Radio," *Popular Radio* 12 (November 1927): 366.

14. John Wallace, "The Listeners' Point of View," *Radio Broadcast* 9 (May 1926): 41.

15. Edgar Felix, *Using Radio in Sales Promotion* (New York: McGraw-Hill, 1927), 89–90.

16. "Hollywood Call to 16-Year-Old Ends Jones and Hare as Team," *New York World Telegram*, 17 February 1940; Brian Rust, ed., *The Complete Entertainment Discography* (New York: Arlington House, 1973), 325–33; Arthur Wertheim, *Radio Comedy* (New York: Oxford University Press, 1979), 7.

17. J. H. Morecroft, "The March of Radio: We Need More Delicacy in Radio Advertising," *Radio Broadcast* 7 (June 1925): 206–7.

18. "What the Listener Likes and How He Likes It," *Radio Broadcast* 11 (Janu-ary 1927): 32.

19. William Peck Banning, *Commercial Broadcasting Pioneer: The WEAF Experi-ment, 1922–1926* (Cambridge, Mass.: Harvard University Press, 1946), 68, 131–39.

20. Pierre Boucheron, "Radio Broadcast Central," *Radio Broadcast* 3 (July 1923): 254–55; Gleason Archer, *The History of Radio to 1926* (New York: American Historical Society, 1938), 213–15, 303. For an early description of WJZ, includ-ing program schedules, see "The WJZ Radiophone Broadcasting Station at New-ark, N.J.," *Radio News* 3 (December 1921): 482, 552, 554, 556.

21. WJZ, 25 May 1923; WJY, 28 July 1923; WJZ, 16 August 1923. Box 98, National Broadcasting Company Papers (hereafter cited as NBC Papers), Mass Communications History Center, Wisconsin State Historical Society, Madison.

22. WJZ, 30 June 1926; WJZ, 3 July 1926; WJZ, 3 September 1926. Box 98, NBC Papers.

23. WJZ, 14 January 1925; WJY, 28 April 1925; WJZ, 5 November 1925; WJZ, 8 July 1925; WJZ, 12 March 1926; WJZ, 18 March 1926; WJZ, 14 March 1926; WJZ, 14 April 1926; WJZ, 5 June 1926. Box 98, NBC Papers.

24. J. H. Morecroft, "The March of Radio: WGY Offers $500 for Prize Radio Drama," *Radio Broadcast* 4 (November 1923): 5–6.

25. WJY, 7 April 1925, Box 98, NBC Papers.

26. Mark Woods, "The Reminiscences of Mark Woods," Oral History Research Office, Columbia University, New York, 9.

27. Banning, *Commercial Broadcasting Pioneer*, 90.

28. Woods, "Reminiscences," 4.

29. Banning, *Commercial Broadcasting Pioneer*, 146.

30. Banning, *Commercial Broadcasting Pioneer*, 154; Woods, "Reminiscences," 9.

31. Banning, *Commercial Broadcasting Pioneer*, 90, 147; Woods, "Reminiscences," 25.

32. While NBC often denied the distinction between the red and the blue networks, most listeners recognized it, at least in the network's first years. See Phillips Carlin, "The Reminiscences of Phillips Carlin," Oral History Research Office, Columbia University, New York, 12.

33. Jim Walsh, "Favorite Pioneer Recording Artists: The Happiness Boys, Billy Jones and Ernie Hare," *Hobbies* (March 1959): 36; "Billy Jones Dies: Early Radio Star," *New York Times*, 24 November 1940. On the favorable aspects of radio publicity, see Gwen Wagner, "What Price Radio Popularity?" *Radio Age* 5 (May 1926): 28–29, 49.

34. Carlin, "Reminiscences," 10.

35. Banning, *Commercial Broadcasting Pioneer*, 148; "Silver Masked Tenor," 17 March 1926, sound recording, R76-0335; "Clicquot Club Eskimos," June 1927, sound recording, R76:0338, Museum of Broadcasting, New York; "Silver Masked Tenor Becomes Deputy Sheriff," *Radio World* 9 (19 June 1926): 18; Herbert Devins, "A Glimpse behind the Mike During the Palmolive Hour," *Radio Revue* 1 (December 1929): 27, 29, 48; Frank Arnold, *Broadcast Advertising: The Fourth Dimension* (New York: J. Wiley and Sons, 1931), 177–80; Francis Chase, *Sound and Fury: An Informal History of Broadcasting* (New York: Harper, 1942), 158; "Goldy and Dusty," *Radio Broadcast* 8 (November 1925): 33. For a regional variation, see the account regarding WFAA, Dallas, in Lera McGinty, "Who's the Red-Headed Girl?" *Radio Age* 4 (February 1925): 35, 58.

36. Arnold, *Broadcast Advertising*, 181–84; John Wallace, "The Listeners' Point of View; The Ipana Troubadours," *Radio Broadcast* 9 (September 1926): 391; "Bristol Meyers Company," Box 1, Folder 7, James Papers; "Radio Gave Gypsy Violinist Chance To Become Famous," *Radio Revue* (January 1930): 29–30.

37. Two advertising agencies claimed to have represented the National Carbon Company in starting the program, but the agencies probably became involved only later. See Robert H. Rankin, "Broadcasting in America," *Broadcast*

Advertising (September 1929): 10–12, 23–24; Ralph Hower, *The History of an Advertising Agency: N. W. Ayer & Son at Work, 1869–1949* (Cambridge, Mass.: N. W. Ayer & Son, 1949), 166.

38. George C. Furness, "Program Pioneers: The Eveready Hour," *Radio News* 11 (December 1929): 509.

39. Francis Chase, *Sound and Fury: An Informal History of Broadcasting* (New York: Harper, 1942), 24; Julia V. Shawell, "Eveready Hour," *Radio News* 9 (May 1928): 1218, 1273.

40. Chase, *Sound and Fury*, 25; John Dunning, *Tune In Yesterday: The Ultimate Encyclopedia of Old-Time Radio, 1925–1976* (Englewood Cliffs, N.J.: Prentice-Hall, 1976), 187.

41. Furness, "Program Pioneers," 581. For changes in the program, see "What the Broadcasters Are Doing: Eveready Hour Is Program Pioneer," *Radio Age* 5 (June 1926); "The Good and Evil of Musical Scenarios," *Popular Radio* 11 (January 1927): 98.

42. Furness, "Program Pioneers," 582.

43. Shawell, "Eveready Hour," 1273–74; Furness, "Program Pioneers," 582–83.

44. Jerry Hoffman, "The Thrill of a Lifetime: The Wedding of Wendell Hall" *Radio World* 5 (14 June 1924): 15; "Adventure in the Air: How It Feels To Be Married by Radio," *Popular Radio* 6 (August 1924): 211–12. See also scrapbooks and correspondence in Wendell Hall Papers (hereafter cited as Hall Papers), Mass Communications History Center, Wisconsin State Historical Society, Madison.

45. Detroit, 25 March 1924; St. Louis, 22 March 1924; Rock Island, Ill., 21 March 1924; Detroit, 22 March 1924; Silvis, Ill., 21 March 1924. Box 1, Hall Papers.

46. Furness, "Program Pioneers," 510.

47. Robert E. Hutchinson, "Stopping the Leak in Storage-Battery Advertising," *Electrical World* 83 (28 June 1924): 1355–56.

48. As examples of many similar advertisements in various radio magazines, see the following, all of which include listings of when and on what station listeners could hear the Eveready Hour. "Recommend Good Batteries," *Radio Broadcast* 7 (May 1925): 155; "These Eveready Batteries Are the Correct Size for Your Set," *Radio Broadcast* 8 (January 1926): 353; "The Eveready Hour," *Radio Broadcast* 8 (February 1926): 485.

49. National Broadcasting Company, "Making Pep and Sparkle Typify a Ginger Ale: Broadcast Advertising and the Clicquot Club Eskimos," 14 March 1929, Box 3, Folder 6, James Papers.

50. R. Daniels, "Should Similar Products Be Advertised Collectively?" *Printer's Ink* 148 (12 September 1929): 48; "Four Distinct Campaigns for 3 Closely Related Products: Clicquot Club," *Printer's Ink Monthly* 21 (July 1930): 35, 108, 111;

"Limited Production as a Selling Feature: Clicquot Club Ginger Ale," *Sales Management* 14 (30 June 1928): 1163; "Why Clicquot Club Sometimes Runs Homely Advertisements," *Printer's Ink* 151 (12 June 1930): 100.

51. Orrin Elmer Dunlap, *Radio in Advertising* (New York: Harper and Brothers, 1930), 201.

52. P. M. Boggs, "But You Can't Sell Ginger Ale in Winter," *Printer's Ink* 132 (30 July 1925): 25–26.

53. Kimball quote in Banning, *Commercial Broadcasting Pioneer*, 149. On the agency rebate, see Frank Weston, interview by Edwin L. Dunham, 16 August 1965, Broadcast Pioneers Library (hereafter cited as BPL), Washington, D.C.

54. National Broadcasting Company, "Making Pep and Sparkle Typify a Ginger Ale," 4, 6.

55. Arnold, *Broadcast Advertising*, 87.

56. Thomas A. DeLong, *The Mighty Music Box: The Golden Age of Musical Radio* (Los Angeles: Amber Crest Books, 1980), 49; National Broadcasting Company, "Making Pep and Sparkle Typify a Ginger Ale," 14; *Clicquot Fox Trot March: Featured by the Clicquot Club Eskimos under the Direction of Harry Reser*, sheet music, BPL.

57. Arnold, *Broadcast Advertising*, 181.

58. Ibid., 182.

59. DeLong, *Mighty Music Box*, 48–49; "Harry Reser Recalls: Leader of Big Radio Band Contrasts Early Broadcast with TV Work," undated newspaper article, BPL; Brian Rust, ed., *The American Dance Band Discography, 1917–1942*, vol. 1 (New Rochelle, N.Y.: Arlington House, 1977), 310–12.

60. Myers to Witmer, 10 June 1933, Box 16, Folder 58, NBC Papers.

61. Myers to Witmer, 13 November 1932, Box 8, Folder 9, NBC Papers.

62. Quotation from Canadian listener in Bill McNeill and Morris Wolfe, *Signing On: The Birth of Radio in Canada* (Garden City, N.Y.: Doubleday, 1982), 66. Articles about the Happiness Boys include Vera Connolly, "Bagging the Radio Lions," *The Delineator*, September 1930, 60–63; "Gag Creation Placed on Basis of Business by 'Mike' Comedians," 15 January 1930, newspaper article, William Hedges Collection, BPL; "Let the 'Happiness Boys' Help You!" *Radio Age* 4 (January 1925): 28, 46; Lucille Husting, "The Happiness Boys—Billy Jones and Ernie Hare," undated magazine article, National Broadcasters' Hall of Fame, Freehold, N.J.; "Pinchhitting for Hare: Ernie's Marilyn Sings On in the Hare Tradition," *Radio Guide* (24 November 1939): 2, 18. For mentions of the Happiness Boys by other performers, see Jim Walsh, "Favorite Pioneer Recording Artists: The Happiness Boys," *Hobbies* (May 1959): 30. Listener letters to Jones and Hare are described in "Billy Jones Dies: Early Radio Star," *New York Times*, 24 November 1940; "Ernie Hare Dies: Early Radio Star," *New York Times*, 10 March 1939; Jack Gaver and Dave Stanley, *There's Laughter in the Air: Radio's Top Comedians and*

Their Best Shows (New York: Greenberg Publishers, 1945), 3. For "working on my second million," see John Carl Morgan, Ernie Hare's nephew, interview with author, 28 June 1983.

63. William Boyd Craig, "Candy, a Billion Dollar Muddle," *Nation's Business* 15 (August 1927): 17–20; "Much Interest in Candy Advertising," *Printer's Ink* 137 (23 December 1926): 88; V. P. Connolly, "Candy Industry Needs 'Dr. Advertising,'" *Advertising and Selling* 14 (2 April 1930): 34–35, 65; A. L. White, "Candy Making Develops into an Important Industry," *Dun's International Review* 52 (February 1929): 35–37, 48; R. W. Johnson, "Surveys of Merchandising Trends in the Confectionary Field," *Sales Management* 10 (3 April 1926): 488–89; "Too Much Competition on Poor Quality," *Printer's Ink* 138 (10 March 1927): 103–4; Henry Burwen, "Advertising Takes a Product out of the 'Free Deal Class,'" *Printer's Ink* 123 (28 June 1923): 57–60, 64; "How Some Successful Advertisers Got Their Start," *Printer's Ink* 125 (15 November 1923): 53–56; Otto Y. Schnering, "Without Advertising, Baby Ruth Was a Failure—With Advertising, It Succeeded," *Printer's Ink* 139 (5 May 1927): 17–20, 25; "Candy Manufacturer Samples His Product among Brides," *Printer's Ink* 119 (8 June 1922): 28; Louis Wheelock, "How the Candy Industry Will Be Advertised; Details of the New Association Campaign To Increase Candy Consumption," *Advertising and Selling* 8 (November 1926): 36, 70–71.

64. John Moody, *Moody's Manual of Investments and Security Rating Service* (New York: Moody's Investor Service, 1926), 1532–35; Moody, *Moody's Manual of Investments and Security Rating Service* (New York: Moody's Investor Service, 1930), 3155.

65. A description of the first script appeared in "Hollywood Call to 16-Year-Old Ends Jones and Hare as Team," *New York Telegraph*, 17 February 1940. The evolution of the program was discussed in John Carl Morgan, interview with author, 28 June 1983.

66. Felix, *Using Radio in Sales Promotion*, 162.

67. Heywood Broun, "It Seems to Me," *The World*, 1 April 1925, Box 1, Folder 6, James Papers.

68. John DiMeglio, "Radio's Debt to Vaudeville," *Journal of Popular Culture* 12 (Fall 1979): 228–35.

69. Robert Toll, *Blacking Up: The Minstrel Show in Nineteenth-Century America* (New York: Oxford University Press, 1974), 54–57, 169–79; Douglas Gilbert, *American Vaudeville: Its Life and Times* (New York: McGraw-Hill, 1940), 4.

70. Albert McLean, *American Vaudeville as Ritual* (Lexington: University of Kentucky Press, 1965), 106–37.

71. "Down at the Old Swimming Hole," Billy Jones and Ernie Hare, sound recording, Edison 50841, August 1921; OKeh 4375, c. July 1921. See also Jim

Walsh, "Favorite Pioneer Recording Artists: The Happiness Boys, Billy Jones and Ernie Hare," *Hobbies* (April 1959): 36.

72. "In the Little Red Schoolhouse," Edison 50962, c. April 1922; "Down by the Old Apple Tree," OKeh 4756, c. January 1923; Edison 51106, c. January 1923; "Just a Little Old Schoolhouse," Edison 52050, c. June 1927; "Shout Hallelujah! Cause I'm Home," Edison 52333, c. June 1928.

73. "Open Your Arms, My Alabammy," Edison 51131, c. January 1923; "Down Where the South Begins," Edison 51333, c. March 1924; "How's Your Folks and My Folks (Down in Norfolk Town)," Edison 51618, c. August 1925; Victor, 19739, 1 July 1925; "I Would Rather Be Alone in the South," Victor, 19826, 21 July 1925; OKeh 40520, 14 September 1925; "Stay Out of the South," Edison 52236, c. February 1928.

74. William Leuchtenberg, *The Perils of Prosperity, 1914–32* (Chicago: University of Chicago Press, 1958), 225–29.

75. "Don't Bring Lulu," Edison 51555, April 1925; "No One Knows What It's All About," Edison 51454, c. November 1924; "Hooray for the Irish!" Vocalion 15285, c. January 1926; "Me No a Speak Good English," Edison 51322, c. March 1924; "In the Little Red School House," Edison 50962, c. April 1922; "From De Ol Home Town," Edison 51199, c. October 1923.

76. "Pardon Me While I Laugh," Edison 51624, c. September 1925; "King Tut," Edison 51155, April 1923; "Henry's Made a Lady out of Lizzie," Victor 21174, 4 January 1928; Edison 52200, c. January 1928; "When Lindy Comes Home," Victor 20741, 14 June 1927; "Mr. Hoover—Mr. Smith," Victor 21607, 24 July 1928; Edison 52367, c. August 1928. See also Carl Scheele, liner notes, "Henry's Made a Lady out of Lizzie," *Come Josephine in My Flying Machine: Inventions and Topics in Popular Song, 1910–1929*, New World Records, NW233.

77. "Twisting the Dials," Victor 35953, 31 October 1928 and 12 November 1928. See also Wertheim, *Radio Comedy,* 9; *Phonograph Monthly Review* 3 (January 1929): 142.

78. "Branded Men and Women: Pioneers Who Paved the Way and Paid with Personal Oblivion," *Radio Guide* 1 (3 March 1932): 1. See also K. Trenholm, "If Radio Is To Survive It Must 'Hitch Its Wagon to a Star,'" *Radio Revue* 1 (December 1929): 12–14.

79. "Branded Men and Women," 13.

80. On the "Interwoven Pair," see NBC Sales Manual, Box 5, Folder 4, James Papers. The Interwoven Sock program had a CAB rating of 22.0, according to Harrison Summers, *A Thirty Year History of Programs Carried on National Radio Networks in the United States, 1926–56* (Columbus: Ohio State University Press, 1958), 20. On the "Best Food Boys," see "Jones and Hare Sign Long Term Contract with Best Foods, Inc.," *Broadcast Advertising* 4 (March 1932): 44.

81. "Branded Men and Women," 13.

82. G. W. Johnston to Frank E. Mason, 18 February 1932, Box 11, Folder 19, NBC Papers.

83. "Cities Service: On the Air," undated pamphlet, Class 134, Clark Collection, NMAH.

84. Jessica Dragonette, *Faith Is a Song: The Odyssey of an American Artist* (New York: David McKay, 1951), 19.

85. Dragonette, *Faith Is a Song*, 105, 172–83; Dunning, *Tune In Yesterday*, 135; Amy Henderson, *On the Air: Pioneers of American Broadcasting* (Washington, D.C.: Smithsonian Institution Press, 1988), 117–18.

86. J. Fred McDonald, *Don't Touch That Dial: Radio Programming in American Life, 1920 to 1960* (Chicago: Nelson-Hall, 1979), 28; Dunning, *Tune In Yesterday*, 527–28; Frank Buxton and Bill Owen, *The Big Broadcast, 1920–1950* (New York: Viking, 1972), 264.

87. Roland Marchand, *Advertising the American Dream: Making Way for Modernity, 1920–1940* (Berkeley: University of California Press, 1985), 168.

88. Dale Howard Ross, "The 'Amos 'n' Andy' Radio Program, 1928–1937: Its History, Content, and Social Significance" (Ph.D. diss., University of Iowa, 1974), 67. See also Wertheim, *Radio Comedy*, 35–36.

89. For a discussion of the program's supposed popularity with black listeners, see H. P. W. Dixon, "Amos 'n' Andy," *Radio News* 11 (April 1930): 951. For more on the protests, see McDonald, *Don't Touch That Dial*, 27, 341–43; Arnold Shankman, "Black Pride and Protest: The Amos 'n' Andy Crusade," *Journal of Popular Culture* 12 (Fall 1978): 236–52; Ross, "The 'Amos 'n' Andy' Radio Program," 243–69.

90. Ross, "The 'Amos 'n' Andy' Radio Program," 105. See also McDonald, *Don't Touch That Dial*, 342.

91. Gertrude Berg with Cherney Berg, *Molly and Me: The Memoirs of Gertrude Berg* (New York: McGraw-Hill, 1961), 174–94.

92. "A Brief Study of the Appeal and Popularity of 'The Goldbergs,'" 25 July 1932, Box 13, Folder 58, NBC Papers.

93. W. W. Templin to Niles Trammell, 9 March 1932, Box 13, Folder 58, NBC Papers.

94. "A Brief Study of the Appeal and Popularity of 'The Goldbergs,'" NBC Papers.

95. "Daniel Starch, Ad Analyzer, at 95," *New York Times*, 10 February 1979; Ann Evory, ed., *Contemporary Authors* (Detroit: Gale Research, 1979), 519.

96. Daniel Starch, "A Study of Radio Broadcasting," 1928, Box 8, Folder 4, James Papers.

97. Daniel Starch, "Revised Study of Radio Broadcasting," 1930, p. 31, Divi-

sion of Electricity, National Museum of American History, Smithsonian Institution, Washington, D.C.

98. Carroll Carroll, *None of Your Business: Or My Life with J. Walter Thompson (Confessions of a Renegade Radio Writer)* (New York: Cowles Book Company, 1970), ix.

99. Talk by E. P. H. James, 16 February 1933, 1, Box 5, Folder 4, James Papers.

100. Ibid.

101. Carroll, *None of Your Business*, x.

102. McDonald, *Don't Touch That Dial*, 40.

103. Dunning, *Tune In Yesterday*, 178–79; Eddie Cantor with Jane Kesner Ardmore, *Take My Life* (New York: Doubleday, 1957), passim.

104. Cantor, *Take My Life*, 31–32.

105. DiMeglio, "Radio's Debt to Vaudeville," 232.

106. McLean, *American Vaudeville as Ritual*, 106–37.

107. Carroll, *None of Your Business*, 278; McDonald, *Don't Touch That Dial*, 118–20. For a description of working in radio joke factories, see Arnold Auerbach, *Funny Men Don't Laugh* (Garden City, N.Y.: Doubleday, 1965). For a fictional account of the same experience, see Herman Wouk, *Inside, Outside* (Boston: Little, Brown & Company, 1985).

108. McLean, *American Vaudeville as Ritual*, 118. Irving Howe contends that Jewish immigrant comedians were especially drawn to vulgarity; see Irving Howe, *World of Our Fathers* (New York: Harcourt, Brace, Jovanovich, 1976), 558. A different view of Jewish humor can be found in Paul Buhle, "The Significance of Yiddish Socialism," in Paul Buhle, ed., *Popular Culture in America* (Minneapolis: University of Minnesota Press, 1987), 38–45.

109. John Royal to Bertha Brainard, 12 December 1932, Box 7, Folder 6, NBC Papers.

110. John Royal to Bertha Brainard, 31 May 1933, Box 7, Folder 6, NBC Papers.

111. Cantor, *Take My Life*, 213. For a description of Cantor's clowning for the few people in the studio and their difficulty in refraining from "prohibited laughter," see "Backstage in Broadcasting," *Radio News* 13 (January 1932): 603.

112. Cantor, *Take My Life*, 213.

113. Even Ed Wynn, who based much of his comedy on puns and crazy voices, had problems with a completely nonvisual medium. See Wertheim, *Radio Comedy*, 87–112.

114. Carroll, *None of Your Business*, 10.

115. John Karol to William Hedges, 4 June 1964, William Hedges Collection, BPL; Archibald M. Crossley, "Mr. Crossley Writes Us a Letter," *Broadcast Adver-*

tising 3 (May 1930): 6, 30; R. B. Robertson, "A.N.A. Survey Replete with Errors," *Broadcast Advertising* 3 (April 1930): 5, 38.

116. A. W. Lehman, "Introduction," *Ten Years of Program Analysis* (New York: Cooperative Analysis of Broadcasting, 1939).

117. Crossley, Inc., "The Invisible Audience: First Comprehensive Four-Month Report of a Nation-Wide Recording of National Advertisers," n.d., BPL.

118. Crossley, Inc., *Cooperative Analysis of Broadcasting: Second Year—Seasonal Report, July to October Inclusive* (New York: Association of National Advertisers, 1932); idem, *Cooperative Analysis of Broadcasting: Third Year Report, March 1932–February 1933* (New York: Association of National Advertisers, 1933); idem, *Cooperative Analysis of Broadcasting: Third Year Program Report #25, For Period Ending 25 March 1932* (New York: Association of National Advertisers, 1932); idem, *Cooperative Analysis of Broadcasting: Third Year, Station Area Studies* (New York: Association of National Advertisers, n.d.), BPL.

119. Crossley, Inc., *Cooperative Analysis of Broadcasting: Second Year,* 16.

120. E. P. H. James, "Measuring Broadcast Audiences," 28 October 1964, William Hedges Collection, BPL.

121. Biel, "The Making and Use of Recordings in Broadcasting before 1936," 15, 32, 228–33; Rosen, *The Modern Stentors,* 38; T. S. McClary, "Electrical Transcription for Broadcast Purposes," *Radio News* 13 (January 1932): 564.

122. Herman S. Hettinger, *A Decade of Radio Advertising* (Chicago: University of Chicago Press, 1933), 45. See also J. R. Poppele, "Some Practical Facts about Transcriptions," *Broadcasting* (15 October 1932): 7; E. C. Rayner, "Using the 'Wax Chain' in Broadcasting," *Broadcast Advertising* 1 (May 1929): 8–9.

123. Barry Golden, "Some Views on Electrical Transcription," *Broadcasting* (1 September 1932): 7; M. A. Hollinshead, "Electrical Transcription," in Neville O'Neil, ed., *The Advertising Agency Looks at Radio* (New York: D. Appleton and Company, 1932), 108–21; J. R. Spadea, "A Defense of Transcriptions," *Broadcast Advertising* 3 (January 1931): 9, 48; Jarvis Wren, "Recorded Programs vs. Networks," *Advertising and Selling* 15 (11 June 1930): 27, 74; M. A. Hollinshead, "Recordings: Their Place in Broadcasting," *Broadcast Advertising* 4 (July 1931): 24; Preston H. Pumphrey, "Spot versus Chain Broadcasting," in O'Neil, *The Advertising Agency Looks at Radio,* 127–30.

124. "Making Pep and Sparkle Typify a Ginger Ale," 6. See also "Harry Reser Recalls," undated newspaper article, BPL; Thomas A. Delong, *The Mighty Music Box: The Golden Age of Musical Radio* (Los Angeles: Amber Crest Books, 1980), 49–50; Myers to Witmer, 10 July 1933, Box 16, Folder 58, NBC Papers; Myers to Witmer, 13 October 1932, Box 8, Folder 9, NBC Papers.

125. McClary, "Electrical Transcriptions for Broadcast Purposes," 564–55, 619–20; Richard Patterson to David Sarnoff, 27 September 1933, Box 21, Folder

49, NBC Papers; Richard Patterson to David Sarnoff, 4 October 1933, Box 21, Folder 49, NBC Papers.

126. On the announcement, see "For the Record: A Brief Historical Note on the Mechanical Reproduction Announcement Requirement," *Journal of Broadcasting* 4 (Spring 1960): 119–22; Hettinger, *A Decade of Radio Advertising*, 155–56. On possible audience reaction, see Wren, "Recorded Programs vs. Networks," 27; Hollinshead, "Electrical Transcriptions," 109.

CHAPTER 5. DRUNK AND DISORDERLY: THE BACKLASH AGAINST BROADCAST ADVERTISING

1. James Rorty, *Order on the Air* (New York: John Day, 1934), 7.

2. Susan Douglas, "Amateur Operators and American Broadcasting: Shaping the Future of Radio," in Joseph Corn, ed., *Imagining Tomorrow: History, Technology and the American Future* (Cambridge, Mass.: MIT Press, 1986), 35.

3. Clayton R. Koppes, "The Social Destiny of Radio: Hope and Disillusionment in the 1920s," *South Atlantic Quarterly* 68 (Summer 1969): 364.

4. *For a Genuine Radio University* (Los Angeles: Pacific Western Broadcasting Federation, 1930), 1, Warshaw Collection of Business Americana, Archives Center, National Museum of American History, Smithsonian Institution, Washington, D.C.

' 5. On the Truth in Advertising movement, see Daniel Pope, *The Making of Modern Advertising* (New York: Basic Books, 1983), 202–26. On the 1920s efforts at reforming advertising, see Otis Pease, *The Responsibilities of Modern Advertising: Private Control and Public Influence, 1920–1940* (New Haven, Conn.: Yale University Press, 1958), 44–115. On the uneasy alliance between consumers and the New Deal, see Ellis W. Hawley, *The New Deal and the Problem of Monopoly* (Princeton, N.J.: Princeton University Press, 1966), 76–79, 198–204. On the 1930s consumer movement, see Roland Marchand, *Advertising the American Dream: Making Way for Modernity, 1920–1940* (Berkeley: University of California Press, 1985), 312–15, as well as Stuart Chase and F. J. Schlink, *Your Money's Worth: A Study in the Waste of the Consumer's Dollar* (New York: Macmillan, 1927) and Arthur Kallet and F. J. Schlink, *100,000,000 Guinea Pigs: Dangers in Everyday Foods, Drugs, and Cosmetics* (New York: Grosset and Dunlap, 1933).

6. Gerald Carson, *The Roguish World of Dr. Brinkley* (New York: Rinehart and Company, 1960), 146; see also 87–105, 142–53.

7. Erik Barnouw, *A Tower in Babel: A History of Broadcasting in the United States to 1933* (New York: Oxford University Press, 1966), 168. On W. K. Henderson,

see Joseph Pusateri, *Enterprise in Radio: WWL and the Business of Broadcasting in America* (Washington, D.C.: University Press of America, 1980), 65–78.

8. Fourth National Radio Conference, *Proceedings of the Fourth National Radio Conference and Recommendations for Regulation of Radio* (Washington, D.C.: Government Printing Office, 1925), 18.

9. John Wallace, "The Listeners' Point of View: Communication," *Radio Broadcast* 9 (May 1926): 39. See also Stuart Chase, "An Inquiry into Radio," *Outlook* 148 (18 April 1928): 617.

10. Jack Woodford, "Radio: A Blessing or a Curse?" *Forum* 8 (March 1929): 169.

11. Bruce Bliven, "How Radio Is Remaking Our World," *Century* 108 (July 1924): 149. See also James C. Young, "How Will You Have Your Advertising?" *Radio Broadcast* 6 (December 1924): 245.

12. "So This Is Advertising!" *Radio Broadcast* 7 (May 1925): 83.

13. Federal Radio Commission, *Commercial Radio Broadcasting: Report of the FRC in Reply to Senate Resolution 129*, 72d Cong., 1st sess. (Washington, D.C.: Government Printing Office, 1932), 14.

14. Philip Rosen, *The Modern Stentors: Radio Broadcasters and the Federal Government, 1920–1934* (Westport, Conn.: Greenwood Press, 1980), 110–12; Lawrence F. Schmeckebier, *The Federal Radio Commission: Its History, Activities, and Organization* (Washington, D.C.: Brookings Institution, 1932).

15. Public Law No. 195, 70th Cong., 28 March 1928. For contemporaneous accounts of the allocation process see J. M. Herring, "Equalization of Broadcasting Facilities within the United States," *Harvard Business Review* 9 (July 1931): 417–29; "Davis Amendment Criticized," *Air Law Review* 1 (January 1930): 117–20; Edgar Felix, "Federal Radio Commission: Equalization of Broadcasting Facilities among Zones," *Air Law Review* 2 (April 1931): 260–62.

16. James Rorty, "Free Air: A Strictly Imaginary Educational Broadcast," *The Nation* 134 (9 March 1932): 281.

17. B. B. Brackett to T. M. Beaird, 15 December 1931, General Correspondence, National Association of Educational Broadcasters Papers (hereafter cited as NAEB Papers), Mass Communications History Center, Wisconsin State Historical Society, Madison. See also Rosen, *Modern Stentors*, 168–69; Barnouw, *A Tower in Babel*, 218; B. B. Brackett to Armstrong Perry, 13 January 1933, NAEB Papers.

18. J. C. Jensen to B. B. Brackett, 16 May 1930, NAEB Papers.

19. S. E. Frost, Jr., *Education's Own Stations* (Chicago: University of Chicago Press, 1937), 4–5.

20. B. B. Brackett to Armstrong Perry, 27 April 1931, NAEB Papers. See also B. B. Brackett to Armstrong Perry, 13 January 1933, NAEB Papers.

21. "Commercial Broadcasters To Intensify Lobby," *Education by Radio* 2 (10 March 1932): 38.

22. J. C. Jensen to Wallace White, 5 April 1927, Wallace White Papers (hereafter cited as White Papers), Library of Congress, Washington, D.C.

23. "An Appraisal of Radio Advertising Today," *Fortune* 6 (September 1932): 27. See also "Radio Advertising Headed for $150 Millions in 1931," *Business Week* (12 August 1931): 10.

24. Pusateri, *Enterprise in Radio*, 128.

25. Rosen, *Modern Stentors*, 168.

26. Carl Joachim Friedrich and Jeannette Sayre, *The Development and Control of Advertising on the Air* (Cambridge, Mass.: Harvard University Press, 1940), 16–22.

27. James Rorty, "The Impending Radio War," *Harper's* 163 (November 1932): 714, 723.

28. Frank Hill, *Tune in for Education: Eleven Years of Education by Radio* (New York: National Committee for Education by Radio, 1942), 22; James Rorty, *Our Master's Voice: Advertising* (New York: John Day, 1934), 271.

29. Charles Culver and J. C. Jensen to Wallace White, 5 May 1926, White Papers.

30. Evan Carroon, "Financial Report for 1929," March 1930, NAEB Papers.

31. B. B. Brackett to R. C. Higgy, 29 May 1930, NAEB Papers. See also B. B. Brackett to E. E. Ross, 29 June 1933, 25 February 1932, and 29 June 1933, NAEB Papers.

32. Charles Culver to Wallace White, 5 May 1926 and 17 May 1926, White Papers.

33. Charles Culver to Wallace White, 19 May 1926, White Papers; J. C. Jensen to Wallace White, 21 March 1927 and 5 April 1927, White Papers.

34. T. M. Baird to H. J. Baldwin, 1 February 1934; B. B. Brackett to I. D. Weeks, 9 February 1933; C. C. Dill to B. B. Brackett, 13 February 1933; Joseph F. Wright to B. B. Brackett, 13 February 1933; A. M. Harding to B. B. Brackett, 18 March 1930; Carl Menzer to Harold G. Ingham, 22 August 1934. All with NAEB Papers.

35. Hill, *Tune in for Education*, 21–22.

36. Ibid., 52.

37. "National Committee on Education by Radio," *Education by Radio* 1 (25 June 1931): 80; "Child's Reaction to Movies Shown: Youthful Emotions More Stirred Than Adults' Payne Fund Study Reveals," *New York Times*, 25 May 1933, section 4, p. 7.

38. Tracy F. Tyler, *An Appraisal of Radio Broadcasting in the Land-Grant Colleges and State Universities* (Washington, D.C.: National Committee on Education by Radio, 1933).

39. Tracy F. Tyler, *Radio as a Cultural Agency: Proceedings of a National Conference on the Use of Radio as a Cultural Agency in a Democracy* (Washington, D.C.: National Committee on Education by Radio, 1934).

40. Hill, *Tune in for Education*, 13–14.

41. Armstrong Perry, *Radio in Education: The Ohio School of the Air and Other Experiments* (New York: Payne Fund, 1929), 13, 18; Joy Elmer Morgan, "Radio in Education," in Martin Codel, ed., *Radio and Its Future* (New York: Harper and Brothers, 1930), 78. For a similar experiment in New York, see Fred Siegel, "Teaching School by Radio," *Popular Radio* 5 (February 1924): 146–51.

42. *For a Genuine Radio University*, 26–27, 49–55, 58. For another view of the possibilities of using radio in education, see Percy Mackaye, "The University of the Ether," *Popular Radio* 5 (January 1924): 37–40.

43. On the "practical solution," see F. H. Lumley, "Introduction," *Education on the Air: Fifth Yearbook of the Institute for Education by Radio* (Columbus: Ohio State University, 1934), vii–viii. On the connection between the institute and the Ohio school system, see B. H. Darrow, "The Purpose of the Ohio School of the Air," in *Education on the Air: First Yearbook of the Institute for Education by Radio* (Columbus: Ohio State University, 1930), 197–203; R. C. Higgy, "Educational Broadcasting from Ohio State University," in *Education on the Air: First Yearbook of the Institute for Education by Radio* (Columbus: Ohio State University, 1930), 257–58.

44. Jerome Kerwin, *The Control of Radio* (Chicago: University of Chicago Press, 1934), 20–23.

45. Ibid., 24.

46. Ibid., 26–27.

47. For "education must come from above," see Kerwin, *The Control of Radio*, 11. For "all the evidence is not in," see ibid., 24. For the futility of complaints, see ibid., 25.

48. "James Rorty, 82, A Radical Editor," *New York Times*, 26 February 1973, 34.

49. Daniel Pope, "His Master's Voice: James Rorty and the Critique of Advertising," *Maryland Historian* 19 (Spring/Summer 1988): 12.

50. Rorty, *Our Master's Voice*, 266–67.

51. Rorty, "The Impending Radio War," 714–15.

52. Rorty, "Free Air," 282; Rorty, *Order on the Air*, 28–30.

53. On NCER, see Rorty, *Our Master's Voice*, 273; on publishers, see Rorty, *Our Master's Voice*, 267.

54. Giraud Chester, "The Press-Radio War: 1933–1935," *Public Opinion Quarterly* 13 (Summer 1949): 257; George E. Lott, Jr., "The Press-Radio War of the 1930s," *Journal of Broadcasting* 14 (Summer 1970): 275; Paul White, *News on the Air* (New York: Harcourt, Brace and Company, 1947), 30–49; A. A. Shecter with Edward Anthony, *I Live on the Air* (New York: Frederick A. Stokes, 1941), 1–16; "Broadcasters and Newspapers Make Peace," *Newsweek* 2 (23 December 1933): 18; "Controversy between Radio and Press," *Literary Digest* (29 September 1934): 5.

55. For a look at one aspect of radio news in the 1930s, see David Culbert,

News for Everyman: Radio and Foreign Affairs in Thirties America (Westport, Conn.: Greenwood Press, 1976).

56. "Free Press Radio Campaign Backed by 726 Newspapers," undated newspaper clipping, Box 4, NBC Papers.

57. H. O. Davis, *The Empire of the Air* (Ventura, Calif.: Ventura Free Press, 1932), 91–92. See also 90–106.

58. H. O. Davis to Charles A. Webb, 5 January 1932, Folder 5, Box 15, NBC Papers.

59. H. O. Davis to H. L. Williamson, 25 September 1931, Box 4, NBC Papers.

60. H. O. Davis to Gene Huse, 8 August 1931, Folder 5, Box 15, NBC Papers.

61. H. O. Davis to "Publisher," 1 December 1931, Folder 5, Box 15, NBC Papers.

62. On his suggestions to publishers, see H. O. Davis, "The Radio Advertising Problem: Suggestions for the Conduct of Local Campaigns by Individual Publishers," 2 November 1931, Box 4, NBC Papers. On coordinating educators and publishers, see H. O. Davis to Thomas F. Clark, 21 January 1932, Folder 5, Box 15, NBC Papers.

63. H. O. Davis to Gene Huse, 8 August 1931, Folder 5, Box 5; H. O. Davis to L. Lea, 8 August 1931, Box 4; H. O. Davis to A. R. Williamson, 21 October 1931, Box 4; H. O. Davis to "Editor," 11 December 1931, Box 4; H. O. Davis to "Editor," 24 December 1931, Box 4. All with NBC Papers.

64. Lloyd Yoder to Don Gilman, "Your letter of introduction to Walter Woehlke," 30 September 1931, Box 4; Don Gilman to M. H. Aylesworth, "Walter Woehlke–Ventura Free Press," 1 October 1931, Box 4; David Sarnoff to M. H. Aylesworth, 21 October 1931, Box 4; Glenn Tucker "Confidential Memorandum," 20 October 1931, Box 4; M. H. Aylesworth to David Sarnoff, 23 October 1931, Box 4; Gene Huse to J. B. Maylard, 1 February 1932, Box 4; J. B. Maylard to Gene Huse, 19 February 1932, Folder 5, Box 15; Gene Huse to Frank Mason, 23 February 1932, Folder 5, Box 15. All with NBC Papers.

65. Owen D. Young, Statement, "The First Meeting of the Advisory Council of the National Broadcasting Company," 1927, Broadcast Pioneers Library (hereafter cited as BPL), Washington, D.C.

66. Report of the Chairman, Committee on Education, "Committee Reports, Advisory Council of the National Broadcasting Company," Fourth Meeting, 1930, 27–31; Report for the Committee on Education, "Committee Reports, Advisory Council of the National Broadcasting Company," Sixth Meeting, 16 February 1932, 23–30; Report of the Chairman, Committee on Education, "Committee Reports, Advisory Council of the National Broadcasting Company," Seventh Meeting, February 1933, 34–39. All with BPL.

67. Herman S. Hettinger, *A Decade of Radio Advertising* (Chicago: University of

Chicago Press, 1933), 291. On CBS and for a network view in general, see Stanley Kaufman, "Radio and Its Present Relation to Education," *Radio News* 15 (November 1933): 265–66, 312.

68. Report of the Chairman, Committee on Education, "Committee Reports, Advisory Council of the National Broadcasting Company," Fifth Meeting, 1931, 23, BPL.

69. Ibid.

70. "NACRE Devotes Session to Advertising on Air," *Broadcast Advertising* 5 (June 1932): 28–29; Rosen, *The Modern Stentors*, 166. See also Report for the Committee on Education, "Committee Reports, Advisory Council of the National Broadcasting Company," Sixth Meeting, 16 February 1932, 24–25, BPL; Report of the Chairman, Committee on Education, "Committee Reports, Advisory Council of the National Broadcasting Company," Seventh Meeting, February 1933, 35–36, BPL; "Dr. Nicholas Murray Butler Heads New Educational Series," *Radio Digest* 27 (November 1931): 19.

71. Henry Adams Bellows, "Commercial Broadcasting and Education," NACRE press release, 22 May 1931, Box 4, Folder 49, NBC Papers; "NACRE Assembly," *National Association of Broadcasters News Bulletin*, 9 April 1932, BPL; "Proposes National Radio Institute," *National Association of Broadcasters Reports* 1 (27 May 1933): 54, BPL.

72. Bellows, "Commercial Broadcasting and Education," 3.

73. "NACRE Devotes Session to Advertising on the Air," *Broadcast Advertising* 5 (June 1932): 129. See also Merle S. Cummings, "The Schoolmaster's Radio Voice," *Radio News* 13 (September 1931): 194–95, 240–41.

74. "Second Annual Assembly NACRE Closes," *National Association of Broadcasters News Bulletin*, 21 May 1932, BPL; Bellows, "Commercial Broadcasting and Education"; "NACRE Devotes Session to Advertising on the Air," *Broadcast Advertising*.

75. Rorty, "Free Air," 281.

76. Kerwin, *The Control of Radio*, 25.

77. B. B. Brackett to W. H. Bateson, 6 November 1931, NAEB Papers. See also B. B. Brackett to T. M. Beaird, 2 February 1932, NAEB Papers.

78. William Hedges, "Broadcast Education Should Be Commercially Sponsored," *Broadcast Advertising* 3 (September 1930): 33–34; "Debate Handbook Soon Ready," *NAB Reports* 1 (25 November 1933): 229, BPL.

79. Friedrich and Sayre, *The Development and Control of Advertising*, 8–9. See also "Commission Warns Broadcasters to Eliminate Offensive Advertising," *Broadcast Advertising* 4 (January 1932): 18, 20; David R. Mackey, "The National Association of Broadcasters: Its First 20 Years," vol. 1, 104–20, unpublished manuscript, BPL.

80. For example, "The Empire of the Air," *National Association of Broadcasters*

News Bulletin, 16 January 1932, BPL; "The Campaign Goes On," *National Association of Broadcasters News Bulletin*, 14 May 1932, BPL.

81. David R. Mackey, "The Development of the National Association of Broadcasters," *Journal of Broadcasting* 1 (Fall 1957): 321.

82. William S. Paley, *Radio as a Cultural Force* (New York: Columbia Broadcasting System, 1934), 1. See also 5, 9, and 17.

83. Radio Act of 1912, Public Law 64, 62d Cong., 13 August 1912.

84. *Congressional Record*, 70th Cong., 2d sess., 1 March 1929, 4865.

85. H. Rept. 1886, 69th Cong., 1st sess., 27 January 1927; S. Doc. 200, 69th Cong., 1st sess., 31 January 1927.

86. Lawrence Lichty, "The Impact of FRC and FCC Commissioners' Backgrounds on the Regulation of Broadcasting," *Journal of Broadcasting* 6 (Spring 1962): 99.

87. Act of 28 March 1928, Statute Law 373.

88. *Congressional Record*, 70th Cong., 1st sess., 10 March 1928, 4488–89; see also 3373–74, 4486–4500, 4508–9, 4562–90, 5155–75.

89. H. Rept. 2106, 72d Cong., 2d sess., 25 February 1933.

90. S. Rept. 1045, 72d Cong., 2d sess., 11 January 1933.

91. Schmeckebier, *The Federal Radio Commission*, 47ff.

92. "Broadcasting Is Subject of Senatorial Investigation," *Broadcast Advertising* 4 (February 1932): 160.

93. "Commission Warns Broadcasters To Eliminate Offensive Advertising," *Broadcast Advertising* 4 (January 1932): 18.

94. S. Res. 129, 72d Cong., 1st sess., 12 January 1932.

95. *Congressional Record*, 72d Cong., 1st sess., 12 January 1932, 37.

96. Report of the President of the National Broadcasting Company, "Reports of the Advisory Council of the National Broadcasting Company," Sixth Meeting, 16 February 1932, 15, BPL.

97. "Investigation Begins," *National Association of Broadcasters News Bulletin*, 16 January 1932, BPL.

98. "Broadcasting Is Subject of Senatorial Investigation," 18.

99. "Commercial Broadcasters To Intensify Lobby," *Education by Radio* 2 (10 March 1932): 38.

100. Paul F. Peter to Donald Withycomb, "FRC Questionnaire to All Stations," 20 January 1932, Folder 82, Box 9, NBC Papers; Paul F. Peter to Howard Milholland, "Program Bulletin to Stations: Federal Radio Commission's Questionnaire," 21 January 1932, Folder 82, Box 9, NBC Papers.

101. "Commercial Broadcasters To Intensify Lobby," 38.

102. Joseph Wright to B. B. Brackett, 29 November 1932, NAEB Papers; "To Members of the Association of College and University Broadcasting Stations," 1 March 1932, NAEB Papers.

103. S. Res. 270, 72d Cong., 1st sess., 1 June 1932.

104. "Broadcasting Is Subject of Senatorial Investigation," 16; Federal Radio Commission, *Commercial Radio Broadcasting: Report of the FRC in reply to Senate Resolution 129, Seventy-Second Congress, First Session,* (Washington, D.C.: Government Printing Office, 1932), 38–39.

105. FRC, *Commercial Radio Broadcasting,* 33.

106. Ibid., 14.

107. Ibid., 36–37.

108. Ibid., 37.

109. H.R. 12845, 72d Cong., 1st sess., 8 June 1932; "Bill To Fix Advertising Rates," *National Association of Broadcasters News Bulletin,* 2 July 1932, BPL; H.R. 8759, 72d Cong., 1st sess., 2 February 1932.

110. *Congressional Record,* 71st Cong., 3d sess., 17 February 1931, H.R. 11635, 5205–6.

111. *Congressional Record,* 72d Cong., 1st sess., 8 January 1932, H.R. 7253, 1555; *Congressional Record,* 72d Cong., 1st sess., 15 January 1932, S. 3047, 1997; "Labor Seeks a Clear Channel," *Education by Radio* 2 (April 1932): 57–60; "Labor Fighting for Channel," *National Association of Broadcasters News Bulletin,* 19 March 1932, BPL.

112. *Congressional Record,* 72d Cong., 1st sess., 25 January 1932, 2598.

113. John H. MacCracken, "The Fess Bill for Education by Radio," *Education by Radio* 1 (19 March 1931): 21–22; *Congressional Record,* 71st Cong., 3d sess., S. 5589, 8 January 1931, 1614; Rosen, *Modern Stentors,* 170; Rorty, "Free Air," 280–83; Bernard Schwartz, *The Economic Regulation of Business and Industry: A Legislative History of U.S. Regulatory Agencies,* vol. 4 (New York: Chelsea House, 1973), 2464.

114. "Broadcasting from the Editor's Chair," *Radio Digest* 27 (September 1931): 54; "Lawyers Attack Wave Grab! Standing Committee of Bar Association Vigorously Assails Fess Bill and Calls Attention to Menace in Setting Aside Channels for Special Interests," *Radio Digest* 27 (September 1931): 19–21, 96; H. A. Bellows, "Chaos," *Radio Digest* 27 (November 1931): 18, 95.

115. Sol Taishoff, "Powerful Lobby Threatens Radio Structure," *Broadcasting* 6 (15 May 1934): 5; Pusateri, *Enterprise in Radio,* 167–69; R. Franklin Smith, "A Look at the Wagner-Hatfield Amendment," in Harry Skornia and Jack William Kitson, eds., *Problems and Controversies in Television and Radio* (Palo Alto, Calif.: Pacific Books, 1968), 171; Robert McChesney, "Crusade against Mammon: Father Harney and the Debate over Radio in the 1930s" *Journalism History* 14 (Winter 1987): 118–30.

116. Rosen, *Modern Stentors,* 168.

117. For the bill that Hoover vetoed, see H.R. 7716, 72d Cong., 2d sess., 1 March 1933, 5397. On Hoover's role in radio regulation, see Edward F. Sarno,

Jr., "The National Radio Conferences," *Journal of Broadcasting* 13 (Spring 1969): 189–202; C. M. Jansky, "The Contribution of Herbert Hoover to Broadcasting," *Journal of Broadcasting* 1 (Summer 1957): 241–49.

118. Arthur Schlesinger, *The Coming of the New Deal* (Boston: Houghton Mifflin, 1958), 558–59. For a view of Roosevelt that portrays him as a more active participant in the passage of the Communications Act, see Robert McChesney, "Franklin Roosevelt: His Administration and the Communications Act of 1934," *American Journalism* 5 (1988): 204–29.

119. For Roosevelt's call for a new communications bill, see S. Doc. 144, 73d Cong., 2d sess., 26 February 1934. For early debate on a combined communications commission, see *Congressional Record*, 70th Cong., 2d sess., 1 March 1929, 4859. For surprise over the easy passage of the Communications Act of 1934, see Schwartz, *Economic Regulation*, 2373–76.

120. Communications Act of 1934, Public Law 416, 73d Cong., 19 June 1934, section 1.

121. Radio Act of 1927, Public Law 632, 69th Cong., 23 February 1927, section 9; Communications Act of 1934, section 303f. See also "Administrative Control of Radio," *Harvard Law Review* 49 (June 1936): 1333; Keith Masters, "The Present Status of Radio Law: A Survey," *John Marshall Law Review* 1 (1936): 211; P. M. Segal and Harry P. Warner, "Ownership of the Broadcasting Frequencies: A Review," *Rocky Mountain Law Review* 19 (February 1947): 111–22.

122. Schwartz, *Economic Regulation*, 2429.

123. Communications Act of 1934, sections 311, 313, 314.

124. Ibid., sections 302, 307.

125. Schwartz, *Economic Regulation*, 2488.

126. Erik Barnouw, *The Golden Web: A History of Broadcasting in the United States* (New York: Oxford University Press, 1968), 26.

127. Smith, "A Look at the Wagner-Hatfield Amendment," 176.

128. Barnouw, *The Golden Web*, 25–28.

129. "Supplementary statement by the National Association of Broadcasters regarding the amendment to H.R. 8301, to the Committee on Interstate and Foreign Commerce of the United States House of Representatives," Box 4, William Hedges Papers, Mass Communications History Center, Wisconsin State Historical Society, Madison.

130. Schwartz, *Economic Regulation*, 2504.

131. Communications Act of 1934, sections 302, 307.

132. Communications Act of 1934, section 315.

133. Hawley, *The New Deal and the Problem of Monopoly*, passim.

CONCLUSION

1. John Cheever, "The Enormous Radio," in *The Stories of John Cheever* (New York: Knopf, 1978), 41.

2. Frederic Wakeman, *The Hucksters* (New York: Rinehart and Company, 1946); Herman Wouk, *Inside, Outside* (Boston: Little, Brown & Company, 1985).

3. R. LeRoy Bannerman, *Norman Corwin and Radio: The Golden Years* (Tuscaloosa: University of Alabama Press, 1986).

4. Historian David Culbert contends that between 1938 and the attack on Pearl Harbor, "radio emerged as the principal medium for combating isolationism in America" and that "radio commentators played a major role in creating a climate of opinion favorable to an interventionist foreign policy though they did not directly make foreign policy." David Culbert, *News for Everyman: Radio and Foreign Affairs in Thirties America* (Westport, Conn.: Greenwood Press, 1976), 5–6.

5. Holly Cowan Shulman, *The Voice of America: Propaganda and Democracy, 1941–1945* (Madison: University of Wisconsin Press, 1990).

6. Samuel Brylawski, "Armed Forces Radio Service: The Invisible Highway Abroad," in Iris Newsom, ed., *Wonderful Inventions: Motion Pictures, Broadcasting and Recorded Sound at the Library of Congress* (Washington, D.C.: Library of Congress, 1985), 333–44.

7. Ibid., 335.

8. Alan Havig, "Frederic Wakeman's *The Hucksters* and the Postwar Debate over Commercial Radio," *Journal of Broadcasting* 28 (Spring 1984): 187–99.

9. Relying on specialized programming, radio "escaped direct competition with television and found it could profit without the evening audiences." Peter Fornatale and Joshua E. Mills, *Radio in the Television Age* (Woodstock, N.Y.: Overlook Press, 1980), 16–17.

10. Fornatale and Mills note that "the transistor . . . became a major weapon in radio's struggle against television." Fornatale and Mills, *Radio in the Television Age*, 18.

11. David Marc, *Demographic Vistas* (Philadelphia: University of Pennsylvania Press, 1988).

12. Ken Barnes, "Top 40 Radio: A Fragment of the Imagination," in Simon Frith, ed., *Facing the Music* (New York: Pantheon, 1988), 8–30.

13. J. Fred MacDonald *One Nation under Television: The Rise and Decline of Network TV* (New York: Pantheon, 1990), 52.

14. Erik Barnouw, *The Sponsor: Notes on a Modern Potentate* (New York: Oxford University Press, 1978), 41–58; MacDonald, *One Nation under Television*, 141–46.

15. MacDonald, *One Nation under Television*, 200.

16. Ibid., 201; Barnouw, *The Sponsor,* 68–73.

17. For an overview of the new video technologies, see William J. Donnelly, *The Confetti Generation: How the New Communications Technology Is Fragmenting America* (New York: Henry Holt, 1986), 77–172.

18. Ken Auletta, *Three Blind Mice: How the TV Networks Lost Their Way* (New York: Vintage Books, 1992), 461.

19. Most historians of broadcasting have written that radio, despite a few dissenting voices, became commercialized just after the establishment of the networks because advertising provided a solution to broadcasting's problems. For an example of this interpretation, see John W. Spalding, "1928: Radio Becomes a Mass Advertising Medium," *Journal of Broadcasting* 8 (1963–64): 31–44.

20. Warren Susman, "Communication and Culture: Keynote Essay," in Catherine L. Covert and John D. Stevens, eds., *Mass Media between the Wars: Perceptions of Cultural Tension, 1918–1941* (Syracuse, N.Y.: Syracuse University Press, 1984), xviii, xx–xxi. On "progress talk," see John Staudenmaier, S.J., *Technology's Storytellers: Reweaving the Human Fabric* (Cambridge, Mass.: MIT Press, 1985), chap. 5.

21. Michael Schudson, *Advertising, the Uneasy Persuasion: Its Dubious Impact on American Society* (New York: Basic Books, 1984), 164.

22. R. Franklin Smith, "A Look at the Wagner-Hatfield Amendment," in Harry Skornia and Jack William Kitson, eds., *Problems and Controversies in Television and Radio* (Palo Alto, Calif.: Pacific Books, 1968), 176, 178.

INDEX

A & P Gypsies, 97, 102, 103, 117, 128
Action for Children's Television, 10
advertising: history of, 5; indirect, 70–71,
    74, 76, 79, 99, 106, 117, 128–29, 166; of
    radio receivers, 15, 102; restrictions on,
    102, 147; and spot advertisements, 90–91,
    129; on television, 2, 3, 9, 163
—on radio: agency participation in, 81–86,
    118–19, 156; campaign for, 72–81; code
    of ethics for, 141; and consumerism, 78,
    87, 92; development of, 41, 59, 63,
    65–92; distrust of, 2–3, 8, 68; fees for,
    147; as inevitable, 4, 165; nonprofit alter-
    natives to, 4, 8, 126, 130–31, 132, 148; op-
    position to, 10, 63, 68–71, 73, 125–53,
    158–59, 167; purpose of, 2, 9, 62; spon-
    sors of, 2–3, 98–111
Advertising and Selling, 74
agricultural commodity prices, 20–21, 67
Alexanderson alternator, 43

Allen, Fred, 119
Allen, Gracie, 113, 119
Allen, Ida Bailey, 89, 90
Allen, Woody, 162
amateur radio operators. *See* ham radio
American Association of Advertising Agen-
    cies, 75, 116, 146
American Broadcasting Company (ABC),
    158
American Medical Association, 128
American Newspaper Publishers Associa-
    tion (ANPA), 137
American Radio Association (ARA), 69
American Radio Relay League (ARRL), 13
"American School of the Air," 140
American Society of Composers, Authors,
    and Publishers (ASCAP), 40
American Telephone & Telegraph (AT&T):
    fees for wire lines, 135; radio station
    owned by, 100–102; regulation of, 35;

sales of radio time by, 63, 98; and wired
networks, 34, 42, 43, 46, 47, 50, 52–58
"Amos 'n' Andy," 91, 99, 114–15, 156
AM spectrum, 160, 162
Armed Forces Radio Service (AFRS), 156,
157–58
Arnold, Frank, 73–74, 77, 80, 87, 107
Associated Press (AP), 137
Association of College and University
Broadcasting Stations (ACUBS), 132–33,
135, 141
Association of National Advertisers (ANA)
Radio Committee, 121
audience: changes in listening habits, 18–
19, 94; constructed by advertisers, 6, 7; as
"invisible guests," 76, 77; letters to radio
stations from, 7, 96, 116; as makers of
popular culture, 6–7; market research on,
160–61; national, 20–31; on-air reactions
of, 121; in radio studio, 120–21; ratings
systems for, 9; reaction to radio performers, 109; in rural areas, 20–26; study of,
6–7, 135–36; surveys of, 7, 94, 96, 97, 99,
112, 116–17, 121–22; unresponsiveness
to, 9; and voluntary listener contributions, 65, 66, 161
audion, 13–14, 34, 53, 160
Auletta, Ken, 164
Aunt Sammy, 89, 91
Australia, radio stations in, 61
Aylesworth, Merlin, 114, 139

"Bakelite Hour," 101
Banning, William Peck, 52, 53–54
Barnouw, Erik, 66, 151
baseball, 27, 29
Beaudino, Joe, 51, 52
Bedell, Theodore, Jr., 16
Benny, Jack, 119
Berg, Gertrude, 114, 115
"Best Food Boys," 112
Better Business Bureau, 128
Bliven, Bruce, 129
Boggs, Carl, 3–4

Booth, Edwin, 30
Bourdon, Rosario, 113
boxing, 28–29
"Breyer Hour," 101
Brice, Fanny, 158
Brinkley, John R., 128
Bristol Loud Speakers, 19
British Broadcasting Corporation (BBC),
135, 158
Broadcast Advertising (magazine), 75, 77, 82,
84, 145, 146
Broun, Heywood, 109–10
"Brunswick Hour of Music," 101
Brunswick Symphony Orchestra, 101
Brylawski, Samuel, 157, 158
"Buescher Saxophone Hour," 101
Bureau of Broadcasting, 65
Burns, George, 113, 119
"Butterick Fashion Talk," 101

"Camel Caravan," 158
Canada, radio stations in, 62
Canadian Broadcasting Commission
(CBC), 62
Canadian National Railroad, 62
Canadian Radio Broadcasting Commission,
62
Cantor, Eddie, 113, 118, 119–21
Cantor, Ida, 120
Carnegie Corporation, 140
Carroll, Carroll, 117, 118, 121
Carty, John J., 53
Celler, Emmanuel, 70
censorship, 120, 152
"Charlie McCarthy," 158
Chase, Stuart, 128
"Chase and Sanborn Hour," 119, 158
Cheever, John, 154, 155, 162
Chicago: radio programming in, 18. *See also*
radio stations, individual
Chicago Federation of Labor, 148
Chicago Opera Company, 95
Christiansen, Martin "Red," 104
"Cities Service Concerts," 113

City College of New York, 74
classical music, 26, 53–54, 96–97
Clicquot Club Eskimos, 79, 97, 102, 103, 105–8, 123, 167
Collier's (magazine), 32
Columbia Broadcasting System (CBS), 63, 84, 90, 122, 131, 137, 140, 142
Columbia Phonograph Record Company, 63
"Columbia Workshop," 156
"Comedy Caravan," 158
"Command Performance," 157–58
Communications Act of 1934, 7, 8, 9, 59, 126, 127, 142, 149–51, 167
Conrad, Frank, 14, 51
consumerism: and brand-name consciousness, 80, 106; development of, 128, 131; fed by television, 1–2; goals of, 128; and radio advertising, 78, 87, 92
Cooley, Charles Horton, 32
Coolidge, Calvin, 55, 56
Cooperative Analysis of Broadcasting (CAB) project, 121–22
Corporation for Public Broadcasting (CPB), 161
Correll, Charles, 114, 115
Corwin, Norman, 156, 157
country music, 23–26, 31
Couzens, James, 145
Crocker, Betty, 89, 90
Crosby, Bing, 158
Crosley, Powel, 41, 134
Crossley, Archibald, 121
Crossley, Inc., 121–22
Curti, Merle, 79
Czitrom, Daniel, 4, 5, 31–32, 34

Damrosch, Walter, 130
Danielian, N. R., 56–57
Daniel, Pete, 25
Davis, Edwin, 60, 61, 143, 144
Davis, H. O., 137–38, 139, 142
Davis, H. P., 50
De Forest MR-6 receiving sets, 15
De Forest vacuum tubes, 53

Dewey, John, 32
Dill, Clarence, 145, 151
Dillon, T. J., 40
District of Columbia Circuit Court of Appeals, 144
Douglas, Susan, 5, 13, 127
Dragonette, Jessica, 113
Dunlap, Orrin, 74, 78, 80, 84
DX'ers (distance fiends), 15

Edison Ensemble, 112
educational programming, 20, 22, 67, 88–89, 127, 129–30, 133, 139–42, 146–47, 167. *See also* schools, radio stations owned by
Electrical Supply Jobbers Association, 45
Empire of the Air, 137
England, radio network in, 61, 77, 135
Erbstein, C. D., 46
ethnicity, 10, 30, 63, 114, 116, 120
"Eveready Hour," 97, 102, 103, 104–5

fan clubs, 9
"Fanny Brice–Frank Morgan," 158
Federal Communications Commission (FCC), 126, 142, 150–52, 160, 163, 167
Federal Radio Commission (FRC), 60, 123, 128, 130–31, 133, 142–49
Felix, Edgar, 74, 76
Fess, Simon D., 148
"50 Questions," 101
First National Radio Conference (1922), 38, 70
"Fleischmann Hour," 113–14
"Flit Soldiers," 112
Flonzaley String Quartet, 104
FM spectrum, 160, 162, 167
Folwell, A. H., 11
Food and Drug Administration (FDA), 127–28
Fortune (magazine), 63, 131
Fort Worth Barn Dance (WDAP), 26
Foster, Stephen, 104
Fourth National Radio Conference (1925), 47–48, 69, 71, 128, 132

Freedman, David, 120
Furness, George C., 104

gender: of early radio DX'ers, 16, 87; of
ham radio operators, 13; in radio pro-
gramming, 7, 73, 81, 86–92
General Electric (GE), 43–44, 47, 49, 50,
52, 56, 58, 59, 63, 101
General Mills, 90
Germany, radio stations in, 61
Glenn, Otis F., 148
Goldsmith, Alfred, 47, 48
Goldy and Dusty (Gold Dust Twins), 97,
103, 112, 117
Goodrich, B. F., Company, 102
Goodrich Silver Masked Tenor, 103, 112
Gorn, Elliot, 27
Gosden, Freeman, 114, 115
Gramsci, Antonio, 3–4
"Grand Ole Opry," 23, 26
Green, Col. Edward, 55

Hall, Stuart, 4
Hall, Wendell, 104–5
ham radio, 12, 13–14, 20
"Happiness Boys," 93, 94, 97–99, 102, 103,
108–12, 117, 118, 167
Harding, Warren G., 55
Hare, Ernie, 93, 98–99, 102, 103, 109–13
Harney, Father John, 148–49
Hatfield, Henry, 149, 151
Hawley, Ellis, 152
Herbert, Victor, 107
Hettinger, Herman, 74, 79, 81
Hill, George Washington, 159
Hindle, Brooke, 4
Hooper, C. F., 122
Hoover, Herbert, 38, 41–43, 47–48, 52, 66,
70–71, 149
"Housekeeper's Chat, The," 89
Houseman, John, 157
Hower, Ralph, 81
"How Far Have You Heard?" (contests),
15–16, 19

Institute for Education by Radio, 135
interference, 18–19, 46, 47, 48, 51
"Interwoven Pair," 112, 117
Ipana toothpaste, 80–81, 97, 102, 103

jazz, 25, 26, 96–97, 127
Jessel, George, 119
Jones, Billy, 93, 98–99, 102, 103, 109–13
J. R. H. receiving sets, 15
Judson, Arthur, 63

Kallet, Arthur, 128
Kaltenborn, H. V., 156
Kent, Atwater, 96, 97
Kern, Stephen, 32
Kerwin, Jerome, 135–36, 141
Kimball, Earl, 106
Kincaid, Bradley, 25
King, Larry, 161
Koppes, Clayton, 127

La Guardia, Fiorello, 60, 147
Lasker, Albert, 114
Lears, T. J. Jackson, 78, 87
leftist politics, 127, 132, 136–37, 138
legislation: Communications Act of 1934, 7,
8, 9, 59, 126, 127, 142, 149–51, 167; Public Broadcasting Act of 1967, 161; Radio
Act of 1912, 142; Radio Act of 1927, 59,
60, 61, 130, 133, 142, 145, 147, 148, 149,
150
Limbaugh, Rush, 161
Lipsitz, George, 24
liquor advertising, 131
Lubar, Steven, 4

McClelland, George, 104
MacDonald, J. Fred, 163
McLean, Albert, 119–20
McNamee, Graham, 104, 106
Marc, David, 161
Marchand, Roland, 5, 78, 88
Marconi Wireless Telegraph Company,
43, 44
Marvin, Carolyn, 34–35

Mason, Frank, 139
Massachusetts Institute of Technology, 50
"Maxwell Hour," 97
"Maxwell House Program," 158
Metropolitan Opera broadcasts, 53–54, 130
Minneapolis Tribune, 40
minstrel shows, 110, 115
monopolies, natural, 35
Morgan, Frank, 158
Morse code, 13, 14
municipalities, radio stations owned by,
    66–67
Munn, Frank, 112
Murrow, Edward R., 157

National Advisory Council on Radio in Edu-
    cation (NACRE), 140–41
National Amateur Wireless Association, 28
National Association of Broadcasters
    (NAB), 74, 75, 82, 85, 140–42, 145–46,
    148, 152
"National Barn Dance," 23, 25
"National Biscuit Co. Band," 100
National Broadcasting Company (NBC):
    affiliates for, 122; ban on electrical tran-
    scriptions at, 123; control of, 59; daytime
    broadcasting at, 91; educational program-
    ming at, 140; establishment of, 58, 97,
    101, 102; and FRC survey, 145, 146;
    news department at, 137; profitability of,
    63, 118, 131; publicity for, 44; support
    for radio advertising at, 72, 73, 80–82, 84,
    106, 108, 112, 114–16, 139; and wired
    networks, 62–63
National Carbon Company, 104–5
National Committee on Education by
    Radio (NCER), 133–34, 136, 146
National Education Week, 146
National Electric Light Association, 55
"National Farm and Home Hour," 130
"National Homemaker's Club, The," 90
National Public Radio (NPR), 161
National Radio Conferences, 38, 41–43,
    46–48, 51, 69, 70–71, 128, 132
national radio service: audience for, 20–31;

desire for, 2, 8, 11–12, 13–20, 30; develop-
    ment of, 31–36, 165
National Recovery Administration, 127
natural monopolies, 35
NBC National Advisory Council, 140
"Negro radio," 159
networks: nontechnological factors influ-
    encing, 57–63; resistance to, 8; role in
    national radio, 2, 167; by shortwave re-
    broadcasting, 39, 42, 43, 44, 48–52; by su-
    per-power transmitters, 38, 39, 41, 42,
    43, 44–48, 58; technological options for,
    38, 39, 42–44; technology of, 8; on televi-
    sion, 163–64; wired, 39, 42, 43, 46–47,
    49, 52–57, 59, 61, 129, 165
newspapers: advertising in, 85; opposition
    to radio networks, 126, 131, 132, 137–39;
    as radio sponsors, 40
news wire services, 33, 137
New York Band Instrument Company, 101
New York City: radio programming in, 17,
    29. *See also* radio stations, individual
"New York Edison Hour," 101
New York Herald, 33
New York Times, 70, 74, 116
nonprofit radio programming, 4, 8, 126,
    130–31, 132, 148
Norfolk Daily News, 139

Office of War Information, 157
Ohio School of the Air, 134
Ohio State University Bureau of Educa-
    tional Research, 135
Oliver, Paul, 103, 112, 117
O'Neill, Neville, 74–75, 82
opera, 26, 53–54, 95, 97, 130
Outlook (magazine), 70
Owen, Tom, 25

Pacific-Western Broadcasting Federation,
    134
Paley, William, 63, 142
Palmer, Olive, 103, 112, 117
Palmolive Company, 103, 112, 117
Park, Robert, 32

Paulist Fathers of New York City, 148
Payne Fund, 133, 135
Pearl, Jack, 119
Pease, Otis, 87
"people meters," 9
Pepsodent toothpaste, 114, 115, 116
performers: fees for, 40, 82–83, 100; qualifications of, 103; types of, 94
Peterson, Anna J., 88
Pittsburgh Courier, 115
Podeyn, George, 106
Pope, Daniel, 85, 136
Popenoe, Charles, 50
Popular Radio (magazine), 26, 75, 98
Press-Radio Bureau, 137
Printer's Ink (trade journal), 69
programming: advertising agency production of, 83, 118–19; of commercial entertainments, 29–30; of community events, 95; as cultural historical text, 6; dramas, 156; early, 14, 17, 94–98; educational, 20, 22, 67, 88–89, 127, 129–30, 133, 139–42, 146–47, 167; and electrical transcriptions, 122–23; factors influencing, 8, 37–39, 63–64; fee (proposed) for listings of, 65; funding of, 39–41, 65–68, 165; interference in transmission of, 18–19, 46, 47, 48, 51; local, 19, 30, 42, 51; mass versus specialized interests in, 9, 31, 159–61; musical, 21, 22–26, 40, 53–54, 94–95, 96–97, 159–61; national, 11–12, 20–31; political, 152; prerecorded, 122–23, 158; provided by federal government, 21–22; purpose of, 9; regional, 8, 10, 21, 22, 23, 30, 54, 61, 63, 99; religious, 53, 95; rigidity of, 9; rural, 20–26, 31, 61, 144; and "silent nights," 17–18; soap operas as, 91; specialization of, 159–61; of sporting events, 26–29, 53, 95; on television, 163; transitional, 111–17; urban, 22, 31, 60–61; vaudeville in, 8, 30, 55, 98–99, 103, 105, 110, 116, 117–22
Public Broadcasting Act of 1967, 161
public utilities, as model for radio regulation, 150

quacks, 128
quiz show scandals, 163

racial segregation: in radio programming, 7, 24, 25–26, 63–64, 115, 159
radio: distortion of its own history, 4; as a fad, 68–69; federal regulation of, 33, 35–36, 58, 59–62, 125, 126, 142–53; influence of television on, 5, 9, 155, 159; local system of, 12, 144; merchandising of, 83–84, 107; privatization of, 35; specialization in, 159–61; transportation metaphors for, 33, 46, 77. *See also* advertising, on radio; national radio service; programming; radio stations
Radio Acts: of 1912, 142; of 1927, 59, 60, 61, 130, 133, 142, 145, 147, 148, 149, 150
Radio Age (magazine), 21, 68, 97
Radio Broadcast (magazine), 12, 14–19, 28, 38, 46, 49, 50, 54, 56, 65–67, 69, 95–99, 129
Radio Corporation of America (RCA), 35–36, 38, 40–50, 56–59, 63, 100, 139
Radio Digest (trade journal), 148
Radio Guide (magazine), 112
Radio Music Fund Committee, 67
radio networks. *See* networks
radio programming. *See* programming
radio receivers, 14, 15, 16–17, 18–19, 25, 37
Radio Revue (magazine), 2
radio sports announcers, 29
radio stations: announcement of call letters of, 14–15; early sponsorship of, 39–40, 66–68, 98–111, 166; management of, 95–96, 144; super-power transmitters for, 38, 39, 41, 42, 43, 58
—individual: KDKA (Pittsburgh), 14, 51–52, 53, 55, 101; KFKB (Milford, Kans.), 128; KFKX (Hastings, Nebr.), 50, 51–52; KGO (Oakland), 50, 51; KSD (St. Louis), 55; KYW (Chicago), 55, 88, 95, 101; WBZ (Springfield, Mass.), 101; WCAP (Washington, D.C.), 55, 56; WCCO (Minneapolis), 90; WCFL (Chicago),

148; WDAF (Kansas City, Mo.), 55; WDAP (Fort Worth), 23, 26; WEAF (New York City), 43, 53–54, 55, 56, 58, 63, 67, 98, 99, 100, 101–2, 104, 105, 106, 109; WEAO (Ohio State University), 134; WFAA (Dallas), 55; WGN (Chicago), 114; WGY (Schenectady, N.Y.), 49–50, 55, 101; WHB (Kansas City, Mo.), 67; WHN (New York City), 58; WJAR (Providence, R.I.), 55, 56; WJY (New York City), 99, 100–101, 102; WJZ (New York City), 40–41, 50, 58, 88, 99, 100–101, 102, 112; WLS (Chicago), 23, 25; WLW (Cincinnati), 134; WLWL (New York City), 148; WMAF (South Dartmouth, Mass.), 55; WMAQ (Chicago), 99, 114; WNYC (New York City), 66–67; WOR (New York City), 89; WRC (Washington, D.C.), 101; WSB (Atlanta), 23; WSM (Nashville), 23
radio talk shows, 9, 161
radio time: early, 96; standardization of, 84–85, 119
"radio trust," 36, 41, 42, 58, 60, 99
Radio World (magazine), 87
railroads, national system for, 32–33, 150
Rayburn, Sam, 152
"Ray-O-Vac Twins, The," 101
Rea, Virginia, 112
Reich, Leonard, 57
Reser, Harry, 106, 107, 108
Rethberg, Elisabeth, 101
"Rise of the Goldbergs, The," 91, 114, 115–16, 156
Rockefeller, John D., Jr., 140
rock 'n' roll, 159, 160, 162
Rodgers, Jimmie, 25
Roosevelt, Franklin D., 127, 149–50, 157
Rorty, James, 125, 131, 132, 136–37, 141
Rothafel, S. L. "Roxy," 55
Roush, Ted, 21
Royal, John, 120
royalties, payment of, 40
"Royal Typewriter Hour," 112
"Royal Typewriter Salon Orchestra," 101

"Sam 'n' Henry," 99, 114
Sarnoff, David, 37–47, 50, 139
Schlink, F. J., 128
schools, radio stations owned by, 66, 126, 130–36, 138, 140–41, 144, 161. *See also* educational programming
Schudson, Michael, 5
Sears-Roebuck, radio station of, 25
Second National Radio Conference (1923), 38
Sevareid, Eric, 157
Sheehy, Russell, 16
Shirer, William, 157
Shulman, Holly Cowan, 157
"silent nights," 17–18
Smith Brothers cough drops, 102
soap operas, 91
Soviet Union, radio stations in, 61
spot advertisements, 90–91, 129
Standard Brands, sponsorship by, 118
Starch, Daniel, 116–17, 121
static. *See* interference
Strasser, Susan, 72
Strong, Walter, 46
Suppé, Franz von, 108
Susman, Warren, 166

talk radio, 9, 161
taxation, 65, 67
technology, 162; and gender, 13, 16, 86, 87; and nationalism, 31–33; and technological determinism, 4–5
Tector, Crystal D., 87
telegraph, 33, 34, 35, 54
telephone: acceptance of, 34–35; Kingsbury Commitment in, 34; long-distance transmissions by, 34; national system of, 35; radio stations connected by, 43, 53–54
television: advertising on, 2, 3, 9, 163; consumerism fed by, 1–2; development of, 163–64; impact on radio industry, 3, 9, 155, 159
theme songs, 98
Third National Radio Conference (1924), 38–39, 41, 42, 43, 46, 51, 70